goal that can justify the killings of millions of people; nuclear possession, nuclear threats and nuclear (first) use is criminal and the so-called balance of terror is just that: terrorism, terrorism so much bigger than any Al-Qaeda or ISIL.

This book tells you just why and how people in these murky buildings have gone MAD and continue the madness inside institutions that defy democratic transparency and in which the people live in their own world. Not without reason does MAD also stand for Mutually Assured Destruction: Omnicide!

Dr. Paul H. Johnstone's amazing insider account should be enough to make everyone on earth demand total abolition. His daughter's framing of this uniquely important piece of contemporary history is brilliantly written, thanks to her own immense knowledge and devotion to a moral, peaceful world.

This book deserves the largest possible readership worldwide. Translate it! Let it enter every relevant university course! And let it be used to nonviolently force the Military-Industrial-Media-Academic Complex (MIMAC) to surrender. After all, in the name of civilisation, humanity has abolished cannibalism, slavery, absolute monarchy and child labor.

It's time to end the nuclear era. A nuclear-free world is possible. A MAD world is not."

—DR. JAN OBERG, Director,
Transnational Foundation for Peace and Future research
www.transnational.org

From MAD to Madness

Inside Pentagon Nuclear War Planning

A Memoir by
PAUL H. JOHNSTONE

with Commentary by
DIANA JOHNSTONE

Clarity Press, Inc

In-house editor: Diana G. Collier
Cover: R. Jordan P. Santos

Library of Congress Cataloging-in-Publication Data

Clarity Press, Inc.
2625 Piedmont Rd. NE, Ste. 56
Atlanta, GA. 30324 , USA
http://www.claritypress.com

TABLE OF CONTENTS

Part II: Imagining Doomsday

Part III: The Critical Incident Studies

FOREWORD

For two decades Paul H. Johnstone worked in the upper echelons of US intelligence. For Air Force Intelligence, the Joint Chiefs of Staff, and the Office of the Secretary of Defense, he devised ways of estimating the military capabilities of potential enemies, and ways of estimating the kind of targets and their locations that, if destroyed, would most damage an enemy's capacity to continue at war. The task of estimating the damage from nuclear war eventually brought the realization of the futility of nuclear warfare.

Johnstone's work in assessing the survivability of nuclear war is as significant and compelling today as when it was written decades ago. Indeed, it is more significant and more compelling. The atomic bombs that President Truman ordered dropped on two Japanese cities were powerful weapons, but they are popguns compared to the thermo-nuclear weapons of today. Moreover, subsequent American presidents—John F. Kennedy, Richard Nixon, Jimmy Carter, Ronald Reagan—worked to reduce tensions with the Soviet Union and formulated a war doctrine that relegated nuclear weapons to a retaliatory role. Reagan working with Soviet president Gorbachev removed the threat of nuclear holocaust by ending the Cold War.

Today the situation is far more dangerous than during the Cold War period. From the Soviet collapse in 1991 came the belligerent neoconservative doctrine of US world hegemony. This doctrine has resulted in violations by Washington of critical agreements made with Moscow. The Clinton regime violated the agreement that in exchange for Moscow's acceptance of the reunification of Germany, NATO would not move one inch to the East and established NATO bases on Russia's border. The George

W. Bush regime violated the anti-ballistic missile treaty and made arrangements for establishing ABM bases on Russia's border with the lame justification that the bases were to protect Europe from non-existent Iranian ICMBs. The Obama regime launched a direct attack on Russia with the goal of evicting Russia from its Black Sea naval base by overthrowing the democratically elected government in Ukraine and installing a puppet government.

Washington, lost in hubris, thought that the Russian government would take the dismissal of Russian interests lying down. When Russia stood up for her interests, Washington began the demonization of Russia's President Vladimir Putin. A constant stream of lies and threats have been issued by Washington, the result of which is to convince Russia that the American and European populations are being prepared for war with Russia.

It is as if Washington has forgotten all of the learned lessons of Johnstone's work—the uncertainties of intelligence, the unpredictability of the course of events, the overwhelming extent of mutually sustained damages. Let us review some of these lessons.

The demand for quantification required the production of numbers that often were only guesses. Consequently, command decisions generally rested on "intelligence" arranged to support the decisions. As Johnstone puts it, "Doctrine was more convincing than evidence."

The world of intelligence is less a world of facts than "a dominant mood" that more than "acute reasoning" determines decisions. Essentially, intelligence is formed from beliefs. So controlling beliefs is the key.

The long view is absent, and current obsessions dominate. Those who question the obsessions and reigning political passions "are either ignored or slandered as fools, even traitors." America's anti-Communist obsession "led us to oppose, and therefore make enemies of, anti-colonial, nationalistic revolutionary movements in all parts of the world that, had we not opposed them . . . could readily have been not our enemies but our friends."

The ability of the military/security complex to create the Cold War out of the Russian Threat owed much to America's anti-communist obsession. This paragraph from Johnstone's memoir gives the flavor of the time:

> The prevailing Pentagon presumption was that at almost any time the Russians would unleash their hordes upon Western Europe. In the Air Force Directorate of Intelligence, a Special Studies Group had been set up by General C.P. Cabell (who later moved over to CIA and was chief of operations there at the time of the 1961 Bay of Pigs fiasco, although it was Richard Bissell who was directly in control of that operation). This Group was charged with writing most of the long range strategic think-pieces for the Directorate. It was headed by Steve Possony, a Hungarian émigré who professed to be an expert on Communism in general and the Soviet Union in particular. Steve was the first of several Central European émigrés I met in the next few years who passed as experts on Communist Europe and who had at least some small influence on strategic thought and the formation of American policy. Others were Strausz-Hupé, Kissinger, Brzezinski and many lesser lights such as Leon Gouré and Helmut Sonnenfeldt. In every case I felt they were thinking, consciously or otherwise, not as Americans but as representatives of a lost cause in their native land, and I always believed they were used by the military because their 'obsessions' were so useful. The one product of Possony's group that I most distinctly remember was an annual appraisal of the strategic situation. And the reason I remember it, perhaps, is that every year that appraisal forecast a massive Russian land attack on Western Europe the following year. Several of us began to laugh about it after a while, but the forecast was always intoned

awesomely and with superficial plausibility. I do
not know whether many people who heard the
briefings really believed the forecasts. I suspect
many doubted it would really be next year, and
thought it more likely the year after that or even
later. But even doubters approved the forecast
because, they reasoned, it was better to err in this
direction than to minimize the danger. Above all,
it was good to say things that emphasized the need
for strong defenses."

And bigger budgets.

I knew Possony. He was my colleague at the Hoover
Institution on War, Revolution, and Peace at Stanford University.
Emigres from the Baltics and Eastern Europe were successful in
setting themselves up as Soviet experts in the post-World War II
era. They were strongly anti-Soviet and succeeded in creating the
impression of a dire threat that did not exist until Washington's
hostile actions created it. In the 21st century Washington has
repeated its folly with its creation of the "Muslim threat" now
superceded by the re-creation of the "Russian threat."

Washington's fear of a Soviet nuclear attack was
intensified by a Rand Corporation study by Albert Wohlstetter, an
inspiration for the film, Dr. Strangelove. The study postulated a
successful Soviet attack on the US Strategic Air Command that
stripped the US of its nuclear capability. Johnstone reports: "To
say it was convincing is a gross understatement."

No one noticed that Wohlstetter's study assumed that
everything worked perfectly for the Soviets, "with perfect weather,
no operational foul-ups, no advance warning. Above all, the study
assumed such an insensate desire on the part of the Soviets to attack
us that they would voluntarily accept the enormous risks that such a
gamble would inevitably involve. Perhaps one factor that made us
so ready to accept the idea of a surprise, pre-emptive Soviet attack
as the way the inevitable war would come was a lingering Pearl
Harbor complex. And the dominant notion was that the Soviets were

bent on world conquest. Almost never was there any suggestion that Soviet arms were in any way defensive, or that the Soviets feared us. Ours was a psychology, perhaps not unlike theirs, of awaiting and bracing for an attack to be launched on us by an irreconcilable enemy. Of course we did not know then that the authors of this study were to go on to be the midwives of the 'missile gap' scare following Sputnik, and then founders of the Committee on the Present Danger in the seventies."

Johnstone provides an abundance of historical information from his own experience that shows that intelligence often consists of emotional preconceptions. The history itself is fascinating, the details, the personages, and the difficulty of ever arriving at intelligence that justified high confidence. Observing the failure of Washington's Vietnam War policies, Johnstone wrote the Pentagon Papers. Daniel Ellsberg without authorization released the Pentagon Papers in 1971, thereby helping to bring the Vietnam War to an end.

In 1960 when the CIA brought word of a split between China and the Soviet Union, the reaction of many in the intelligence community was that either the CIA had gone "soft on Communism," a charge later leveled at President John F. Kennedy, or had been taken in by an orchestrated ruse by the Chinese and Soviets to put the US off guard. In other words, American intelligence was so delusional that it could not take advantage of the break between the two communist powers. It was 12 years later that President Richard Nixon had the vision and courage, despite conservative protest, to go to China and normalize relations between the US and the People's Republic of China. In my considered opinion it was Nixon's action in ending the cold war with China that caused the CIA to terminate his presidency with an orchestrated scandal concocted by the CIA asset, the *Washington Post*.

As US intelligence struggled with understanding the consequences of nuclear war, policymakers began moving the weapons out of the useable category. The US strategy of countering Soviet superiority in conventional forces with US nuclear forces was recognized as a path to mutual suicide. Nuclear weapon use was constrained by Mutually Assured Destruction (MAD). This doctrine made nuclear weapons a guarantor of non-use. As each side possessed nuclear weapons, the destructiveness of these weapons became a deterrent to their use.

As Diana Johnstone makes clear in her brilliant introduction and postscript to her father's memoir, in the early 1990s, following the Soviet collapse, the American neoconservatives in pursuit of their ideology of US hegemony resurrected nuclear weapons as useable weapons of war. The Obama regime has authorized a trillion dollar expenditure for nuclear weapons, and US war doctrine has elevated nukes from a retaliatory role to pre-emptive first strike. US President Reagan and Soviet President Gorbachev eliminated the risk of Armageddon by negotiating the end of the Cold War. The neoconservatives in pursuit of their goal of US world hegemony have resurrected the possibility of nuclear war. The neocons have taken us from MAD to madness.

President Truman's decision to use atomic bombs on Hiroshima and Nagasaki was a political decision, not a military decision. Diana Johnstone reports that senior US commanding officers, including Eisenhower, MacArthur, Hap Arnold, and Admiral William Leahy opposed, in the words of Admiral Leahy, "the use of this barbarous weapon" which "was of no material assistance in our war against Japan. The Japanese were already defeated and ready to surrender."

Diana Johnstone makes the important point that the destructive power of the weapon made Truman "euphoric with the possession of such power" and gave him the confidence to start the Cold War by reneging on agreements he had with Stalin, thus creating distrust. Eisenhower's conclusion was that Truman's use of the atomic bomb ruined the prospect of peace with Russia. In the place of peace was the prospect of Armageddon and the dangers to American democracy from the rising power of the military/industrial complex.

This mistake has now been repeated, and Russia's trust in Washington has been again destroyed, bringing the risk of Armageddon upon us for a second time.

Will luck also be with us this time? As I write the CIA and Pentagon are in the White House seeking presidential authorization to attack Syrian and Russian forces in Syria. Russian President Putin has withdrawn from the plutonium agreement citing "the threat to strategic stability posed by the hostile actions of the US toward Russia." Carl Gershman, who heads the neoconservative propaganda ministry, the US taxpayer-financed National Endowment for Democracy, has called on Washington to "summon the will" to remove Putin from the Russian presidency.[1]

The Cold War was responsibly managed and brought to an end by Reagan and Gorbachev once the destructiveness of nuclear weapons was understood. In contrast, today we are experiencing rising levels of tension between nuclear powers stemming from the neoconservative drive for US world hegemony. We are in a far more dangerous situation than the Berlin Crisis and Cuban Missile Crisis in the early 1960s. Washington is guilty of reckless and irresponsible aggression toward the other two major nuclear powers, Russia and China. Compared to the care taken during Paul Johnstone's era, Washington today appears to be insane.

—PAUL CRAIG ROBERTS
October 11, 2016

THE DANGEROUS SEDUCTION OF ABSOLUTE POWER

by Diana Johnstone

The Spirit of the Times

I have a lasting memory of being with my father in a Chevy Chase drugstore that day in August 1945 when he saw the headlines on a newsstand announcing that the first atomic bomb had been dropped on Japan. I was too young to know what it meant, but my father's reaction made a lasting impression. I understood only that something deeply wrong had happened to the world, casting a dark shadow across the future.

That moment was certainly the real beginning of the story that my father Paul Johnstone tells in his memoirs.

At that moment in Chevy Chase he was back in the United States after spending time in India and Sri Lanka (Ceylon, then) as chief of the Far East Enemy Division of the Bureau of Economic Warfare. In that capacity, he had been involved in evaluating Japanese enemy targets, which is evidently why he was hired years later by the Pentagon to evaluate Air Force targets during the Cold War. But Hiroshima had changed the nature of targeting dramatically, and that is the story my father tells in his memoir. It was certainly the dread and revulsion he felt on that day in August 1945 that endured and grew, inspiring him in his last years to record his experience in the Pentagon.

It took the attack on Pearl Harbor to tear Paul Johnstone from his work in the Department of Agriculture to a field that was far from his initial interests and aspirations.

Paul Howard Johnstone was born in Colorado on April 10, 1903, grew up in Minnesota and died on October 16, 1981 in Fairfax County, Virginia, not so very far from the Pentagon where he worked during the last 20 years of his long career in Government service.

His career was in many ways exemplary of the transformation of the dominant American Zeitgeist in his lifetime. America turned from farming to bombing as the basis of its industrial economy, from the land to the air. Starting with World War II, the United States centered its massive manufacturing capacity on the buildup of military strength, primarily conquest of the air. The ideal of a prospering agrarian society gave way to the ambition of "victory through air power", domination of the planet by bombs, missiles, drones. And with that change, America has turned from "cultivating its own garden", in the broadest sense of the term, to reshaping the rest of the world.

From the Land

The family of Paul Johnstone's pioneer maternal grandparents, the Howards, left their upstate New York farms to seek more land in the West. Some of his relatives went to Colorado, some all the way to Washington State. His mother, Maude, met his father, Bruff, while visiting relatives in Colorado, where Paul was born, before returning to the Howard clan in Minnesota. Most of the family left farming for business, whereas Paul headed for academic studies, with the intention of teaching and writing.

By early 1933, he was in Europe, doing research in Paris and Heidelberg when Franklin D. Roosevelt took office as President of the United States and Adolf Hitler took power in Germany. His doctoral thesis on the relationship between farming and ideology was published in 1937 as "Turnips and Romanticism". About that time, Paul Johnstone joined the "brain trust" men and women in the Department of Agriculture.

In his autobiographical essay, *The Prime of Life,*[1] his colleague Gove Hambidge wrote: "Paul is a historian in the Bureau of Agricultural Economics, looks like a Frenchman — tall, swarthy, black-mustached — and was once in fact a professor of French. Shrewd historical analyses and good writing got him a welcome in the Department. He belongs to the school that approaches history from the standpoint of the cultural patterns of common people, institutional economics, and psychology — a viewpoint that is becoming more and more important in American thinking."

However much he may have looked like a Frenchman to Gove Hambidge, Paul Johnstone was an American Midwesterner, who caught fish through the ice of Minnesota lakes in his boyhood, briefly played professional baseball as a teenager, and could hit a rabbit in his asparagus patch with a stone thrown from a good thirty meters away. Philosophically, he considered himself a Voltairian, and appropriately devoted his retirement to cultivating his own garden until felled by a stroke among his rose bushes.

The Prime of Life describes a sunny Saturday in Washington D.C. in May, 1940, when Department of Agriculture intellectuals gather after a morning of work to play horseshoes at the Chevy Chase home of the author. The book bears witness to a time of enthusiasm in the life of the U.S. Government when the best and the brightest were brought together not to make war, nor to find advantages for themselves, but to build a more human and efficient society.

"Among these public servants with whom I work there are people who represent almost every branch of science and art," Hambidge wrote. "They are here because the problems that must be met by government today demand every kind of knowledge and talent."[2]

That was a time, in the Great Depression, when the "free market" as it is called, meaning financial speculation, had totally failed society and left the country in a shambles of bankrupt businesses, soup kitchens, hobos and Okies wandering desperately in search of a living. The government under Franklin D. Roosevelt was trying to pick up the pieces and rebuild the country to benefit the people.

Nothing perhaps was more central to the New Deal and its spirit than the Department of Agriculture under Henry Wallace,[3] an innovative Iowa agronomist who was perhaps the most progressive visionary in the Roosevelt cabinet. The Department of Agriculture was very far from being either a collection of special interests or a welfare agency. On the contrary, it was above all a many-faceted endeavor to use scientific advancement to raise farm productivity and with it the nation's economic development.

Hambidge wrote:

> If research was to be applied systematically
> to agriculture, as it had to be to feed the cities,
> the job could be done only by government, as a
> public service.
> This necessity was fulfilled. The Department of
> Agriculture and a full complement of agricultural
> colleges and experiment stations were created to
> fulfill it — not primarily for the sake of farmers, as
> everyone thought, but because the growth of modern
> industry and the character of modern civilization
> demanded increasing efficiency in agriculture.[4]

Some 75 years later, it is worth observing that such activities as irrigation and genetic research, then pursued as public services, have since been turned over to private transnational corporations primarily motivated by profits rather than the public interest. The worldwide conflicts over Monsanto products illustrate this change. Scientific research continues, but profit margins rather than public welfare have become the guiding criteria.

Hambidge wrote that his colleagues were forced to take broad views, to see through special interests and weigh them constantly in the balance with the public welfare.

> The net result is that a remarkably large number
> of them, it seems to me, become capable of
> extremely sharp and shrewd appraisals. Yet
> many are idealists, too, and hard fighters for

what they believe in. Relatively few, in my experience, have an exaggerated idea of their own official importance, and many have a great deal of fundamental humility. [...]

You cannot be with these public servants intimately or long without feeling that something has happened to them because they are public servants. They work for something far beyond personal gain — for something long-lasting and fundamental — or the general welfare, in fact.[5]

This active enthusiasm in working for the public good was accompanied by a deep aversion to war. This sentiment was based on a conviction that enlightenment, science and progress were leading to an era of peace. Gove Hambidge wrote: "Europe accepts war as part of the eternal order, the only way to avoid things that are worse. [...] But I have a feeling of certainty that Americans, a different people, will act some day on the simple conviction, which they feel deeply, that the most intolerable thing in the modern world is the wholesale slaughter of men by men, and will take the lead in ending it."

These were the thoughts of an American writer in 1940. A year later, the United States went to war and has, with a few intervals, stayed there ever since.

Within a very short time, the Zeitgeist was reversed.

To the Air

In the nineteen thirties, the country was suffering from mass poverty. The national capital was dominated by a spirit of concern for the public welfare and hope in human progress. The spirit of those times was expressed not only in song, in literature but in famous photos that brought out the innate dignity of impoverished sharecroppers and men in breadlines, all wearing hats. That was "the age of the common man". Those who were stranded by the collapse of capitalism were not "losers", they were human potential, they represented hope for a better future. In the nation's capital, the government's effort was directed toward improving human life.

Within a few years that was turned around. All efforts were directed toward killing the enemy. The change was not evident immediately, but it turned out to be lasting. Jobs were created, and while much of the rest of the world was devastated by war, America prospered. For the United States, war brought unprecedented wealth and power.

Some of the idealism of the New Deal was transferred into the war effort against the Axis Powers, viewed as a unique manifestation of absolute evil. But this marked a profound philosophical shift away from the New Deal's pragmatic humanism, full of doubt and innovation, toward a rigid self-righteous Manichaeism that suits the militarization of society. Since it was "the good war", war was good.

Peace-loving Henry Wallace, by then Roosevelt's third vice president, was put in charge of the Board of Economic Warfare, set up ten days after the Japanese attack on Pearl Harbor. Some time thereafter, Paul Johnstone left the Department of Agriculture for the Bureau of Economic Warfare, where he became chief of the Far East Enemy Division. That was his first step toward the Pentagon. The ploughshares were truly transformed into swords, for a long time to come.

No Turning Back

At the end of the war, Paul Johnstone briefly attempted to get back to his prewar activities on behalf of agriculture. He spent three years in Sacramento working for the Bureau of Reclamation, before it became clear that the irrigation works were going to be taken over by agribusiness rather than by the family-size farms originally meant to be the main beneficiaries.

In 1948, Dr. Johnstone was sent to Shanghai to serve as economic adviser to the Nationalist Government of Chiang Kai-Shek. It was clear at that time that any economic aid would end up in the foreign bank account of one or another corrupt official. On a visit to Guangxi province, he observed the total destitution of the rural population, where all the trees had been burnt for fuel. He arranged to ship water buffalo from nearby Hainan Island to

Guangxi, thus skirting around government corruption and providing the peasants with transport, traction, milk, fertilizer and fuel in the form of buffalo dung.

In the streets of Shanghai, he witnessed popular hostility to the Chiang regime and to its American supporters. Crowds turned their backs on an official parade. He was spat upon by strangers. The experience was a lesson in the limits of U.S. influence in Asia — and the world.

He returned to the United States as Mao's forces were about to capture Shanghai in May 1949. It was at this point that, after some hesitation, largely for family reasons, he refused foreign assignments and went to work for the Pentagon.

In 1981, my father gave me the handwritten copy of this memoir when he was literally on his deathbed, asking me to make it public. I did not succeed at the time, yet now, 35 years later, this document seems more pertinent than ever.

The Fog of War Planning

Dr. Johnstone's memoir illustrates the fog of war planning. The top decision-makers want simple facts and figures on which to base their decisions, and the experts and analysts are ordered to produce them. This book shows how this works, and how far from reality the whole process really is. The political leaders want a certainty that is impossible to obtain. The best brains and most knowledgeable experts are put to work to predict the unpredictable, and only a simplified executive summary ever reaches the top. Some of the conclusions are breath-taking: "the general consensus has been that while a nuclear exchange would leave the U.S. in a seriously damaged condition, with many millions of casualties and little immediate war supporting capability, the U.S. would continue to exist as an organized and viable nation, and ultimately would prevail, whereas the USSR would not."

This basic situation has not changed. Nuclear weapons are still there and analysts are still analyzing how to use them. This story is the story of attempts to answer unanswerable questions.

It illustrates why carefully planned wars cannot ever turn out as planned.

Dr. Johnstone was keenly aware of these uncertainties. As an historian and literary scholar, he deplored the illusion among certain social scientists that all they needed was adequate data to be able to predict human behavior, even during such an unprecedented disaster as nuclear war. In his experience, he found a shared skepticism among physicists and mathematicians. He made an effort to promote evaluations of past crises, precisely to make it clear to decision-makers how easily things could go wrong. His studies here of crises in Laos and Berlin show how easily events can get out of hand. The latest and most thorough of these crisis studies was the review of American involvement in Vietnam ordered by McNamara, titled *The Pentagon Papers* after it was divulged to *The New York Times* by Daniel Ellsberg. Dr. Johnstone was one of the authors of *The Pentagon Papers*.

The public release of *The Pentagon Papers*, as Dr. Johnstone observed, led to a "general tightening of security". This is seen today in the brutal official treatment of Chelsea Manning and other whistleblowers. The public is not supposed to know of the dangers to which our armchair strategists are ready to expose the world, including Americans themselves. We can be sure that today, similar studies are being undertaken to plan for use of the trillion dollars worth of nuclear weapons planned for production over the next thirty years. The best-case-scenario war hawks are certain to believe that we can employ "tactical" nuclear bombs four times more powerful than the one that destroyed Hiroshima, and yet still "continue to exist as a viable nation", assuming that our hypothetical Russian or Chinese adversaries back down — something neither of those nations is famous for. Nuclear escalation? "We shall prevail."

A cautious leader may realize the dangers and hold back, whereas an arrogant and insouciant leader convinced of "exceptional" America's divine mission to lead the world may believe what he or she wants to believe and forge ahead into the perilous unknown, under the impression of possessing the facts and foreseeing the future.

Nuclear War: America's Self-Made Dilemma

The United States decision to use their newly acquired atom bombs to destroy two Japanese cities was a momentous decision. A great war was ending, but that decision meant that the end of one war was the beginning of others, and above all a continuation of the war mentality. World War II had shifted the U.S. bureaucracy away from domestic economic and social progress toward destroying enemies regarded as totally *evil*.

The totality of atomic destruction was justified by the totality of Japanese evil. Although the war was already won, Hiroshima was justified to many Americans above all by the notion that "the Japanese deserved it". This justification persists to this day.

From now on, all our enemies must be totally evil, and thus the proper target of total destruction. Because, as soon as one thinks in terms of total destruction, the enemy must be totally evil in order to deserve it. This is the mindset that necessarily prevailed as the Pentagon engaged in planning nuclear war. It spread throughout the whole political class.

The decision to destroy Hiroshima and Nagasaki was a political, not a military, decision. The targets were *not* military, the effects were *not* military. The attacks were carried out *against* the wishes of all senior commanding officers, who at the time considered that wiping out cities was not the sort of war they had been taught to wage in the military academies. Admiral William Leahy, chairman of the Joint Chiefs of Staff, wrote in his memoirs that "the use of this barbarous weapon at Hiroshima and Nagasaki was of no material assistance in our war against Japan. The Japanese were already defeated and ready to surrender..." General Eisenhower, General MacArthur, even General Hap Arnold, commander of the Air Force, were opposed. Japan was already devastated by fire bombing, facing mass hunger from the U.S. naval blockade, demoralized by the surrender of its German ally, and fearful of an imminent Russian attack. In reality, the war was over. All top U.S. leaders knew that Japan was defeated and was seeking to surrender.

Indeed, Nagasaki was bombed haphazardly, three days after bombing Hiroshima with a uranium bomb, just to see how a plutonium bomb worked. In this case, the means justified the ends.

President Harry S. Truman was meeting with Churchill and Stalin in the Berlin suburb of Potsdam when secret news came that the New Mexico test of the atomic bomb was a success. Observers recall that Truman was "a changed man", euphoric with the possession of such power. While more profound men shuddered at the implications of this destructive force, to Truman and his "conniving" Secretary of State, James Byrnes, the message was: "Now we can get away with everything."

They proceeded to act on that assumption — first of all in their relations with Moscow.

In response to months of U.S. urging, Stalin promised to enter the Asian war three months after the defeat of Nazi Germany, which occurred in early May 1945. It was well known that the Japanese occupation forces in China and Manchuria could not resist the Red Army. It was understood that two things could bring about Japan's immediate surrender: Russia's entrance into the war and U.S. assurance that the royal family would not be treated as war criminals.

Both these things happened in the days right after the bombing of Hiroshima and Nagasaki.

But they were overshadowed by the atom bomb.

And that was the point.

That way, the U.S. atom bombs got full credit for ending the war.

But that is not all.

The demonstrated possession of such a weapon gave Truman and Byrnes such a sense of power that they felt free to abandon previous promises to the Russians and to attempt to bully Moscow in Europe. In that sense, the bombs on Hiroshima and Nagasaki not only gratuitously killed hundreds of thousands of civilians. They also started the Cold War.

A most significant observation on the effects of the atomic bomb is attributed to General Dwight D. Eisenhower. Shortly after Hiroshima, Eisenhower is reported to have said privately:

> Before the bomb was used, I would have said yes,
> I was sure we could keep the peace with Russia.
> Now, I don't know. Until now I would have
> said that we three, Britain with her mighty fleet,
> America with the strongest air force, and Russia
> with the strongest land force on the continent,
> we three could have guaranteed the peace of the
> world for a long, long time to come. But now, I
> don't know. People are frightened and disturbed
> all over. Everyone feels insecure again.[6]

As supreme allied commander in Europe, Eisenhower had learned that it was possible to work with the Russians. U.S. and USSR domestic economic and political systems were totally different, but on the world stage they could cooperate. As allies, the differences between them were mostly a matter of mistrust, matters that could be patched up.

The victorious Soviet Union was devastated from the war: cities in ruins, some twenty million dead. The Russians wanted help to rebuild. Previously, under Roosevelt, it had been agreed that the Soviet Union would get reparations from Germany, as well as credits from the United States. Suddenly, this was off the agenda. As news came in of the successful New Mexico test, Truman exclaimed: "This will keep the Russians straight." Because they suddenly felt all-powerful, Truman and Byrnes decided to get tough with the Russians.

Stalin was told that Russia could take reparations only from the largely agricultural eastern part of Germany under Red Army occupation. This was the first step in the division of Germany, which Moscow actually opposed.

Since several of the Eastern European countries had been allied to Nazi Germany, and contained strong anti-Russian elements, Stalin's only condition for those countries (then occupied by the Red Army) was that their governments should not be actively hostile to the USSR. For that, Moscow favored the formula "People's Democracies," meaning coalitions excluding extreme right parties.

Feeling all-powerful, the United States sharpened its demands for "free elections" in hope of installing anti-communist governments. This backfired. Instead of giving in to the implicit atomic threat, the Soviet Union dug in its heels. Instead of loosening political control of Eastern Europe, Moscow imposed Communist Party regimes — and accelerated its own atomic bomb program. The nuclear arms race was on.

This was both predictable and predicted, notably by the very scientists whose work had made the atom bomb possible. Danish Nobel Prize winning physicist Niels Bohr, whose achievements included the early modern model for the atom and the Copenhagen interpretation of quantum mechanics, made a quiet but determined effort to warn against using atomic power as a weapon. Supported by Justice Felix Frankfurter, Bohr managed to speak personally first to Roosevelt and then to Churchill in 1944, warning that the Anglo-Americans could not keep the secrets of nature from others, in particular not from Russian scientists, and urging them to seek an agreement with the Russians to prevent military use of atomic power. All he gained was dismissal by Churchill, who didn't like his unkempt hair and even suggested that the eminent scientist should be arrested for espionage.

General Leslie Groves, in charge of the Manhattan project, easily convinced Truman's chief advisor, James Byrnes, that the Anglo-American monopoly would be preserved because, he claimed, the Russians had no uranium. This objection found its answer in the June 11, 1945 Report of the Committee on Political and Social Problems, signed by seven Manhattan project physicists[7] at the University of Chicago Metallurgical Laboratory ("The Franck Report"):

> the probability that no large reserves of uranium will be found in a country which covers 1/5 of the land area of the earth (and whose sphere of influence takes in additional territory), is too small to serve as a basis for security.

"In Russia, too," the Franck Report observed, "the basic facts and implications of nuclear power were well understood in 1940, and the experiences of Russian scientists in nuclear research is entirely sufficient to enable the to retrace our steps within a few years, even if we would make all attempts to conceal them."

The decision-makers, Groves and in the end, Byrnes and Truman, dismissed such concerns with disdain. Although many of the key scientists were European exiles, the American politicians grasped their discoveries and accomplishments as unique American accomplishments that could be hidden from the rest of the world.   Only "spies" could threaten the U.S. monopoly.

In vain the scientists warned that "the success we have achieved in the development of nuclear power is fraught with infinitely greater dangers than were all the inventions of the past." The only protection from these dangers can come from "the political organization of the world".

They argued that "In the absence of an international authority which would make all resort to force in international conflicts impossible, the nations could still be diverted from a path which must lead to total mutual destruction, by a specific international agreement barring a nuclear armaments race." This prospect requires U.S. refusal to launch the atom bomb against the Japanese, setting the example of refusal to use the power of the atom as a weapon of mass destruction. "If no efficient international agreement is achieved, the race of nuclear armaments will be on in earnest not later than the morning after our first demonstration of the existence of nuclear weapons."

Considering that dropping America's first atomic explosive on Japanese cities could have no significant military impact on a war that was ending, the scientists insisted that the issue be weighed very heavily by the highest political leadership of this country. "If we consider international agreement on total prevention of nuclear warfare as the paramount objective, and believe that it can be achieved, this kind of introduction of atomic weapons to the world may easily destroy all our chances of success," they wrote. "It will be very difficult to persuade the world that a nation which was capable of secretly preparing and suddenly releasing a weapon, as indiscriminate as the rocket bomb and a million times more destructive, is to be trusted in its proclaimed desire of having such weapons abolished by international agreement."

The scientists thus raised the crucial issue of *lack of trust*, which has been at the heart of the United States approach to the world ever since. By unleashing atomic destruction without serious warning,[8] the United States government illustrated to the world its own untrustworthiness. How could other countries ever feel safe once the United States had shown its readiness to unleash atomic death on a country whose great cities were already in ashes and whose population faced starvation?

Except for General Leslie Groves, who as head of the Manhattan Project had a personal stake in demonstrating that he had "done the job", the decision to bomb was made not by military men but by politicians. The decision essentially reflected the dominant political culture of the United States and its attitude toward other peoples: an attitude of profound mistrust, unless they are white and English-speaking, like the British. The common expression is, "all they understand is force". This attitude is profoundly dehumanizing, and amounts to treating other human beings as less than dogs.

Of course, trust should not be blind. It is built on experience and exchange, on mutual self-interest, which would have applied in avoiding nuclear destruction. It needs safeguards and rules. But in their mood of virtuous omnipotence, the men in charge failed to see any point in proving trustworthiness: mere strength should be enough for the U.S. to get its way with others.

The Russians in 1945 were our allies in a terrible war. For all their differences, they were human beings willing to reach agreements in the interests of preventing yet another devastating war. They had felt the full brunt of World War II, and this experience, foreign to the American continent, won their full adherence to peace efforts. At this point, their allies in Washington exploded two atomic bombs on heavily populated urban areas, figurative "in your face" actions — designed to show who is boss. A way of saying, "all you understand is force".

Not the newly discovered structures of the atom, but this attitude — this denial of the humanity of others — is the basic cause of seventy years of fear and fantasy, of paranoia and preparation for nuclear war...that has never ended.

Fantasy World

The world Paul Johnstone entered in 1949 was a fantasy world.   Men with no particular malice were devoting their professional lives to the technical difficulties posed by a vast fantasy of the total destruction of an Evil Enemy.

The Cold War had replaced the New Deal. The imaginative efforts of the U.S. government brain trust were henceforth centered on "thinking about the unthinkable".

All depended on a "Soviet threat" to "destroy our way of life" that was scarcely more real than the afterlife of the Pharaohs, for which Egyptians built the pyramids. Great fantasies can produce vast human constructions.

The Johnstone memoir illustrates the nature of the Cold War. Reformist policies in Iran and in Guatamala were interpreted as "Soviet threats", leading to U.S-instigated coups overthrowing the democratically elected presidents of those countries. Such extraneous events that had nothing to do with the USSR were seen as signs of the need to prepare for nuclear war against the communist enemy.

Today it is widely admitted that the Soviet threat was largely imaginary. Stalin had long since given up on "world revolution". The international Russian peace campaign was sincere, but dismissed in the United States as hostile propaganda.

Throughout this period there was a huge invisible lacuna in the official imagination: thinking about how to make peace. That is what a Cold War is about; even though we are at peace, we do not think about preserving peace, but about making war. Perhaps it is easier, because making war depends precisely on technical skills with material objects, whereas making peace means dealing with fellow human beings. Not so easy. Not as satisfying, if domination is the objective.

Instead, the planners tried to quantify war (with no particular success, by the way), whereas there is no way even to try to quantify peace.

The fantasy of war was fed by the fantasy of threats, often provided by an array of Central and Eastern European exiles harboring historic grudges which they hoped U.S. power might settle to their satisfaction. While the roots of the New Deal were deeply American, the Cold War was largely a continuation of imported vendettas.

But the mindset of American Cold War politicians was very largely an outgrowth of a particularly homegrown dualism, a conviction of being the good guy who must get tough with the bad guy. None of this was favorable to concerted efforts to understand and compromise with "the other side". There are various ways to analyze why that mentality developed. But there it is. It kept the Cold War going and never really wanted to give it up.

It is virtually impossible to imagine what the world would be like if the huge effort of planning for nuclear war had been directed toward finding ways to rule out the possibility, by getting to know "the enemy", understanding their problems, looking for jointly satisfactory solutions. This would have been an equally, if not even more challenging enterprise. We Americans, collectively, were probably not equipped for it. The social sciences are far from able to do the job. It would take human wisdom. Wisdom cannot be quantified. A bureaucracy can produce statistical estimates, but not wisdom.

There are many glimpses of wisdom in the Johnstone Memoir, but they are fighting for life in a hostile environment.

MEMOIR OF A HUMANIST IN THE PENTAGON

by

Paul H. Johnstone

MEMOIR
OF A
HUMANIST
IN THE
PENTAGON

by

Paul H. Johnstone

FOREWORD

FROM BEHIND THE SCENES

From 1949 to 1969 I worked for Air Force Intelligence, the Joint Chiefs of Staff, and the Office of the Secretary of Defense, I helped make estimates of the military capabilities of potential enemies, I helped develop recommendations concerning targets to be attacked from the air in event of war. I helped prepare estimates of the physical damage, and of the cumulative effects of that damage upon the nation sustaining it, that might result from nuclear war.

I participated in attempts to deal with the mind-boggling problems of what our national strategies and military tactics should best be in this age of nuclear weaponry. I helped initiate, and participated in, a series of studies of how high-level command decisions were made in several incidents in which military operations took place during the nineteen sixties. These so-called "Critical Incident" studies were undertaken for the Joint Chiefs, and were based upon information available in their command center. And finally, I wrote the primary draft of one of the studies known as the Pentagon Papers.

I never made a command decision, I never determined a national policy. I doubt that anything I ever did had anything more than the most minor and remote influence upon events. My experience during those two decades of dealing first-hand with the grubby, unpublicized, and generally secret minutiae underlying national policies and actions taught me much that I would never have known otherwise. Things can look very different from behind the scenes than from the audience, often different even from the impression of the principal actors themselves. As I observe current public consideration of armaments, arms control, strategic policies and posture, it seems clear that little has really changed. The myths and obsessions and posturings are almost exactly the same. And although all of the numbers, many of the names, and some of the areas of dispute are no longer as they were, almost everything of substantial consequence seems essentially as it was ten, twenty, or thirty years ago. And that is what this is all about.

PART I

THE WORLD OF
TARGET PLANNING

Chapter One

AIR TARGETS INTELLIGENCE

In the late summer of 1949 I went to work for the Air Targets Division of the Directorate of Intelligence at the newly established Department of the Air Force. Whatever qualifications I had for intelligence work consisted mainly of three and a half years experience in economic intelligence and strategic target selection during World War II. The Directorate of Intelligence, headquartered in the Pentagon, was composed mainly of four divisions: Estimates, Targets, Requirements, and Policy. The Estimates Division was responsible for order-of-battle intelligence and appraisals of strategic intentions of potential enemies. (Order-of-battle intelligence meant information concerning the size, makeup, disposition, equipment and combat capabilities of military forces.) The Targets Division was responsible for producing the information needed by Plans and Operations (located elsewhere in the Air Force) concerning targets that might be attacked in event of war. The requirements Division was responsible for acquiring the information needed by the Estimates and Targets Divisions, I never knew much about the Policy Division, which was small and staffed mainly by very senior Colonels who seemed never to have much to do, but some of whom I was assigned to help when it came time to present budget estimates to the House of Representatives Appropriations Committee's Defense Subcommittee.

The Air Targets Division's mission was quite accurately indicated by its name: it was responsible for information about targets that might be attacked in event of war. The division was composed of several sections, and the way the work was performed is suggested by the way tasks were divided up and performed by the different sections. There was a **Physical Vulnerability Section**, staffed mainly by engineers of various specialties. Their central task was to develop formulae for estimating the damage to be expected from detonation of weapons of different types and sizes. This was an extraordinarily complicated business. First of all, potential targets ranged in nature from heavily reinforced concrete structures to human beings in the open. Weapons ranged, in those days, from the conventional high explosive and incendiary bombs of World War II vintage to limited numbers of comparatively low yield (kiloton, not megaton TNT equivalent) nuclear weapons. These latter might be airburst at varying heights above the ground with effects varying according to altitude, or surface-burst. Conventional high explosive weapons had blast effects, whose measurement was expressed in terms of "overpressure" in pounds per square inch (psi). This effect tended to follow natural physical laws of decreasing by the cube as distance from the target increased. Potential targets, and important constituent elements of targets if reasonably different from the whole, were assigned Vulnerability Numbers as a measure of their susceptibility to damage from blast. This number was accepted as a guide to the degree and type of damage to be expected from defined levels of overpressure. It was of course recognized that secondary damage from such factors as fire might occur, and in the case of some kinds of targets, even without use of incendiaries, secondary damage could exceed primary damage. This was sometimes referred to as "cannibalism" or, when damage spread to other than targeted installations, "bonus".

A major purpose of making estimates of physical vulnerability was to provide data allowing calculation of the weight of attack required to inflict a desired level of damage to a particular target. However great the uncertainties and complications might have been in developing Physical Vulnerability Numbers applicable to high explosives the problems of providing such formulae were vastly compounded as nuclear weapons gradually became the primary weapons considered for strategic bombing. One complication, known in a general way since the very first observations of damage at Hiroshima and Nagasaki, was the thermal effect. The flash that accompanied the blast was capable of igniting flammable materials even at distances beyond the range of serious blast effects. Another was the instantaneous ionizing effect upon human tissue exposed to the blast, again at considerable distances. And still later, awareness began to develop, first as a result of observation of the mid-Pacific weapons tests, of the great and lingering damage that could result from gamma radiation induced by fallout from surface bursts. The trouble with these complications was that, whereas engineering data did exist which offered some reasonable basis for rough estimates of the capacity of commonly used materials and standard structures to withstand simple forms of stress, the stress from an atomic blast was a two-way affair: first there was pressure outward from the center of the blast, then there was pressure from the opposite direction as air rushed back in to fill the vacuum. As for the thermal, ionizing, and downwind gamma radiation effects, there were practically no guidelines at all. They would be researched, and in time — much time — a lot would be learned about them, although not enough ever, so far as I know, to provide the basis for predictive measurements. So men did what men always do. They calculated what was calculable, as best they could, and generally ignored, or dismissed with mere mention by name, the factors that, however relevant and crucial, were incalculable. Or they would just make a wild guess. One problem was that, whatever the uncertainties, those utilizing the information were rarely in a position to understand its degree of reliability.

There were two other items that accompanied Physical Vulnerability Numbers in assembled target assessment material, although they were not the exclusive product of the Physical Vulnerability Section. One was called DGZ, for Desired Ground

Zero, a somewhat circuitous term used to mean the point on the ground, or the point in the air directly above the point on the ground, at which a detonated weapon was calculated to have maximum destructive effect. Weapons of different types and sizes would have a range of effects depending upon whether they were airburst and if so at what height above the ground, or surface-burst and if so whether exactly at ground level or after penetrating the surface several feet. Also, in the case of installations of any considerable area, very commonly some parts of them were much more vulnerable to damage than other parts, and some parts were much more crucial to the functioning of the whole than others. These calculations referred, of course, not merely to the structures themselves, but to their interior elements, which it was assumed, or at least hoped, were located where they were expected to be. There was another factor: potential targets were often clustered in such a way that probable total damage could be maximized by selecting a DGZ that would result in greatest cumulative damage to multiple targets.

But whether or not such a DGZ was valid depended upon the second item, the degree of accuracy with which weapons might be directed toward targets, expressed as CEP, for Circular Error Probable. CEP was regularly defined as the radius of a circle surrounding an aiming point within which 50% of the bombs would fall. Thus, for instance, a CEP of 1/2 mile meant that it could be assumed that in an average case if one bomb were aimed at the target there was a 50-50 chance it would land somewhere within 1/2 mile of the target, or out of 100 bombs so aimed, 50 would land within 1/2 mile. The common presumption was that this meant random distribution within a perfect circle. The facts were, however, that in such real data as the CEP's were based upon, distribution would most commonly fall longitudinally within an ellipse of varying length, not a circle, more misses being either short of the target or beyond it rather than to one side. Furthermore, like all averages, it was subject to significant deviation in individual cases for unforeseeable causes. The basic presumptions of accuracy came from Operations, and at least in the best case had to be derived from observed performance. But how much this might be affected by the excitement and distractions of combat conditions would of course be anyone's guess.

Nevertheless, such calculations had to be made. It was estimates of this sort along with estimates of comparative strength of opposing forces, of enemy intentions and other intangibles, that provided the foundations for estimates of required force levels, contingency war plans, and peacetime military budgets.

The Target Materials Section of the Air Targets Division performed a function considerably easier to explain. Its sole responsibility was to summarize all essential information on potential targets in a form suitable for Operations (which as time passed increasingly meant the Strategic Air Command). The end product was an almost limitless number of Target Folders, one for each potential target, world-wide. Each Target Folder was replete with charts, topographic data, aerial photos where available, summary verbal and statistical data on the nature, function, and importance of the target, plus data on possible anti-aircraft defenses and notes on identifying landmarks and clues to possible identification by radar. The charts included exact geographical coordinates and recommended DGZs (sometimes alternative DGZs). The Section developed most of its cartographic and graphic materials, but depended largely upon the rest of the division for everything else.

Information was accumulating all the time, often drastically changing earlier assessments, and as a result the target folders were constantly undergoing revisions, while being increased in number as potential targets were newly developed or newly discovered. It was an endless process. In addition, the target folders rapidly became widely used within the entire intelligence community as convenient summaries for quick reference. Collectively they became known as the Bombing Encyclopedia, and as such served as a common means of identification of practically anything that could be located on a map, anywhere in the world, by any groups or agencies concerned with intelligence, and of these there was a surprisingly large and growing number.

Each armed service had its own intelligence service, each had at least one contract organization working for it that used or contributed to military intelligence. The State Department also had an intelligence division. And in the center of things, along with the Central Intelligence Agency, was the National Security Agency where most cryptographic operations were centered.

One early problem that for a while limited the usefulness of the Bombing Encyclopedia arose from the very simple fact that the basic identification of installations was by name. The common practice was to file the folder alphabetically by name. But there were numerous potential confusions of names. Often a single installation had more than one name; often more than one installation had the same name. Sometimes names were changed. Again, an aircraft assembly plant might be filed under the name Tbilisi or Tiflis, a power plant under either Florence or Firenze, and so on. Different sources often referred to the same installation by different names; subsidiary supply depots or branches of industrial plants might carry the name of the mother installation even though a hundred miles apart. In referring to place or installation names from countries not using the Roman alphabet, any of a variety of English spellings might be resorted to.

In addition, much of the time that attention was focused on a single installation, it would he within the context of all installations of its type or capability, and for that reason some system seemed needed to facilitate rapid retrieval of summary information concerning all installations of a given category. In a sense, this did not pose a problem of any great difficulty. Someone suggested that we adapt to our purposes what was called the Standard Industrial Classification. This Standard Industrial Classification, recently developed and published by the Bureau of Labor Statistics, was in effect a system of indexing all economic and industrial goods and services in a manner logically comparable to the Library of Congress or Dewey Decimal System for indexing books. It began with a five digit code, infinitely expandable, so organized that an identifying number could be found for every conceivable product or service of an economy or a nation. Once adopted, as it quickly was, it was only a simple task to gather together all the target folders for air fields in Russia or oil refineries in Iran or coke ovens in Czechoslovakia.

Difficulties developed, however, because for a while this minor success lured some into thinking that the Bombing Encyclopedia could be used as a major source for summary analyses. Always, it seems, there are those who have faith that the names of things tell all, and this was an early era of the rapidly expanding faith in the capabilities of computers, simple though they were then by comparison with the vastly more elaborate computers developed in the next two decades. These enthusiasts felt there must be some way that the summary data expressed by the digital classification of installations could be used as an analytic tool. But there were problems. The classification was by product or service as distinct from capability to produce that product or perform that service. An installation producing one product at one time might be capable, perhaps equally capable, of producing many other products very dissimilar so far as use was concerned. Later, when attempts were made to develop mathematical models of the Soviet economy as a means of estimating Russian economic capabilities (and hence war-making capabilities), even greater difficulties were encountered. Along with the Standard Industrial Classification were elaborate statistics, based upon questions that had been specially included in the 1948 Census of Manufactures, which aimed to show the amount of all inputs and outputs of American industrial establishments that year. The intent was to include everything going into production, everything coming out: labor, capital equipment, materials of all sorts, electric power, fuels, transportation — everything. This was done on a matrix with, originally, a hundred categories (based on the Standard Industrial Classification) supposed to include everything — literally everything — with the input categories in a column on the left side, the output categories, which were exactly the same, in a line across the top, with the inputs of each category from the top entered in the space where the lines and columns intersected, and finally, in the extreme right hand column, the total product, expressed in terms of dollars, each category on the line running from the category on the left. It was an ingenious procedure, first developed by Professor Vassily Leontief of Harvard a decade or so before, and thereafter promoted and elaborated by scores of his disciples as a device for analyzing the interrelationship of parts of an economy as a whole.

Its best advocates recognized it to be still primitive, and possibly never capable of producing anything more exact than insights which should never be trusted for details until examined by other means.

But growth of the input-output matrix idea coincided with the growth of computer technology, which vastly facilitated the computations that were an inherent part of the procedure. The two growing enthusiasms nourished each other. And the enthusiasm was later to become practically irresistible.

The problems of ever making the procedure yield anything beyond helpful insights were enormous, very likely insuperable. There had to be a common denominator for inputs and outputs, and of course this was in dollars, and these fluctuated from year to year within the United States, within groups of industries, even within the most narrowly defined industries. Translating these dollar values into the currency of another country, into rubles for instance, was obviously running the risk of compounding original inaccuracies. Moreover, the categories that were manageable in number were necessarily so gross that often they were meaningless. For instance, within a 100-category matrix, one category was ceramics. And ceramics included items as diverse as sewer pipe, fine porcelains, and heat resistance components for jet engines, along with hundreds of other identifiable items, and the mix of these products within the gross categorization of ceramics varied greatly from one year to another. Thus a number representing the number of dollars worth of electric power or labor or transportation going into the production of a given dollar value of total ceramic production could hardly be safely assumed to be a constant to be depended upon from year to year in this country, let alone transposed into a model of the Soviet economy. Yet that was

the sort of thing that later was to be attempted. And neither the
enthusiasts nor the ignorant ever seemed to learn proper caution.

The rest of the Air Targets Division, with more than half
the total personnel, consisted mainly of several sections each
responsible for analyzing and summarizing intelligence on a
major industrial category or group of related categories deemed of
importance to "war potential". War potential was understood to be
the industrial base upon which capacity to wage war was believed
to depend. Categories included Aircraft, Automotive, Atomic
Energy, Electric Power, Heavy Industry, Machine Tools and Light
Engineering, Transportation, and so on. Each section was supposed
to learn everything possible about the industries assigned to it,
with emphasis on the targetable installations it comprised, the
immediacy of its relationship to military requirements, physical
details relevant to vulnerability, details of productive processes
suggesting key elements, plus other supposed criteria for judging
its vital role as a supplier of the sinews of war. This division
structure faithfully reflected the prevailing doctrine of the strategic
use of air power, and it also reflected even broader concepts of
what high policy and grand strategy should be in an age of world
wars, total wars waged by modern industrialized nations.

Finally there was a comparatively small section called the
Target Intelligence Development Section, whose loosely defined
mission it was to find means of improving the methods used to
perform the functions of the division as a whole. This was to be
done partly by studies performed within the section, partly by
conceiving and monitoring research by outside institutions with
capabilities we lacked. It was as chief of this section that I went to
work for Air Force Intelligence in 1949.

Chapter Two

AIR TARGETS DOCTRINE

Winning a war by denying a potential enemy the underlying economic or general social strength upon which actual combat capability depends is a strategy as old as the institution of organized warfare itself. In different ages and cultures and as military technologies have changed, the specific strategic means have changed. The major factors that were new in this century were the increasing dependence of military power upon a large and elaborate industrial base, and the rapid development and extension of air power. Air power made it possible to strike the enemy rear without first defeating or outflanking his defenses on the ground.

The idea that wars could he fought and won by strategic bombing was a doctrine developed during World War II before there were any nuclear weapons. The Germans had pursued a strategy of terror and general disruption, first against Poland, then against Britain. When the British mustered strength to strike back, they followed more or less the same strategy with saturation bombing of industrial and urban areas. When later we joined the British with our Liberators and Flying Fortresses, we sought basically to be selective, claiming a capability for "precision bombing", and testing a theory that somehow there must be a comparatively limited number of industrial targets that, by themselves, comprised a critically essential element of the enemy's "economic war potential". The theory was that there must be, somewhere, an Achilles tendon, a linchpin or cotter key, upon which the entire war economy depended, and whose destruction would cause the entire structure to collapse. Once this foundation was destroyed, the armed forces' ability to carry on effective resistance would be undermined. The problem was to discover that critical vulnerability, and then destroy it.

To that end, we had established in 1943 two blue ribbon, inter-service inter-agency committees, one in Washington, one in the Office of Economic Warfare at the American Embassy in London, to develop recommendations concerning which enemy installations constituted the hoped-for Achilles heel. There was a considerable amount of communication and cooperation between the two committees, but the London Advisory Bombardment Committee addressed itself primarily to Nazi Germany, the Washington group primarily to Japan.

These committees were staffed by a wide variety of engineers, economists, industrial experts of many kinds, securities analysts, academicians of various stripes, lawyers, and sundry others. All of those I had known were notably bright and enthusiastic for their task. In London there were many from the Office of Strategic Services and the Board of Economic Warfare as well as others drawn in by the Embassy for one or another specialized task or field of knowledge. The Washington group was headed by a distinguished Boston lawyer and was centered in the bowels of the military establishment. I was never a member of either committee, but was well acquainted with their work partly because several industry intelligence experts, who for a time worked in the division I then headed, served directly on the committees and even had substantial influence on bombing policies. One of these was a former Wall Street analyst named Larry Harris, who was long charged with being the BEW expert on enemy machine tool and antifriction bearing industries, and whose work contributed to the choice of targets in Germany that led to the costly raids on Schweinfurt. Another was Dr. Joseph Z.

Schneider, an industrial chemist who had been long employed by Skoda as a coke oven specialist until he escaped to Scandinavia just ahead of the Nazi occupation of Czechoslovakia, and whose Teutonic eloquence concerning the easy destructibility of coke ovens and the primary indispensability of coke and coke oven by-products probably contributed to the fact that the targets assigned for the first B-29 raids on North China and then Japan included coke ovens.

The committees had no power to decide strategy, but they made recommendations which, for a time at least, were evidently seriously considered if not always followed out completely. Those of us who were privy to the activity used to joke that every industry expert ended up recommending the industry he was specialized in as the Achilles heel. We joked this way, but I do not remember that during the war we ever questioned the theory. We believed it, but reasoned, as evidence mounted that German production of particular items showed no sign of slackening despite repeated attacks on production facilities, that damage had been overestimated, or our information on facilities had been incomplete, or some such. At one time or another a dozen industrial categories were decided upon as the Achilles heel, only to be abandoned as a target in favor of some other category when the desired crippling effects did not follow. Among these chosen target systems were aircraft engines, aircraft assembly, machine tools anti-friction bearings, petroleum refineries and synthetic fuels, electric power and railroad marshaling yards. In the case of Germany we ended up bombing so many different target systems that the final effect was hardly distinguishable from what it would have been had we followed the British theory of saturation bombing. Near the end, the notion of the Achilles-heel sort of industrial vulnerability was abandoned by commanders in the field in favor of such holocausts as Leipzig was subjected to. In the case of Japan, that grim disciple of strategic bombardment, Curt Lemay, did not fool around long with selective target systems once he had enough B-29s and bases close enough to Japan to use them. Area bombing was easier and less costly because targets were bigger and incendiaries more destructive than high explosives used alone. (It appears generally forgotten now that in 1943 or 1944 some heretics, who must have had high echelon support to do it, experimented with a replica of a typical Japanese urban area to determine its vulnerability to fire bombs.) And of course we all remember Hiroshima and Nagasaki.

But if by the end of the war we had gone over in practice to area bombing and general destruction with its resultant terror and presumptive demoralizing effect, the theory of selective bombing retained advocates. Undeniably at least some selectivity was called for. Some areas were larger, more populous, more densely packed with industrial capital, more readily destroyed than other areas. None could deny that some industries were of more immediate and critical importance to combat capability than others. (Yet I do remember that one Colonel Bebby of the British Board of Economic Warfare was often quoted by his colleagues to the effect that it was just as disruptive to the Nazis to destroy £.100 worth of overcoats as £100 worth of machine guns because in either case productive resources currently devoted to producing essential war supplies would have to be diverted to replacement of what had been destroyed.) This theory was contradicted after the war by evidence that the Nazi economy had not been so strained, that even during 1944, aircraft production in Germany had increased greatly despite the attacks upon aircraft engine and aircraft assembly plants throughout 1943-44. But on the other hand it was later disclosed that shortage of fuel in 1944 curtailed the use of Nazi combat planes and attacks on refineries and synthetic fuels had perhaps contributed. Also, the Nazi war production chief, Albert Speer, related after the war that he had been deeply concerned when he realized that electric power facilities were being systematically attacked, fearing this would lead to general industrial paralysis and he was immensely relieved when attacks on power plants dwindled just before a critical stage might have been reached and other targets were attacked instead.

So far as strategic doctrine was concerned, the World War II experience did not resolve the issue. A variety of opinions existed within the Air Force and elsewhere. The issue was considered of such importance that immediately after the war, and practically as soon as we could get observers into bombed areas, the very ambitious United States Strategic Bombing Survey was initiated. The USSBS, pronounced "uzzbuzz", resulted in many shelves of monographs that sought to explore every conceivable aspect of strategic bombing, and to a great many, uzzbuzz became a sort of bible. Attempts were made to correlate bomb tonnages dropped with damage done to targets of many kinds (very little correlation was found); to compare estimates of damage made during and immediately after a bombing operation with what appeared to have been the damage when investigators could study the site at more leisure and closer at hand. As might be expected, current estimates of damage were found to have been greatly exaggerated in many cases as far as reduction of production was concerned. Correlations were attempted between actual damage done and effect on production, but this was complicated by problems of defining extent of damage.

Industrial experts of many kinds studied damaged industries, psychologists and political scientists studied what seemed to have been effects upon morale, and so on and on. Much was learned, many findings seemed contradictory, and the most important questions were often those that remained most in doubt, or that fostered the greatest doubts of our ability really to understand the nature of what we were attempting to do.

Not only did current wartime estimate of effects turn out in later examination to have been in many cases in gross error, the various studies of effects upon morale produced almost as many estimates as there were experts studying the problem. However, there was fairly broad agreement that lesser amounts of casualties and damage frequently resulted, at least for a time, in strengthening popular will to resist rather than weakening it. Generally speaking, bombing of German industries producing military end products had had no significant effect upon Nazi military capability until very late in the war when combat capabilities were collapsing for a variety of reasons. By utilizing previously unused productive resources we had not considered, by resorting to many expedients and substitutions we had not anticipated, they had actually increased production of the essential items we sought to deny them. Until the later states of the war, the Nazi economy contained capacities not fully utilized. Contrary to the British assumptions, which we at least partially subscribed to, the Nazi economy had not been strained to the utmost. Accordingly, when military demands were given still higher priority in the later states of the war, an innovative resilience resulted in productive capabilities we had not anticipated, partly because we had assumed the historical productive patterns that we could calculate from past practice and such common sources as the German *Statistisches Jahrbuch* were applicable in extraordinary wartime circumstances. One small example I recall was the case of the anti-friction bearings in one of the most effective of all Nazi weapons, the 88 mm artillery piece. Faced with a shortage of such bearings, resulting in part from our bombing, the Germans reduced the number of them in the gun by about 90% with no appreciable loss of efficiency of this dreaded weapon.

In the many varied studies of effects of bombing on morale — which was a subject of increasing interest as the prospect of very extensive civilian casualties in a nuclear war became a major concern — anything resembling conclusions had to be qualified, for obvious reasons, and the studies served mainly to suggest what factors should be considered in varying circumstances. It was clear enough that no straight-line relationship had been evident between amount of damage or numbers of casualties and morale. Examined with appropriate skepticism, the studies were informative at least in the sense that they refuted some prevailing myths. But they were undertaken, evidently with some expectation of providing answers to questions and their principal accomplishment was perhaps to suggest the almost limitless complexity of the subject. Some studies sought to appear scientific by giving numbers to factors that, once examined, were clearly not defined precisely enough to provide a basis for quantification (the same pressure to ape the physical sciences that for half a century now has propelled so much social science into the practice of counting what has not been defined in countable units in order to provide statistical rather than verbal responses). How could anyone define, and measure, the almost limitless variable circumstances that, demonstrably, altered the behavior of human beings, human beings of diverse backgrounds both individual and cultural, different prior expectations and training, when subjected to the same amount of deprivation or injury or threat? And how measure the damage or threat? And how distinguish between verbal responses to questionnaires and actual behavior? And how define morale in terms applicable for transfer from one people in one situation to other peoples in other situations? Some of the studies pretended to do these things, but who was being fooled?

There is little doubt that USSBS, studied in its entirety, amounted to an almost complete repudiation of any claims to validity of the Air Force doctrine of air strategy. Much has been written about it since, even by many of those who supervised parts of the study, including such as John Kenneth Galbraith, its principal director. It is clear that the overwhelming judgment of all those with a comprehensive view was that the costs and sacrifices devoted to strategic bombing in World War II might have been much more effective if expended on other, more direct goals and strategies. But somehow the lesson was not learned by those who asked for the study so that they might learn from it. Doctrine was more convincing than evidence. And it is hardly unfair to say that USSBS was often used — parts of it — to prove the very things that in effect it disproved. Like the Devil quoting scripture. It took the delayed impact of realizing the vastly greater devastation assured by nuclear stockpiles for World War II strategic bombing doctrine to be gradually abandoned. But that was slow in coming, and one may wonder if later strategies were any more realistic.

Despite the skepticism of many of us about much of the content of USSBS, it contained the best source of information about what happened when rear areas had been heavily bombed, and for that reason it remained one of the two most widely accepted gospels of the New Testament of strategic bombing.

The other gospel was the strategic target selection discipline developed during World War II by the Advisory Bombardment Committee. Again there were many among us who held serious reservations, but there seemed to be no alternative, though major qualifications began to seem necessary as awareness grew of the new considerations required as we learned more about the effects of nuclear weapons.

It was a logically attractive procedure I had admired during the war, and that had been taken over, unreservedly, by Air Force Intelligence in the period following the war. By this procedure, every industry or resource of a potential enemy that appeared to have any importance in providing materiel important to military operations was examined, as critically and minutely as available information allowed, with particular attention to a series of carefully worked out criteria. Major factors thus examined were: *Importance* to combat capability, with emphasis on *indispensability* to combat capability and *immediacy* in the sense that denial would result in immediate rather than long term or delayed effect; *Substitutability* and *Recuperability*, meaning whether effects of loss could be avoided by substitution or altered practice, or mitigated by rapid repair; *Location*, meaning simply could the target be reached with available weapons; *Vulnerability*, meaning susceptibility to damage by air attack. There were of course many aspects of these major factors. For instance, if a secondary target were located close enough to a primary target to suggest it would sustain probable damage if the primary target were attacked, this added to the attractiveness of the primary target by the promise of what we called "bonus damage". As weapons became larger and more plentiful, this became an ever larger and broader consideration, including, as just one example, skilled labor.

However logical, the procedure clearly had not always worked out as expected. That could be explained away as the result of faulty or incomplete information. But if one looks at ideas as the product of circumstances, it seems that all this may be viewed as an application of the doctrine of "economic war potential", a strategic concept that was in especially high favor in that era among those who thought about such things. It seems to have been a natural consequence of protracted wars between entire nations in arms, with armed forces dependent for effectiveness upon extravagant expenditure of materiel. It is customary to trace the nation-in-arms phenomenon to the wars of the French Revolution, and indeed one might go to extremes and find cases of totalitarian wars between ancient peoples and tribal conflicts of almost any age. But something rather new developed during World War I when the most economically and technologically developed nations fought a war of attrition over an extended period in which much or most of the nation not actually engaged in combat was mobilized to provide the continuous logistic support upon which the military forces were absolutely dependent. Defeating an enemy in time of war by destroying economic war potential was the military application of the concept. Preventing renewal of aggression by a defeated enemy, after a war had been won, by preventing development of a large economic war potential, was its political application. The Treaties of Versailles at the end of World War I had sought to prevent renewal of German aggression by forbidding rearmament, but that had not worked, we thought, because we had not enforced the ban on rearmament by depriving Germany of the basic economic capacity to rearm (economic war potential), an oversight that permitted Hitler to rearm Germany very rapidly when, later, he dared defy the disarmament provisions of the treaties.

In World War II we sought to destroy the economic war potential of Nazi Germany by strategic bombing, but while that effort had contributed to the defeat of the Nazis, it was still highly debatable how much it had contributed, and even whether that much effort might have been more advantageously expended otherwise. The case of Japan raised different and perhaps even more compelling questions concerning the effectiveness of strategic bombing. Navy critics argued that the Japanese war economy was disrupted more by the strangulating effects of blockade than by destruction of production facilities; and so far as identification of the cause of Japan's surrender was an issue, on the one hand it was known that the Japanese had on rational grounds decided at high levels, early in 1944, that they could not win the war and should seek the earliest opportunity to end the war and thereby cut their losses. On the other hand, their precipitate surrender in August 1945 appeared induced more by the indiscriminate destruction and terror from the firebombing followed by Hiroshima and Nagasaki than by any problem of war materiel.

Economic War Potential Doctrine Applied to Occupation Policies

Regardless of past experience, the prepossessions of the age compelled us to give prime attention to "economic war potential". Thus our earliest post-war plans for our defeated enemies focused upon depriving them for the foreseeable future of the economic base needed to produce modern weapons. From the beginning of active occupation planning for Germany and Japan, in what became known as the Morgenthau Plan for Germany and its counterpart for Japan, the primary emphasis was upon economic control measures that would end up by insuring that these aggressor nations would in the future lack the economic war potential upon which military power for future aggressions would have to be based. The methods employed in trying to determine what key industries should be controlled, or prohibited entirely, were very similar to the methods of analysis employed by the ABC during the war, and by those of us doing target analysis following the war. This I knew very well because I had lived in the very midst of that planning from mid-December 1944 to late summer, after the Japanese surrender in August.

I had spent most of the year 1944 in India and Ceylon, where I was engaged in economic intelligence work as chief of the Joint Intelligence Collection Agency (JICA) for the American command of the China-Burma-India (CBI) theater, and as American representative for economic intelligence to the British Army of India and to the Southeast Asia Command (SEAC) from mid-summer on. When I rotated from this job to my job back in Washington, where I was chief of the Far East Enemy Division of the Foreign Economic Administration (which had originated as the Board of Economic Warfare), I found that whereas the entire work of the division had previously been devoted to supplying intelligence for military operations and plans, the greatest demand now was for information for the use of our occupation forces once the war was ended. For almost every definable industry or economic enterprise, indeed for almost every definable aspect of society, studies were wanted which would provide both the facts of the existing order and the policy guidelines concerning how goods and resources and facilities and municipalities should be administered.

Midway during my service in the Far East the FEA had undergone a vast reorganization, part of it reflecting the changing concerns that progress in the war had led to. My new boss, whom I had never seen before, was Henry Fowler, known then to all who knew him not as Henry but as "Joe", who was later to become Secretary of the Treasury under President Lyndon Johnson. His boss, in turn, was Leo T. Crowley, a conservative middle western utilities executive who had previously been head of the Federal Deposit Insurance Corporation, and was shifted by President Roosevelt to the reorganized Federal Economic Administration to heal a rift that had developed between Milo Perkins, a liberal New Dealer Texan, and Jesse Jones, a highly conservative Texan who headed the Reconstruction Finance Corporation, and organization called upon to finance some of the overseas purchases of strategic commodities such as rubber, quinine, bauxite and several alloying metals. Vice President Henry Wallace had been Chairman of the original Board of Economic Warfare, and he had brought Milo Perkins in from the Department of Agriculture to be the active administrator. Perkins was an ebullient hell-for-leather type who in hindsight it seems was destined surely to clash with Jones. BEW operations included not only intelligence, but procurement of materials critically important to the war effort that were available abroad, and also a lesser but more debatable function, preclusive purchasing (such as trying to buy up the Swedish output of bearings to prevent the Nazis from getting them). What the merits of the case were I'm in no position to judge. Most of my informants were among those very loyal to Perkins and antagonistic to Jones (and to Crowley as well). They summarized their judgment of the dispute by citing a case — whether true or not I do not know — that when Jones was informed that a great fire had destroyed a warehouse in which natural rubber had been stored, rubber being one of the vital items in very short supply, Jones' response was, "So what, it's fully insured."

Immediately upon my return to the States to take over the Far East Enemy Division, I was hailed into Fowler's office to be told how things had changed and how we were to operate from there on out. Briefly the message was that the military intelligence services, especially the Special Branch of Army Intelligence and the ONR, had developed such a high level of competence that they no longer needed much help from civilian agencies, but that the services were urgently in need of manuals and guides that would serve them as they established military government in territories they would occupy as our forces drove the enemy back. Military government officers were already being trained, by the hundreds, at the University of Virginia and elsewhere, for their future tasks in conquered enemy territory, and texts were needed for their immediate instruction as well as manuals to be followed once they took over from the Military Police. The counterpart to my division, the European Enemy Division, was already heavily engaged in such activities for Germany and Italy. Fowler and Crowley were in constant touch with Treasury, which clearly implied that Treasury was the source of policy guidance. General policy was already decided, or at least assumed. Germany's economic war potential was to be so reduced that Germany would never again be capable of military aggression, and there would be a large and continuing job of economic policing long after hostilities were ended. I was asked to sit in on major meetings on Germany to see how things were handled on that end, and was to accept the principles and policies I learned from those meetings as guidance on how things were to be handled for Japan.

I accepted all this without any serious question at first. Much of what we were to do in the future followed the lines of what we had done in the past. Just which industrial and economic capacities did Japan need for her war effort? Just how much annual steel production did Japan need as a minimum requisite to sustain her *civilian* economy? Where were there actual or potential bottlenecks where industrial output might be regulated or military production prevented? I attended meetings almost constantly in Fowler's office, most of them attended by representatives from Treasury as well as people from the European Enemy Division. Some meetings were attended by engineers and executives from private American firms interested in or with special knowledge of German industrial processes. Meanwhile I accepted many requests for studies concerning Japan to be made by experts in my division. The story is too long to recount fully here, but the deeper I got into the substance beneath the generalities, the more I found myself raising what seemed unanswerable questions about the whole process. We were to suggest occupation programs that would encourage a truly democratic government in Japan, while at the same time seeing to it that the Japanese level of living was not higher than that of the neighboring lands she had conquered and occupied. This of course meant that the Japanese would have to lower their living standards considerably, while embracing a new democracy. We were asked what should be done with the Zaibatsu, with rural land tenure, with municipal governments, police, even the Emperor. It was obvious enough that much or even most of the material we were being asked to provide amounted to guidance on the execution of political policy, but there was no explicit guidance available anywhere as to what the political policy was. Finally, some time in May or June of 1945, I tried to find out who, in either the White House or the State Department, was to be looked to for authority concerning occupation policy for Japan, and found there was nobody, really.

There was just one man in State who was considered to have any responsibility for occupation policies in Japan, a man recently transferred to State from his spot as a Japanese expert for OSS. All he could do was refer me to SWNCC — the State-War-Navy Coordinating Committee. SWNCC was housed in the Pentagon, and was the source of many or most of the requests we were receiving for occupation manuals. Theoretically there was State Department participation, but SWNCC was responsive to the Joint Chiefs of Staff, and looked upon their task as military — not political. Military occupation was just something the military did between the time combat ended in an area and the function of government was turned over to civilian authority. Whatever you did during this interval had no lasting political significance, except, in this case, the significance of the Morgenthau Plan, which had somehow become national policy during the last ailing days of Roosevelt and the near interregnum of Truman's first months as President. There simply was never any serious and informed consideration at high levels in Washington of what our long-term goals should be, or of how our early occupation policies might influence the later course of events — no consideration, that is, except in the little clique in Treasury that settled on the Morgenthau Plan, and in the absence of concern or leadership from either the White House or State, managed somehow to make it the initial occupation policy of the United States.

It was this SWNCC group that was requesting occupation manuals on every conceivable aspect of occupation. It seemed abundantly clear that as you wrote occupation manuals you were expressing the operational aspects of occupation *policy*, but there was no overall guide to occupation policy — just the Morgenthau Plan, which of course never lasted long anywhere. But such were our instructions. And I remember sitting in on the final drafting, sometime in March, of the basic directive for the occupation of Germany. Those drafting the final document, in Joe Fowler's office, were a small group from our Office of Foreign Economic Administration, and representatives from Treasury. No one from State, no one from the White House. But out it went. (Later there was a flurry about this, because these initial policies greatly facilitated the Soviet policy of stripping Germany of all conceivable industrial equipment, and Harry Dexter White and others in Treasury who were involved were suspected of Communist affiliation. I was never generally inclined to sympathize with such allegations, but I always believed there was substance to these, mainly because two or three of those who worked most assiduously for Fowler on all this were widely reputed to be extreme left-wingers. As for Fowler, I think his only interest was in policies that would assure the greatest jurisdiction for the agency he headed.)

I spent many hours in conference with the senior people in my division examining the problem of applying the Morgenthau Plan to Japan, and most of them shared my deep misgivings. I tried to induce Fowler to reconsider the problem, but he was fully absorbed with Germany, intent on getting a large jurisdiction in post-conflict affairs, and so impatient with any questioning that he would not listen. His only advice amounted to saying that the military government asked for these studies, we were following the same policies we had laid out for Germany, and that was that. At a later juncture I wrote him a long, carefully considered memo wherein I argued that our punitive economic policies were unnecessary, self-defeating, and even impossible to administer. Above all they were aimed entirely in the wrong direction, because with the territorial and other losses it was already assured Japan would sustain, the power in the Far East we should worry about in the future was not that of Japan, but of China and Russia. I do not know whether Fowler even read that memo. He was being the big shot, too busy and ambitious to stop and think. I later left that job in protest, which was a high water mark of innocent futility, I suppose. In practice, the Morgenthau Plan never really got off the ground in Japan, nor even in Germany, so utterly impossible it was in reality. Yet those in high positions who espoused it without question moved on to greater glory.

Somehow this concept of economic war potential was commonly associated in those days with the notion that some nations are inherently aggressors, while others, also inherently, are peace-loving. Even the prestigious and intellectually respectable Brookings Institution published, in 1944, a slender book entitled *The Control of Germany and Japan* written by Brookings president Harold G. Moulton and an equally distinguished French co-author, Louis Marlio, which in all seriousness addressed itself to the problem of preventing resumption of aggression by those inherently war-loving nations after they had been defeated. The book began with a chapter entitled "Some Lessons of Experience" which sought to put the problem in historical context by reviewing the failure of the Versailles treaty to prevent Germany from rearming and resuming her inherent warlike ways. Despite appropriate skepticism concerning the effectiveness of preventing renewed aggression by economic controls, there was never a hint that the future might bring changes in political alignments. In the very effort to put the subject into historical perspective, the authors fell into the trap of projecting current preoccupations into the indefinite future. Implicitly throughout the book, and explicitly in Dr. Moulton's summary chapter on "Alternative United States Policies", the only potential future enemies considered were Germany and Japan. This view was set forth flatly, in a lame attempt at historicity, following a birds-eye squint at the rise of Germany and Japan as world powers coincident with the relative decline of the French army and the British navy as keepers of the peace, in these words:

> In the present century two developments have
> completely altered the picture. The first is the rise
> of two volcanic nations, one in Europe and one in
> Asia, with clear aspirations for world domination
> and backed by the manpower, industrial
> resources and military organization to bring these
> aspirations within the realm of reality.

In fairness to Dr. Moulton it must be said that he was merely reflecting the attitudes of all but a very few in our western world. We in the United States have never seemed capable, officially at least, of the long forward view. Almost always we see current issues as the dominant issues for all time to come, and current alignments of friends and foes as eternal alignments.

Current obsessions dominate, and those who, knowing the transiency of so many political passions, question them, are either ignored or slandered as fools, even traitors. Thus those who questioned the Draconian aspects of the Morgenthau Plan for Germany and its extended application to Japan were frequently answered with the accusatory question, "Oh, so you want a soft peace!" And those who suggested that instead of committing the United States irrevocably to either side in the civil war in China, we "let the dust settle" before any such commitment, or who were so bold as to suggest that Chinese Communists, once in power, might not forever remain merely part of a completely monolithic structure dominated by Moscow, were either driven into obscurity or hounded from office. Instead of a really rational foreign policy with a long forward view of where our national interests lay, we have had an anti-Communist obsession that has led us to oppose, and therefore make enemies of, anti-colonial, nationalistic revolutionary movements in all parts of the world that, had we not opposed them (often by lending support and tying our fortunes to the most oppressive, despotic and generally unsavory regimes, such as those of Trujillo in the Dominican Republic, Batista in Cuba, and Shah Reza Pahlavi in Iran), could readily have been not our enemies but our friends.

I once asked Paul Nitze, who had long experience in the Policy Planning group in State, for a time as its chief, why that group had not attempted truly long-term studies to serve as guides to current policies, and Paul replied that it seemed a good idea but they had always been too busy putting out fires for any such luxury.

Some Problems and Methods

Most people know very well that the secondary definition of intelligence is, as one dictionary puts it, "the gathering of secret information, as for police or military purposes". And if they follow current events, whether in time of peace or cold war or war, they are informed, generally with never so much as a blink, what potential enemy strengths and intentions are, often down to fine detail. The public forms opinions of national security, prospects of war or peace, of victory or defeat, on the basis of such disclosures. The Congress and the Executive frame budgets and policies on the basis of what intelligence organizations tell them, which of course is generally more detailed than the information openly available.

I believe that, to anyone who has been deeply immersed in it and then has had the privilege of viewing it with some measure of detachment, military intelligence must seem a world of flickering light, dark shadows, mood music and whispered rumors half heard against trumpeted accompaniment proclaiming dire threats that imperil us from outer darkness. Shapes are partly perceived at best, most commonly merely implied, often not seen at all, and often what you think you see is really not there at all. There are always some things you know you know, but you never know how many things there are that you have no evidence even to suspect. You do not know how much of what you see is deliberately staged to mislead you.

What is seldom realized is that there is always a dominant mood that determines, more than the sharpest senses or the most acute reasoning could do, what you decide is out there and what is going on. Like all the world and all experience, it is kaleidoscopic, and the figures and designs you make out of the bits and pieces that flit before your eyes are mainly what you thought you'd see before you looked.

Always of course there are the true believers. The images immediately before their eyes are God's own truth. It's a matter of right or wrong, bright sunlight or utter darkness. Then there are those not fully convinced nor deeply caring, who find it least troublesome to see what others say they see. Like herded sheep they may once in a while say "baa", but though they may distrust the direction they are driven in, they feel reassured following the path forced on them by the pressure of the bodies next to them.

That is the way it used to be, in the fifties and sixties, and I know no reason to believe the world of intelligence is in essence any different in the eighties. Most of the specifics of military intelligence have no doubt changed in the last quarter century. But the fundamental process, which involves drawing inferences from evidence that is always incomplete, and characteristically ambiguous, must be the same; and that human element — the inescapable element of hypothesis — must remain the determining factor. It really could not be otherwise. (Though the small minds content with what they know would probably deny it, this as a generality is true even of the physical sciences, as I believe the logicians of science would confirm.) But it is important to see how it works, because only then can one appreciate the nature of the gamble when a decision is based on intelligence estimates.

There are always certain major sources of military intelligence. There is the open literature, ranging from encyclopedias, scholarly and scientific and special publications to periodicals of every kind. There are the reports of foreign service and regular intelligence operatives stationed abroad, some open, some secret, and the observations of travellers abroad, especially those who have served in some technical capacity in enterprises of particular concern. And there is a very considerable world of communications and electronic surveillance intelligence, dubbed Commint and Elint. Elint was comparatively new and unsophisticated in the early fifties, and obviously has developed, in the years since, far beyond anything we even dreamed about in those days. Our preoccupation in target intelligence with economic war potential led us of course to give Soviet armaments industries highest priority in our considerations, and for these we had a major source of information that was unique. This was the intelligence files on Russia captured from the Germans at the end of World War II. These files consisted mainly, so far as we were concerned, of aerial photographs taken from German reconnaissance planes between 1941 and 1943, along with the photo interpretation provided by German intelligence, plus other associated textual information summarizing what the German Oberkommando Ost saw fit to record concerning installations so photographed. Obviously this material was out of date, but our knowledge of Russia generally was so scanty at that time that this was the best we had as a basis to work on, and our own dossiers – target folders – on Russian industrial installations in a great many cases were built upon that German photo recce,[1] as we called it. The problem was to bring it up to date and correct it when necessary with our own current intelligence.

The Foreign Broadcast Information Service (FBIS) monitored open broadcasts on a worldwide basis and published daily, weekly and monthly summaries and translations of items considered significant to the agencies it served. The National Security Agency (NSA), which was the national center for both cryptographic intelligence and the highest levels of encrypted message traffic, monitored and wherever possible decoded the message traffic of other countries judged important enough to be worth the effort. The NSA material was generally useful and often quite revealing. But clearances for it were so restricted that few analysts had access to it. Many were not even aware of it, and there were cases where analysts labored diligently but fruitlessly for months in complete ignorance of NSA data that were unmistakably essential to an understanding of the problem they were struggling with. The NSA had small analytical units following subjects of obvious importance, on which they would produce reports from time to time. But these reports, based mainly on the decoded messages, were generally accurate so far as discrete facts were concerned, but often those discrete facts might reasonably be interpreted in a great many ways, and the reports based on them suffered from lack of the sort of background to be found only in less secret sources.

We had another major source, in the form of a unit operating under the jurisdiction of the Library of Congress, that was engaged solely in abstracting and translating material found in Russian publications. The staff of that unit was composed mainly of Russia émigrés, none of whom had any security clearances, and it was plainly impossible to devise statements of "intelligence requirements" that would be an effective guide to the information we were seeking without revealing information or interests that security regulations forbade us to import to anyone who lacked proper clearances.

Possession of a key item of intelligence by some element of the intelligence community does not by any means assure its effective use. The significance of each bit commonly depends upon its relationship to some other bit. The meaning of the two in combination is sometimes evident only in respect to concerns or purposes that are by no means obvious. One result of this is that it is virtually impossible for those who try to put together and analyze intelligence for its meaning to describe adequately, to those collecting information, just what items of information they need. The result all too often, at the using end, is that the information available in the system never reaches those who might act upon it, or reaches them but is not acted upon because its significance is not understood because other bits of information, necessary to its full understanding, had not been grasped. The most famous example of this was United States failure to understand and act upon the clear-cut fragments of intelligence that, properly understood, would have completely eliminated the element of surprise in the Japanese attack on Pearl Harbor. Less well known is the fact that in 1944 our intelligence knew, by decoding the Japanese diplomatic communications, that the Japanese government realized it could not win the war, was seeking a way to cut losses, and had its delegation in Moscow actively seeking Soviet cooperation in finding a way to end the Pacific war. We also knew that the Russians never advised us of these activities. Had we put these facts together in 1945 at highest levels, it should have suggested considerably different policies with respect to both our Russian allies and our Japanese enemies as hostilities approached an end.

In a typical target system analysis as we operated in the early 1950s, an intelligence analyst would have responsibility for collating and analyzing all intelligence on some particular subject, commonly some category of industry or even, in a few cases, a single industrial complex, as, for instance, the aircraft assembly plant in Tiflis and associate installations. The centerpiece of the intelligence would be the German wartime photography. Photo interpretation would indicate the various functional areas of the installation and the square footage of each. The square footage was a dependable number, the definition of functional areas ranged from probable to dependable, on the basis of photo interpretation, which had been developed into a minor art during World War II. This was brought more or less up to date, and fleshed out by all the other intelligence we could get. We were interested, of course, in current levels and types of activity because the facility might well have been altered, its effort channeled into production of other items. Open sources frequently revealed whether or not major rebuilding or conversion had taken place. Open communications between governmental agencies and with or between the managements of specific enterprises often revealed much about the general nature of the relationships between various installations, and the level of priority accorded the installation under scrutiny. Very commonly all this might disclose, for instance, that the Tiflis plant was indeed still assembling military aircraft, but even so we could not be sure to what degree it was almost purely an assembly plant or to what extent it manufactured some of the components of the final product. Nor could we be sure how much of the total capacity of that plant might be devoted to the production, say, of automotive parts or bicycles, or agricultural machinery. Neither could we be sure of the level of assembly line technology being used, nor did we often know how log the plant had been producing the particular product we believed it was currently concentrating on.

These were no minor deficiencies, because most light engineering plants are capable of varying their product mix a great deal from year to year, and commonly do so to respond to fluctuations in demand. Furthermore, the productivity of an establishment producing a highly complicated final assembly such as an aircraft, as measured by the number of finished units turned out, varies enormously according to the proportion of the final product provided by other plants in the form of sub-assemblies, according to the length of time it has been gaining experience in production of that item, and of course depending on many other variables, such as the assembly line techniques being used, whether retrofits and updating of models (a very important factor in products undergoing almost constant alterations, as military aircraft almost always were) were being done at this particular plant or elsewhere. Such at least are the major variable factors I remember.

In the face of all these uncertainties, it was our job to produce the estimates of the number of aircraft that plant was producing. These estimates were required because they were part of the foundation of final judgments as to how important that particular plant was to the Russians, and how many aircraft the Russians were producing, and therefore how much of a threat the Russians might be if worse came to worst.

The process of making these estimates consisted, in its crucial phase, of calculating the number of pounds of finished aircraft per thousand square feet of productive floor space, then dividing the total weight of production as thus estimated by the estimated weight of the particular model of aircraft we believed the plant was assembling. In a way this was not as far-fetched as it might seem, for at least in a very generalized way it reflected widely accepted practice in industrial engineering. It was commonplace to figure productive capacity in terms of the weight of finished product against productive floor space. Even though it was obvious that this ratio might vary widely among light engineering products of strikingly different nature, there had to be some rule of thumb and we lacked anything better. Above all, we had elaborate records of our own World War II experience in aircraft production in which assembly of finished aircraft was recorded as a function of the productive area allotted to it. We had this data for every American plant, collected and published, if my memory serves, by the War Production Board, and for a few British plants. Even in our own experience, correlation of production to plant area was far from constituting a dependable index, and extrapolation to Russia obviously involved introducing still other potential sources of significant error. But again, there was nothing immediately at hand that was any better, and those who made high policy decisions had to have summary answers. They had many other factors to take into consideration and could not afford the time to consider the details we worried about. It was customary, of course, to express estimates of this sort in highly qualified language. Nevertheless, the higher the echelon of decision, the more naked of qualification the estimate became. I know for a fact that many of the wiser, more experienced individuals at high echelons of decision were characteristically skeptical of most such intelligence estimates, and upon occasion that element of skepticism colored their judgments. But it was also clear that just as we, at the level of the most basic details of information, often had to settle for what we knew were hardly better than mere guesses that conceivably could be grossly misleading, they in their more important posts likewise felt forced by circumstance to act on the basis of information they had no more confidence in than we in ours. But so far as I know, those high officials making great decisions on these matters never publicized the lack of a really solid basis in fact for the decisions we were making.

We did of course take what steps we could to reduce the margins of possible error. We tried to get some idea of how an application to Russian plants under study of what the experts called "the learning curve" might affect our estimates. In principle the learning curve was very simple: a factory beginning production of almost any new product, especially a highly complicated product comprised of many parts and subassemblies, produced very slowly at first and reached full capacity production only after a significant period of learning. This factor had been studied and analyzed by industrial engineers and in the records of our own wartime production there was a great deal of statistical data exemplifying our own experience with getting new factories into full production and getting already established factories into production of articles they had not produced before. However simple the principle, however, close scrutiny of what the statistical data revealed taught us mainly that, in practice, its application in any particular case could be very misleading unless a great deal more was known about the immediate and possibly peculiar circumstances of the case than we could hope to know about many Russian installations. For instance, in our American plants in World War II, the learning curve was found to vary according to the efficiency of suppliers of contracted subassemblies, differences in quality control practices, and the extent to which model changes interrupted what might have been, otherwise, a comparatively smooth and rapid learning curve.

One outstanding example was the record of Liberator bomber production at the Willow Run plant in Ypsilanti, Michigan. Production there was at very nearly peak level from the very beginning, at rates unattained by any other plant producing Liberators, and continued rather uniformly at that level despite model alterations that ordinarily would have caused significant fluctuations in output. Looking into this we found that, although the Willow Run records said nothing about it, the assembly line there had not been put into operation until after Liberators had been in production in other plants long enough to have assembly line kinks ironed out and, above all, they continued turning out the basic model, unchanged, after design alterations were in order, and flew the basic Liberators to other plants for alteration, rather than hold up Willow Run production lines.

As for the validity of extrapolating American or other Western experience to Russian practices, we thought for a while we might have a clue when we got hold of industrial planning manuals issued by Soviet ministries containing procedures and standards Soviet industrial managers were expected to observe. That these included information that would throw light on our problems was evident enough. But there was a problem in that the information was there in such minutiae of detail that it was meaningful only in the context of relevant engineering practices, and Russian engineering practices differed from those we were accustomed to in many respects. Somehow, however, we unearthed a *bona fide* Russian émigré who was an industrial engineer with several years of experience in Russian aircraft plants before his plant had been overrun by the Nazi invasion. Along with others uprooted by the war, he escaped to the West, along with a Ukrainian wife he had met during their search for a new life. We were assured that he was truly a refugee, and very probably not a Russian spy, but we could not get a clearance for him, and therefore could not reveal to him the classified information needed to make the most of his combined talents. Nevertheless we did our best to exploit his knowledge, by placing a contract with the University of North Carolina where he had settled. We turned over to the University, which assumed immediate responsibility for directing the research, our copies of the voluminous industrial planning manuals, and tried to convey the highly particular bits of information we hoped he could glean from them. We were confident that somewhere within those thousands of pages of official guidance there must be answers to the many questions that confronted us when we sought to make sense, in our terms, of the fragments of convincingly hard facts we had concerning the Soviet industries we were trying to measure. But although for about two years I made periodic trips to Chapel Hill, always with one or another analyst specialized in some specific industry or industrial installation, and always with laboriously worked out lists of particular questions we hoped to answer, I cannot remember that we ever had much success. It seemed the information in the manuals was characteristically geared to ways of doing things so different from the American practice that inescapably formed the basis of our own thinking that the analogies on which we based estimates were either of doubtful validity or plainly mistaken. We felt that had we been able to turn over everything we knew, or thought we knew, to our Russian engineer, he could have made sense out of many things that baffled us. But most of the critical details were of a highly secret security classification, and it was impossible at that time to convince our security people to obtain any clearances for him.

As best I now remember, the main thing I learned from all this was that our Russian conformed to the Russian stereotype I had long had in mind. He was unrestrainedly voluble and exuberant in his eagerness to please, excitable, unquestionably bright through his heavy accent, and above all slightly frightening as he drove us around winding roads at breakneck speed in an over-age car he had picked up to celebrate American freedom and luxury, meanwhile talking at the top of his voice to whoever was in the back seat and trying always to face the person he was talking to. His wife had much of the restraint he lacked. She was sturdily built to perform the hard physical labor I supposed Ukrainian women were obliged to perform, and dished out, in their apartment, an abundance of dishes featuring farina, carrots, potatoes and cabbage that did nothing to enhance my impressions of Russian cuisine.

About the time the Korean War was a year old, we began to get captured items of Soviet-built military equipment. Here was what we called "hard intelligence," by which we meant irrefutable, factual information. If we could get enough of it, of the right kind, and properly handled, it promised to answer many of our questions. Captured military equipment is generally prized by many branches of intelligence. First of all, of course, it offers samples of the arms of the enemy, and increasingly, as modern military equipment has become more technologically advanced, and often more important than the forces employing it, every bit of information one can get about the characteristics of enemy weapons is valuable, and can be crucial. For general strategic intelligence, and for order-of-battle intelligence, which is concerned with the specifics of size, disposition, tactics, and strengths and weaknesses of opposing forces, captured equipment can be invaluable. One may learn from it the range and power of weapons, speed and maneuverability and range of aircraft and land vehicles, the types of communications, the strength and distribution of armor, the rate of fire of weapons, even such things as implied logistic requirements.

Our particular interest, however, was in what went under the loose term of "name-plate intelligence". I had had first-hand experience during World War II in the use of nameplate intelligence. From the serial numbers of major components and subassemblies of Japanese aircraft shot down and retrieved over land areas of the Southwest Pacific Theater, we gradually built up, during the years 1942-1944, enough firm information to develop estimates of aircraft production rates on several models, which at war's end had turned out to be remarkably good. We had also learned much about the processes and location of production.

Before we got such nameplates, our "estimates" had in

fact been no better than the wildest guesses, based mainly on nothing better than the intuitive impressions — prejudices would be a better word for it — of American engineers who had had some contact with the Japanese aircraft industry in the years and months before Pearl Harbor. Their testimony had ranged from notions that the Japanese were inherently incapable of designing and manufacturing a warplane of their own (something the performance of Japanese Zeros soon suggested could hardly be true) to wildly exaggerated opinions at the other extreme, which gave the Japanese credit for almost any accomplishment in war production they might undertake. Throughout 1942 the estimates of Japanese combat aircraft production that went into the "economic enclosures" of "situation papers" submitted to the Joint Chiefs of Staff (and sometimes the Combined Chiefs of Staff) had been 10,000 planes per year. That was a nice round figure that was accepted because no one could prove that any other figure was better. Sometime in late 1942 I was pressured by an urgent request from an Army Colonel himself under pressure to make a recommendation concerning allocation of American aircraft to the Pacific Theater, which of course was in competition for supply with the European, North African, and China-Burma-India theaters. It so happened that I had just learned that an Australian Army intelligence officer had begun collecting and photographing nameplates from parts of Japanese aircraft shot down in his area, I told the gentleman that I knew of no way to improve upon the currently accepted guess of 10,000 planes per year unless we could get our hands on the nameplate intelligence being collected in Australia, and also whatever other such materials might be made available in other areas. Very soon after, my little shop began to receive scores of good photos of nameplates and markings, those from Australia plus a few from mid-Pacific areas, and Assam, Northern Burma and Ceylon. I put an ingenious machine tools expert named Norman Meiklejohn, who had a bent for statistical analysis, to work on the incoming material. And not too long after, our estimates of the Japanese war economy based on nameplate and serial number analysis were among the most reliable we made.

Hoping to repeat the experience with Japanese nameplates in World War II, I tried to make a major effort to capitalize in similar fashion on the acquisition of Soviet materiel captured in Korea. It must be understood, of course, that this is far from a simple matter. Most of what is to be found in the war zone are single parts, subassemblies components of many sorts, often damaged and not positively associated with other parts comprising the total piece of equipment. Only in the rarest instance is an entire assembly with its serial number to be found. Serial numbers of components are of course peculiar to their own series, generally without explicit relationship to the serial numbers of other components or to that of the assembly itself. Usually they are coded in some way, although in most cases the code must be simple enough for mechanics to determine readily whether or not the component is suitable for use in the particular model they are working with. Only very rarely are there any dates. (In World War II, we were aided enormously in our analysis of Japanese Zero fighter production by the fact that among the nameplates we recovered were two that amounted to final inspection tags of completed aircraft and were dated. But after the earliest nameplates, we got few that were dated, and very little was uncoded.) Much of the analysis must be a matter of multiple correlation. What one gets in components must be analyzed in consideration of how many of that particular item may be produced in proportion to other components of the completed assembly or to the total number of the completed assemblies it belongs to.

Once alerted to the existence of captured Russian equipment in Korea, we encountered a long series of bureaucratic and jurisdictional hassles in getting access. Control in the field was naturally dominated by intelligence officers preoccupied with the problems of fighting the North Koreans and their Chinese allies, and while they probably understood without being told that almost all captured Russian equipment was of some interest to national intelligence services in Washington, at first there were evidently few if any who had any grasp of how nameplate intelligence might be used or should be gathered. What we wanted were clear photos, made so that all markings or stampings were legible, and with complete identification of what the item was and a notation of its association with any other part or component. We drafted and had sent to the field statements of "intelligence requirements" that embodied the information we thought necessary to enable those collecting captured equipment to satisfy our needs in an efficient manner. But the field was being bombarded with intelligence requirement requests from the headquarters of all three military services, plus the CIA, each with its own functions and questions primarily in mind (though with a considerable evident overlap). To commands under combat pressure the first priority is bound to be order-of-battle intelligence, and requests from distant headquarters half way around the world for items of no obvious immediate value are bound to seem secondary, and may even be regarded as so many starry-eyed boondoggles. There were times when this latter attitude seems to have prevailed.

In addition, there was the problem of the ongoing struggle between the MacArthur Command and Washington. MacArthur and his Chief of Intelligence General Willoughby quite routinely disregarded Washington requests, even upon occasion openly treating them as either useless or suspect. Rumor had it that MacArthur would not grant the CIA a place within his Empire, and that such CIA activities as remained there did so only under cover that the MacArthur command could not penetrate.

Eventually, however, a flow of captured materiel, including nameplates and markings, began to come, mainly after a special group was sent out to guide the collection effort. That group represented all our intelligence services, and acted as well in cooperation with the intelligence services of those European allies who had token forces in the field along with our own. James W. Walker, now a Professor of Mathematics at Georgia Tech, was our unit's representative in that group.

A few photos of markings and nameplates were made in the field, but generally the pieces of captured equipment, if not simply left lying around, were crated and sent back to the States, generally going to engineering research organizations such as Stanford Research Institute in California or the Battelle Memorial Institute in Dayton,

Ohio, where the services had placed contracts for analysis of technical qualities. In no case I can remember had those receiving the material been instructed to photograph or make rubbings or otherwise record nameplates or markings. Their contracts called for them to perform technical analysis, which they plunged into eagerly. After a couple of trips to these places to explain our need, the engineers did their best to satisfy us, though much was lost because the association of related items that might have been possible at the point of collection in the field was no longer possible.

We did get some useful information from the markings, however, mainly in the form of confirming where various subassemblies were either manufactured or given their final inspection. But nothing provided more than the merest hint of production rates of major items. Moreover, it was clear that in most cases, the materiel had been produced several years before and was from a model long since superseded, and that current models and production processes might be very different. Still, it gave us some basis for claiming we had at least an earthy Russian flavor in our guesses. At least we had some hard evidence of what some small details had been a few years before. But those of us who remembered some of the intelligence heroics of World War II were disappointed. We knew from our reading how in World War II Allied intelligence had a very accurate count on the total number of some types of German artillery pieces from nameplate analysis. And some of us could recall the good old days of eager beaver nameplate collection by intelligence men in the field. Whether it is true or not I cannot guarantee, but in 1943 the explanation of how we learned so much so quickly about the numbers and production details of the dreaded Nazi Tiger tank was that an OSS operative named Bill Alexander was reputed to have ripped off the main nameplates of disabled and overrun tanks while they were still hot from burning and stinking of charred corpses inside.

Perhaps what impressed me most from our effort with the nameplates from Korea had little to do with our immediate purposes, but served, rather, as an example of how expectation determined the nature of what one saw, even in the case of consultant engineers who examined physical items in a laboratory. At first, they placed great emphasis on how much more poorly finished many components were than their American components. Or similarly, it was emphasized that because of the design or materials used, certain parts would wear out much faster than comparable parts of American manufacture. For a while, such observations were interpreted as reflecting inferior technology, nothing else. But after a time this initial emphasis was tempered somewhat. They began to say, occasionally, that our manufacturing practice was often to machine things finely where fine finishing served only cosmetic purposes and often to require closer tolerances than were necessary. But when the practical need existed, the Russian practice approximated our own.

A similar shift occurred in judgments of some items initially criticized on grounds they would wear out quicker than ours. They began to say, in some cases, this represented a sort of planned obsolescence: where component or equipment items were parts of assemblies that could not reasonably be expected to survive beyond some short span of use, lesser components were not engineered to outlast the assemblies when to do so would have been more costly. I had no competence to judge the technical validity of these opinions. But it would have been difficult to ignore the influence of sheer custom and even of social ideologies upon judgments that supposedly were purely engineering judgments. At first, the almost automatic assumption was that departures from our own established customs were evidence of inferior practice. Only after long second thoughts did it begin to dawn on at least some of them that there were other ways of doing things that might be just as good.

Chapter Three

PLAYING GAMES
WITH NUCLEAR
WAR

In the early fifties, Air Force Target Intelligence was new, growing, finding its way. Everything was in a state of flux, and over all hung an air of urgency resulting from the threat of the Cold War.

The Cold War Atmosphere

The prevailing Pentagon presumption was that at almost any time the Russians would unleash their hordes upon Western Europe. In the Air Force Directorate of Intelligence, a Special Studies Group had been set up by General C.P. Cabell (who later moved over to CIA and was chief of operations there at the time of the 1961 Bay of Pigs fiasco, although it was Richard Bissell who was directly in control of that operation). This Group was charged with writing most of the long range strategic think-pieces for the Directorate. It was headed by Steve Possony, a Hungarian émigré who professed to be an expert on Communism in general and the Soviet Union in particular. Steve was the first of several Central European émigrés I met in the next few years who passed as experts on Communist Europe and who had at least some small influence on strategic thought and the formation of American policy. Others were Strausz-Hupé, Kissinger, Brzezinski and many lesser lights such as Leon Gouré and Helmut Sonnenfeldt. In every case I felt they were thinking, consciously or otherwise, not as Americans but as representatives of a lost cause in their native land, and I always believed they were used by the military because their 'obsessions' were so useful. The one product of Possony's group that I most distinctly remember was an annual appraisal of the strategic situation. And the reason I remember it, perhaps, is that every year that appraisal forecast a massive Russian land attack on Western Europe the following year. Several of us began to laugh about it after a while, but the forecast was always intoned awesomely and with superficial plausibility. I do not know whether many people who heard the briefings really believed the forecasts. I suspect many doubted it would really be next year, and thought it more likely the year after that or even later. But even doubters approved the forecast because, they reasoned, it was better to err in this direction than to minimize the danger. Above all, it was good to say things that emphasized the need for strong defenses.

This prediction of imminent mass attack by Russian hordes upon freedom's bastions in Western Europe was, so far as I know, the specialty of Possony and company (maybe even they did not believe it, but it was, after all, a living). The general tone was not unlike the orientation briefings that were standard fare in those years for visitors to military bases of almost every sort — at least all of those I visited. These standard briefings were intended to explain the function and organizational status of the particular base or command, and as a one-time teacher I felt they were models of effective pedagogy. There was generally an articulate and accomplished raconteur, commonly a major or lieutenant colonel, armed with well practiced topical jokes for starters, with a baton and a profusion of well executed charts and graphs and diagrams manned usually by a master sergeant. The introductory pleasantries varied from post to post and from time to time, but once these preliminaries were disposed of there was no doubt where the serious business would begin. It would begin with a series of charts, the first being Russia, colored red of course, with its boundaries of 1938, before the Russo-Finnish War and before the annexation of eastern Poland following the Nazi-Soviet pact of 1939 and the outbreak of World War II. Then the red of Soviet Russia would flow into the areas taken from Finland, then from Poland in the 1939 seizure, then the red would move, one nation at a time, to cover the Baltic States, and after that Poland, Romania, Hungary, East Germany, Yugoslavia, Albania, North Korea, Czechoslovakia, China, and what we still called French Indochina. It was a red tide that was gradually overrunning the world. It was monolithic, centrally controlled and directed from Moscow, and the peoples of the areas turned red were Communist automatons, with never so much as a hint that they might have different cultural traditions or social values. The only suggestion of local differentiations was that poverty and hunger and sheer desperation induced human beings to become Communist automatons, which explained why areas in which there was political unrest of any sort were the areas we needed to keep a sharp eye on to prevent a Communist takeover.

It was almost always assumed that any war would be an unlimited war between the United States and our allies on one side, and the USSR and all her European Communist satellite states, plus China and North Korea on the other. The latter two did not count for much in those early days. Indeed the Korean War, although not a general war, was interpreted to confirm what almost everyone took for granted anyway, namely that the entire Communist bloc was a completely monolithic structure, with every major action dictated by Moscow and every slave state acting in concert.

By no means was this sort of presumption confined to the Pentagon. Even such a distinguished and broadly informed intellect as Secretary of State Dean Acheson subscribed to the doctrine. For instance, when in the last week of June, 1950, the North Koreans launched their attack on South Korea and President Truman returned from Missouri for a week of crisis conferences in Blair House, the basic premise of every attempt to understand the gravity of the situation and what our best response should be was that this was a *Russian* ploy and that the dominant question was what role in the overall strategy of Soviet plans for world conquest did this Korean venture play. Nearly twenty years later, when he wrote his State Department memoirs, *Present At the Creation*, Acheson still felt the same way. All this, despite the continued reporting, from 1945 on by our people on the spot, that the hostility of the regimes of both North and South Korea toward each other was so bitter that it was dangerously explosive and might erupt at any time. Our first occupation commander in South Korea had recommended we get out to avoid entanglement in a civil war between the two. And at least up to the time I write this, even though we have poured billions of dollars worth of military aid into South Korea, we have very carefully refrained from providing enough to give such confidence of military victory as to encourage their acknowledged aggressive tendencies.

In our air targeting studies, we regularly assumed that economic resources in satellite states should get the same bombing treatment we planned for those within Russia proper. Thus, if refineries were judged an inviting target, those in Ploesti were ranged along with those in Baku. No difference. Still, I remember the puzzlement of one compassionate Air Force general following a briefing in which estimates were given of the probable incidental casualties among civilians in hypothetical attacks on Hungary or Romania. He asked if it wasn't "immoral" to plan attacks that might kill so many people who were not themselves responsible — it was Moscow that was responsible. I recall no controversy ensuing, although I think everyone thought it unusual to raise such a consideration. What I remember most is that a couple of us who were present, but who said nothing then, commented smugly afterward that what the general had described as a moral question was really a *political* question.

Games and Bonuses

It was about that time that we first began including what we termed "bonus" in our estimates of probable damage from hypothetical attacks. Bonus damage was the damage to everything else, including human beings, of course. Bonus damage was considered a plus in evaluating the desirability of a target, but I cannot remember it ever being judged more than that in those early days. Nor do I remember that population, as such, was ever given serious consideration as a primary target. However, what we called "command and control" or "population control centers" — generally meaning either military headquarters or command posts or government buildings — were generally high on the list. And at times we tried to decide where skilled labor might be located for targeting purposes. We always did try to make some sort of estimate of what casualties would be if specified weapons were directed at specified ground zeros (aiming points). This became a very complicated though highly speculative exercise that I worked at over a period of many years. To me the striking feature of it is that once you became involved it became almost impossible to give attention to the fact that you were dealing with anything but numbers. Numbers, not human beings.

I cannot believe that this reflected any real lack of concern for humane values on the part of those of us engaged in such calculations. Most of those I knew who were engaged in this were essentially gentle folk for whom it was all an exercise one went through, pretending one dealt with potential realities — that was part of the game — yet acting always with a split personality that prevented emotional or ethical consciousness from communicating with one's game-playing concentration.

Generally we are aware of gross illogic only among pariahs or people of exotic cultures, and we assume that consistency of attitudes and values and coherent rationality are the norm. There is little, I suspect, that is more necessary to our very existence than this delusion of coherent rationality. Yet there is nothing more certainly untrue, or more surely irrational.

In the RAND group in Santa Monica, where there was the highest concentration of defense intellectuals anywhere, a fashionable parlor game was *Kriegspiel*, a form of chess reputedly very popular within the old Prussian officer corps. *Kriegspiel* differed from ordinary chess only in that it was played with two boards, a referee and neither player could see the other's board nor know about his opponent's moves beyond what he could infer from referee rulings. If a player lost a piece the referee would remove it from the board, or if a move he proposed was impossible because of the position of the opponent's pieces, the referee would inform him it was impossible without explanation. But he would never know for sure where his opponent's pieces were, or which were remaining, until the game ended. He would keep track of what he *thought* his opponent's pieces were, and where they were, by placement of opposing pieces on his own board. The popularity of the game among Prussian officers was supposedly that it simulated the so-called "fog of war" in which you fight an opponent never fully visible, and in which you never know for sure what or where his forces are or how badly you may have hurt him.

Some of the bright young men at RAND elaborated these principles into what they conceived might be a game more directly related to the atmosphere of a modern air war. It was first intended, I believe, as a training exercise of possible interest to war college officers.

STRAW was an enormously complicated war game between two players, one Red (Russia) and the other Blue (the USA), with an umpire. Each side had a map board representing both his own and his opponent's country, and in each country the military and industrial resources were in place about as it was imagined they would be at the beginning of a real war. All Blue installations were known to Red, but not all of Red's installations were known to Blue. Initial striking forces approximated those credited by intelligence estimates to both sides. Neither could see the opponent's map to know precisely where striking forces were placed, nor how much damage was done from a strike. Red always got off the first strike, intended to be preemptive. On a randomized basis the umpire would announce weather conditions (affecting accuracy), attrition rates (affecting both losses and damage); the attacker would learn the extent of attrition to his own force, but only the side attacked would know what damage had been inflicted. Then the second side would counterattack under similar rules. Attrition rates, abort rates, damage criteria, aiming accuracy, and all other critical details, including of course comparative strength of striking forces, range of effectiveness, location and vulnerability of targets, were in all cases intended to be as representative of reality as possible.

For a couple of years, STRAW was merely a game set up in the RAND offices in Santa Monica and another in the Target Intelligence Division in Washington. Some of the most civilian-minded and almost pacifistically inclined Air Force employees I knew found the game so fascinating they borrowed it to play at home on weekends. It was like Parchesi or Monopoly, and I believe that as we played it we gave the same sort of feeling of reality to our moves as when we tried to calculate the weight of attack necessary to destroy command and control and installations and marshaling yards in Smolensk, aircraft assembly in Tiflis, or tank production facilities in Novosibirsk.

I was never aware of any high level Air Force interest in STRAW in those days. However, in the late fifties, when I had moved into another position, an elaborated SUPERSTRAW played with computers and purported to test various strategies became a major Air Force research project in the bowels of the Pentagon, funded one year with an $8 million budget, even given some publicity by *Time* magazine.

The Rise of Fear

The existence of nuclear stockpiles had a growing influence on air target doctrine. Gradually it became evident that weapons effects should no longer be appraised solely in terms of how much "economic war potential" or military materiel they destroyed or denied, or how many airfields or port facilities were put out of action. Whatever military or industrial installations might be the targets of attack, it became increasingly evident that the probable effect upon these targets would be no greater, possibly less, and possibly less important, than the incidental devastation, disruption and death that would be visited upon civilians and upon civilian society. And as awareness of this likelihood grew, the obvious problem was to find some way to estimate the magnitude of such damage and casualties, and appraise the impact upon the society and the nation of such devastation. It was obviously an impossibly difficult problem for which there could be no real answers. (Neither then nor now, though many good minds have tried to address the question.) But the problem was there. It could not be ignored. And beginning sometime in 1952 I became engrossed in it, gave almost all my time to it, and from then until 1959 first with Air Force Intelligence, then after 1955 with the Weapons Systems Evaluation Group (WSEG) serving the Joint Chiefs of Staff and the Secretary of Defense. Ever since those earliest days there have been both secret and publicized estimates of what devastation nuclear war would result in. I believe the estimates themselves are less significant than understanding the factors used in making them, and the methods by which they are arrived at.

We started in very simply and naively, and added greater knowledge and some sophistication as time passed, but I am not convinced that much improvement resulted because in the enormously complicated problem that it amounted to, everything depended, at every stage along the way, upon many arbitrary assumptions that critically affected the answer. I see no reason to believe these could ever be better than informed guesses.

We began with what we called "cookie cutters". These were graduated concentric rings representing "over-pressure" (force of blast) measured in terms of PSI (pounds per square inch). At the epicenter, everything would be reduced to ashes; from there out destructive force, both to humans and to structures, would diminish. We would apply the formulae of physical vulnerability (PV) numbers to calculate the degree of damage to structures according to their PV number and distance from ground zero, and from this impute the number of dead and wounded assumed to be in various parts of these structures. We would of course have to assume where the people were at the time of the blast, how many were in the open, how many underground, and so on. The

PV numbers would provide a formula for telling how to estimate casualties among those caught in the open, casualties meaning dead and various degrees of being less than fatally wounded. Ordinarily we centered the cookie cutter (as apparently is still the common practice) on the DGZ (the desired ground zero, or target) although we knew of course that a single weapon so aimed had only a 50% chance of detonating within the radius indicated by the assumed Circular Error Probable (CEP) we were working with, which might be a half a mile or more. I do not remember ever assuming more than one weapon to a target, though it would have been entirely reasonable, operationally, to have directed more than one weapon at targets of high importance. Cookie cutters would of course have had to vary according to height of burst, but as I recall we commonly assumed surface burst.

Blast effect was all we tried to take into account at first, although we were aware of both thermal and immediate ionizing effects. We simply did not know enough about them even to try to guess. The Physical Vulnerability people were constantly worrying about thermal effects, because it was demonstrated that flammable materials might be set on fire at distances considerably beyond the range of any significant blast damage, and many special consultants were brought in to advise. But the problem of thermal effects was surrounded by real incalculables, such as the atmospheric quality and humidity at time of blast, and the angle of the waves radiating from the blast. Gamma radiation from fallout of debris from weapons burst low enough for the fireball to touch the earth was for some time ignored, although it was no secret among the initiated. At the Trinity test in 1945 some measurement had been made of fallout around the periphery of the blast area, and the central Pacific tests had provided further evidence of the problem. But something like a muzzle was put on us until 1955.

Through the first half of the decade of the fifties, as the numbers and destructive power of nuclear weapons grew, many questions were stimulated concerning how they might affect our earlier judgments of military strategy. The complex of questions was considerable, and if one looks back now it is easy to conclude that most of us were slow in awakening. But gradually we did perceive that the enormity of devastation likely to result from what we euphemistically called a "nuclear exchange" might call for a complete re-thinking of what a major war might mean. And the first ingredient of a re-thinking was, obviously, a real comprehension of the magnitude of the probable devastation. Estimates were called for, not just of the damage to the physical installations that might be targeted, but of the civilian casualties as well. And after some appreciation grew of their magnitude, the questions began to center on what the cumulative effect upon a society or nation might be. Of course this was a question for which there was no answer. But it was also the question that could not be ignored because it was the reality at the heart of any rational consideration of what a major war involved. One could have no "answers", but perhaps by examining all the ascertainable and relevant facts one could come at least a little closer to understanding what was involved. It was a problem impossible to ignore as well as impossible to resolve.

However conjectural estimates of expected casualties and structural damage might be, appraisals of how such devastation would affect the will and ability of a nation to continue to resist, how it might affect the very structure of the society sustaining it, were equally in demand and of course even more obscure and unpredictable. But it was inevitable that those anticipating the possibility of the sort of war for which we were preparing would want to have some guesses made concerning the likely outcome. Because the question was asked, some response had to be made.

There were two stabs I made at this impossible problem in the early fifties, and I think the sorry outcome of both throws some light on the way our institutions and our people in positions of social responsibility often grope in the dark when matters of such magnitude are at issue.

Some time in the winter of 1952-53, I hit upon the idea that one might approach the problem by proceeding from the hypothesis that in the disaster situation that nuclear devastation would certainly impose, self-preservation would be the first goal of those who survived, and that consequently much could be learned by attempting to quantify the material and labor requirements of mere survival, in an organized way, following reasonably closely the existing customs and divisions of labor. I drew up, as best I could, a list intended to include all the minimum requirements of continuing existence; food, shelter, clothing, medical care, water, restoration of essential services and utilities, policing, etc. I went to every reputable source I could think of to categorize and quantify these bare essentials of continued existence within organized society, and to get data on the minimum amounts of labor and materials needed to supply them. I organized these materials into a series of quite elaborate tables arranged like ledger sheets. Major sources of data were the records of civil disasters and rescue operations both in this country and in other countries. One such source that interested me especially because of its location in the Soviet Union was a Russian account of the way they had handled the aftermath of a major earthquake not long before that almost totally destroyed the city of Ashkabad, on the Iranian border. Generally speaking, I assumed medical care requirements would approximate those the military service counted as necessary in battlefield locations under wartime conditions.

I never had much confidence that my numbers meant what they might seem to mean, yet it did all amount to an honest attempt to get some idea of the magnitude of the relief problems confronting a city in the immediate aftermath of a nuclear attack. (Rural areas I ignored because I did not know what to do with them.) Because I used the accounting device of computing estimated requirements in terms of requirements per survivor (seriously wounded, slightly wounded and unhurt) it was possible to settle upon a number or a proportion whose requirements would exceed the locally available relief resources.

I had often speculated that in any great disaster situation, survivors would act within existing institutions for as long as it was helpful to them to do so, but that when established institutions failed, individual actions would tend to become privatized. Either every individual would act solely to save himself and his family and immediate friends, or else new organizations would be improvised on a highly local basis. In either case the established order would be replaced, at least temporarily, by something else. And that of course could be taken to mean that the established order was overthrown.

It so happened that after I had been working on this long enough to have it in such shape that the intent was evident, I was visited by Clyde Kluckhohn, who was a Professor of Anthropology at Harvard, and at that time Director of the Air Force's Russian Institute there. I tried out my Rube Goldberg Monstrosity, as I called it, on Clyde, apologizing profusely for all its oversimplifications and arbitrary assumptions. He studied it for an hour or two, and then, somewhat to my surprise, certainly my relief, praised it highly as innovative and enlightening. In the succeeding year or two and until his untimely death I came to know and admire Clyde greatly, and I know he understood my reservations about my monstrosity as well as I did. Nevertheless he told many others in his circle of Air Force contacts of my research on the subject, if it can be called that, and I gained confidence to show it to others.

I do not remember that my piece was ever published as a formal study, but it became widely known, and widely used. For a time I tried to refine it and as best I could, I always sought to emphasize that this could not pretend to be more than a highly tentative and very flawed approach. Above all, I tried to emphasize that none of my numbers should ever be taken at face value. Nevertheless, the particular model and particular numbers I had used were such that when total casualties exceeded 40%, the assumed relief requirements exceeded the capacities of the surviving 60%. Within months the word spread that 40% casualties was "the breaking point", and strategic inferences of all sorts were drawn from that. And within the intelligence community, and elsewhere, that conclusion was used by people who never studied the tables or understood how the numbers were arrived at. For several years that 40% figure was accepted as gospel, despite my protests.

People wanted numbers, and they took what was available even though the source of the numbers disclaimed them.

The other incident of that era, and on the same subject matter, that seems to me to reveal something of the nature of people and institutions on whom social responsibilities devolve occurred about a year later. I was more unhappy than anyone else with the research I had attempted in this area, and felt that others should try other ideas. With this in mind, I drew up an ambitious research proposal and took it to a research group at the Massachusetts Institute of Technology led by Max Millikan and including Francis Bator, Ithiel de Sola Poole and others I admired, that I considered the most able and conscientious of any of the academic institutions that might undertake such studies. They had really top flight people in many disciplines, and I knew them well and believed that if a task demanded a talent they lacked they would go out and bring it in from somewhere else. Perhaps the important thing is that after long consideration, Max and M.I.T. declined to accept the contract, on grounds there was little prospect they could accomplish anything worthwhile because the problem was insoluble.

Equally vividly I remember that when Max convened his group to hear, for the first time, what my research proposal was all about, everyone was there at the appointed hour except Walt Rostow. We waited ten minutes or so, then when he did not appear Max asked me to begin my presentation. I had proceeded for perhaps five minutes when the door opened and in came Walt. As I stopped talking Max said to Walt, "Paul has just started, but I think neither he nor the rest of us will object to his starting over. It's a research proposal dealing with the possible cumulative effects of extensive damage from nuclear bombing." Before I could open my mouth to start over, Walt, who had had some minor hand in the U.S. Strategic Bombing Survey, launched into a long discourse on strategic bombing that had nothing whatever to do with what I had come for, but which he presented with an air that seemed to profess all questions were being answered. After an uninterrupted speech of twenty minutes or so, he abruptly said he had another appointment, and departed. In case of doubt, this was the same Walt Rostow who later became President Johnson's Authority on Everything.

It was not solely the military agencies that sought answers to questions about the prospective damage and effects of nuclear war.

I was repeatedly called upon to provide information and estimates to the Office of Civil Defense after it was set up as an agency within the Executive Office of the President. For the latter I provided what passed for appraisals of the effect of hypothetical nuclear attacks upon the United States, and was given a routine Presidential appointment as Executive Reserve Officer. In that capacity I took part in the annual exercises designed to test the working of the national civil defense system under conditions of nuclear attack.

I well remember the first such drill, which occurred, I believe, in the late spring of either 1953 or 1954. On a Friday morning those of us who were Executive Reserve Officers betook ourselves to the top of Mount Weather, a few miles west of Leesburg, Virginia, where there was a large building originally serving as a point from which the old Weather Bureau made meteorological observations, and thereafter for many years was used as a site for government conferences when the conferees wanted to get away from it all. It had been taken over by Civil Defense as the site for the shadow government to operate from in event of nuclear attack. Later a deep underground command center was constructed there, but in 1953 the only preparations for the national exercise was an encampment of a dozen or more large tents, some furnished conference and assembly rooms in the old building, a TV intercom, and communication with the outside world via a telephone line running down the mountain and hooking into the commercial telephone system in Leesburg. We on the mountaintop were supposed to take over administration of the country, or at least be prepared to do so should the city of Washington be heavily damaged. My job was to put together hourly briefings on the damage we had sustained throughout the country and to confer with others concerning steps to be taken in the light of such damage. This was, of course, a national exercise, and Civil Defense officials all over the country had been given data concerning nuclear weapons bursts, and these were to be reported to us according to an exercise schedule prepared in advance. Presumably the officials making the sitings would have determined, by brief visual observation, what the ground zero of each such blast had been, the size of the weapon, and from that made an immediate estimate of the degree of damage inflicted upon key war industries in the vicinity. This was to have been accomplished in a matter of minutes. Accepting these reports as they came in, and of course raising no questions concerning their accuracy, much less that such observations were patently impossible, I was supposed to report to the assembled Executive Reserve Officers that, as of that moment, we had sustained the loss, for example, of 18% of our machine tools industry, 49% of our airframe assembly capacity, 63% of our petroleum refining capacity, and so on. Even this, however, did not attain the highest point of hilarity that the exercise afforded. That climax came as the result of a heavy thunderstorm, with high winds, that struck late that Friday afternoon, just as the hypothetical Russian attack was supposed to have begun. Not only were a couple of our tents blown down and our encampment turned into a sea of mud, but our sole line of communication with the outside world, the telephone line down to Leesburg, was severed, and when, bedraggled, we slopped from our rained-in tents to the assembly in the main building, our Director, Arthur Fleming, came on the TV intercom to apologize for the breakdown of communications and to promise that on the morrow, when service was restored, the exercise would continue as planned.

It is of course easy to ridicule the absurdity of much that was done in response to the dilemma posed by the increasing presence of nuclear arsenals. But I am not aware that anyone, in any place, at any time, proposed anything that amounted to a practical answer to the problem. Those who were sufficiently informed to take the nuclear threat seriously generally realized that, as a practical matter, there was nothing that could be done that would make a great deal of difference if nuclear war really came. But so long as nuclear armaments were building up on both sides, *something* had to be done. You couldn't ignore the matter entirely. So you went through comic opera exercises, such as putting up signs on highways and bridges saying they would be closed in case of enemy attack. At a later date, when emphasis shifted to fallout hazards (partly because we became more aware of fallout, and partly because it was possible to provide at least some protection against gamma radiation), we went in for marking fallout shelter areas, even encouraging construction of private and community fallout shelters. But even this was never more than the merest half-hearted gesture.

In a sense, logic demanded that if you armed to fight nuclear wars, you must take all possible steps to protect yourself while you fought them. Many argued this. But others believed that nothing would make much difference. Still others believed that any program large enough in scale to afford any significant measure of protection would be exorbitantly expensive. And they argued that if you survived such a war the world you returned to from your shelter would be uninhabitable. Others argued that a program sufficient to have any protective effect either could not be "sold" to the people, or, if "sold", would undermine our doctrine of massive retaliation as a national strategy. The common belief during the mid- and late fifties was that President Eisenhower was, for whatever reason, far from convinced that a civil defense program should be undertaken, and that he went along with the least he could get by with to appease the proponents of such a program. In any event, it seems clear that our reaction, as a people, and among those within the government concerned with such matters, accurately reflected our national ambivalence and bewilderment in confronting the dilemma posed by the very existence of nuclear weaponry.

At the start of the fifties, most of my colleagues and others I knew felt reasonably secure in our confidence that the United States itself was in no serious danger. The assumption was always that the danger we faced was an all-out ground attack on Western Europe by Russia and her Eastern European satellites. I cannot remember anyone in those days seriously questioning the prospect that when the attack occurred, we would use what nuclear weapons we had — the inventory was still small — wherever we thought they would do the most good. We followed feverishly, of course, such intelligence as we had on Soviet progress in developing nuclear weapons capability. And there was no question in any minds I was acquainted with that the time was coming when the Russians would have a nuclear capability we would have to reckon with. But possession of a few nuclear weapons of the early 1950s vintage did not pose too great a threat to us in America. There were not only few of them, they were still cumbrous, and above all there were no evident means of delivering them against targets in the United States. The Russians had never gone in for long range bombers as we had, they lacked bases close to the United States from which to launch an attack, and the only imaginable way they could attack us was by one-way missions from a few northernmost bases, and even then they could reach only a fraction of the United States, and by no means many of our Strategic Air Command bases. Against this remote possibility we had a network of early warning radar, stretching from Norway to Greenland to Alaska, constantly being pushed farther north. With such warning of comparatively slow-flying bombers, our interceptors could readily scramble and meet them long before they reached American targets. We, of course, had advanced bases almost completely encircling the Soviets, and in addition, a refueling capability that the Soviets, so far as we knew, had not developed.

But then in 1952 our American defense community was given a rude shock by a secret RAND study masterminded by an extremely bright and very persuasive systems analyst named Al Wohlstetter, with considerable help from, among others, Harry Rowan. To understand the impact of this study it is perhaps necessary to recognize that by this time RAND had already acquired the reputation of being the best of the think tanks that the services used to assist in such research. RAND under its first Director, Frank Kollbaum, had fixed very high standards of brightness and scholarship in selecting its analysts, and its studies, which dealt with a wide range of specialties, from nuclear physics and atomic weapons through electronics and aerodynamics to military applications of economics and the social sciences, were commonly judged among the best that the small and cloistered but influential world of defense studies turned out. And Al Wohlstetter was to become their star performer.

The study assumed a surprise Soviet attack upon all the Strategic Air Command bases in the United States. The entire Soviet long range bomber force, committed to one way missions, would attack us from our unguarded flank. Instead of following the most direct route to the United States, which would expose them to our radar warning system and thus alert our defenses, the attacking planes would all fly south over the seas where there was no such warning system, then sweep northward, approaching our SAG bases from the south, where there was also no warning system, and proceed to destroy our entire strategic air force before we knew what was going on. To accomplish this, the Soviets would have to commit practically all of their heavy bombers, and, because none had sufficient range to reach U.S, targets otherwise, it was assumed they would develop a capability to re-fuel in flight, although they would still lack fuel to return. Instead, after dropping their bombs, they would seek haven in Mexico or Cuba or some other neutral territory.

Recalling the study today, it stands out as a *tour de force* of improvised plausibility. The data and figures about types and capabilities of planes and weapons, abort and attrition rates, bombing accuracy, damage probability — all such ingredients of standard studies of air operations — were impressively documented, graphically presented, and eloquently expounded. To say it was convincing is a gross understatement. After the hour and a half or two-hour briefing presented to Defense Department officers and officials, replete as it was with charts and tables and graphs and an assistant briefer always there pointing his baton to the spot or the number to be emphasized, you came away shivering in your boots and wondering if that plane overhead preparing to land at National Airport might really be, not a DC-3 from Chattanooga but a Russian Bear or Bison preparing to unload its bomb.

One problem with the study, which so far as I know was scarcely mentioned by anyone at the time, was that it assumed everything worked perfectly, with perfect weather, no operational foul-ups, no advance warning. Above all, the study assumed such an insensate desire on the part of the Soviets to attack us that they would voluntarily accept the enormous risks that such a gamble would inevitably involve. Perhaps one factor that made us so ready to accept the idea of a surprise, pre-emptive Soviet attack as the way the inevitable war would come was a lingering Pearl Harbor complex. And the dominant notion was that the Soviets were bent on world conquest. Almost never was there any suggestion that Soviet arms were in any way defensive, or that the Soviets feared us. Ours was a psychology, perhaps not unlike theirs, of awaiting and bracing for an attack to be launched on us by an irreconcilable enemy.

Of course we did not know then that the authors of this study were to go on to be the midwives of the "missile gap" scare following Sputnik, and then founders of the Committee on the Present Danger in the seventies. But although that study was vastly too alarmist, it served to accelerate major changes in the way we envisaged a future war, and also in our ideas of what an air target strategy should be. Gradually, very gradually, because in military institutions change is almost always very slow, we became less concerned with a strategy of destroying economic war potential as we had previously considered it, and more concerned, instead, with the immediate and more general impact of a nuclear exchange. Previous concentration on attacking economic war potential assumed a war of attrition. Now, with nuclear weapons, the emphasis shifted to immediate impact, impact that destroyed both nuclear retaliatory capabilities, and the very structure of the national society involved.

In those early years of nuclear weapons and an evolving strategy of massive retaliation, the newly created Air Force had a near monopoly on the weapons, and the Strategic Air Command (SAC) was the most favored of any of the service arms. The 1948-49 economy measures in the Pentagon administered by Defense

Secretary Louis Johnson had hit the Army hardest, the Navy somewhat less, and the Air Force hardly at all. The outbreak of the Korean War in 1950 necessitated a rapid upsurge of spending for all three services, but by the time that war was over, considerable progress had been made in nuclear arms, which placed the Air Force in an ever more advantageous position in contending with rival services for a big share of the Defense Department budget. Getting a larger share of the budget depended significantly upon establishing a capability to use nuclear weapons effectively, or if that could not be done, upon making a plausible case for the usefulness of conventional arms and forces, even in the acknowledged presence of the vastly greater fire-power of nuclears. Over the years this led to many issues between the services, and no doubt still does. It led to nuclear artillery of various types, to submarine-launched missiles, to controversies over which service should provide air-borne close support to ground troops, to inter-service controversy over which branch should be in charge of anti-aircraft and anti-ballistic missile defense. One effort by the Army was to develop a case for the greater utility of conventional ground forces by arguing the limited applicability of nuclear weapons and massive retaliation. Certainly, the increasing evidence of the devastating effects of gamma radiation from ground-burst weapons during the Pacific and Nevada weapons test provided a new element for consideration calling for major study.

PART II

IMAGINING
DOOMSDAY

Chapter One

THE FALLOUT STUDY

On July 14, 1955, the Joint Chiefs of Staff (JCS) and the Defense Department Deputy Director of Research and Engineering issued a directive to the Weapons Systems Evaluation Group (WSEG) to study the "implications of radioactive fallout." This directive led to three formal Secret Restricted Data studies, WSEG number 18 of July 17, 1956, WSEG 22 of June 10, 1957, and WSEG 27 of August 2, 1957. Continuing interest in the subject led to the issuance on February 28, 1958, of a directive to study the "Effect of Civilian Morale on Military Capabilities in a Nuclear War" which was finally completed on October 20, 1959. I was Director of this latter study after serving as Assistant Director of the first three.

WSEG had been set up soon after the Department of Defense was established following World War II. It was housed in the restricted area of the Joint Chiefs of Staff. Each of the services had its own research group: the Operations Research Organization (ORO) for the Army, the Office of Naval Research (ONR) for the Navy, and RAND for the Air Force. But WSEG was inter-service, at the JCS and Defense Department level, and therefore not oriented toward the narrow partisan interest of any particular branch of the services.

It was the custom, when a study was undertaken, to name

a civilian scientist as Project Chief and assign to him one or more officers, of Colonel or Navy Captain rank, from each service, and allow the Project Chief to choose from the pool of civilian scientists, or recruit consultants with special skills from the outside, to assist in the "team research" which would constitute the study. I emphasize the term "team research" because it was still comparatively early in what was to become the booming business of Operations Research (and its scarcely distinguishable twin, Systems Analysis) and there was much promotional hoopla about the value of researchers working together as a team.

At the time the directive for the fallout study was issued, a basic organizational change in WSEG was about to be put into effect. The Eisenhower presidency had, a couple of years before, set up a "Hoover Commission" to study governmental organizations, whose recommendations (among other things) provided a basis for transferring governmental research chores to private, non-profit corporations. The appropriate Congressional Committees had approved such a transfer. A new corporation, the Institute for Defense Analyses (IDA), was to be established to take over the function of WSEG. It would take time to iron out the legal and operational details of all this. Meanwhile, WSEG would continue briefly to operate under Civil Service, then be taken over temporarily by the Massachusetts Institute of Technology, until IDA could be fully established. This arrangement would permit the civilian side of WSEG to operate more freely, uninhibited by Civil Service and other governmental regulations. But functions remained unchanged.

During the summer of 1955, with the directive approved, search for a project leader had led to Professor John Lafayette Magee. John was a physical chemist (physical chemistry deals with the chemistry of the atom and to laymen physical chemists are indistinguishable from atonic physicists) who had been among those working on the first atomic bomb. He had foreseen the problem of gamma radiation from nuclear explosions and had tried to get first measurements of it at the first such explosion ever, the so-called "Trinity" test at Alamogordo in July 1945. He had in fact absorbed 26 roentgens at that time in the course of monitoring the test. He had continued research in related fields in his academic post, and had remained in close touch with scientists in the Atomic Energy Agency, the Livermore Laboratories in California and the Los Alamos group (weapons designers), and the Sandia Corporation (nuclear weapons assemblers). So far as knowledge of the physics of fallout is concerned, it would have been difficult to find a more qualified person to study the subject. But before he had proceeded far in planning the study, John came to the conclusion that there should be some sort of division of the study into two parts.

One part should attempt to develop a better understanding of the nature and scope of fallout from nuclear weapons in wartime. This was something that had never been attempted in a comprehensive and disciplined manner.

But that was only the beginning, because the directive asked for the *implications*. John believed himself competent to address the first part, but the second part concerned matters so foreign to him that he had no confidence in his ability to deal with them.

Somehow or other, mainly because I was known to have made studies of cumulative effects of bombing damage, and had been so bold as to speculate on likely consequences of extensive nuclear devastation, I was invited to join the project to deal with that elusive business of the "implications" of fallout. I joined the project in the fall of 1956, and was almost totally immersed in it for about two years, after the first six months as assistant project leader.

Association with John Magee in a joint intellectual endeavor that stretched each of us to his greatest capacity was for me an enlightening experience. While John was purely a physical scientist, I was, or professed to be, completely the humanist. In this sense we were, according to conventional wisdom, worlds apart. But I felt we had a great deal in common. First of all, and most important, he was a scientist because he was, in his heart, a poet, full of wonder and awe, sometimes penetrating in his insights, but always humble before the phenomena of the universe. He was always learning, always more conscious of the immensity of what he did not know than of what he did know. Always aware of the limits of his own knowledge, he carefully avoided judgment on matters beyond that. He was obviously disdainful of the habit of some scientists to conclude that their knowledge of their chosen field made them experts on all manner of other things, and to deliver pronouncements on subjects they were interested in but knew little about. Although it was easy to see his distrust of anyone who carried emotional fixations into areas where intellect should be dominant, he never argued. He had an abiding belief that controversy impaired judgment, and that human beings seeking to improve their understanding could make progress only if they were free to think things through without worrying about what conclusions the thought process might lead to. As it turned out over the next two years, this was probably an indispensable quality. Because the competing interests of the services, as well as national policies and strategic doctrines, would be affected by the disclosures the project would make, strong outside pressures were ever present. Whatever the outcome, it would tend to favor some entrenched interests and beliefs, and run counter to other entrenched interests and beliefs. It was crucially important, therefore, to convince the interested parties that the study was being conducted with completely honest neutrality, because only by winning that sort of respect was it possible to keep one's thought processes clear of subjective influences that might lead, even unconsciously, into easy paths of judgment to grind axes or avoid unpleasantness.

I feel confident in retrospect that perfect objectivity would have been impossible in that situation from any group. But I do believe that the intellectual atmosphere of that project was as honest as it could have been, and certainly more nearly free from undue influence than any other governmental research project in a highly controversial area that I know anything about.

It takes a long time for a research project of such complexity and magnitude to get under way, and many false starts are to be expected before you decide just how you want to go about it, because you have to learn a great deal through testing various hypotheses before you have any worthwhile ideas about what particular questions it would be best to try to answer. There were almost innumerable possibilities, and one could not test them all. Some time during these preliminaries I concocted a motto which I had the graphics people put on a sign on my wall. It read: "If only I may ask the questions, I care not who supplies the answers."

We had no idea in the beginning what major questions we would try to answer, but it was evident we would have to bring together the best information we could find on the characteristics of fallout, and that is where we started. John would attempt to determine what the probable physical effects would be — physical effects meaning everything up to the point where physics, physical chemistry, meteorology and medical science left off. From there, I would take up the problem of attempting to describe what the damage would be to human beings, to organized society, to national coherence and military capability.

We had three senior Colonels assigned to the project representing the three services, Colonel Joe Renner of the Marines (later to be succeeded by Marine Colonel Jack Dobbins) for the Navy, Colonel Bing Downing for the Army, and Colonel Ola P. Thorne for the Air Force. Officers and civilian analysts assigned to the project were initiated by attending a week-long Atomic Weapons Orientation Course at Sandia Air Force Base next door to the Sandia Corporation just outside Albuquerque. The course presented the basic physics of weapons that had been made and deployed up to then, as well as many movies of detonations with blast and thermal effects from Pacific and Nevada tests. Those attending the Top Secret course usually spent most of one half day in what amounted to the show rooms of the Sandia Corporation, where you could admire and pat sample models of the nuclear weapons built up to that date. On the final day of the course everyone would be taken to visit the weapons storage site in the mountain east of Albuquerque. If you had flown into town from the East, and were sitting on the right side of the plane, you did not need the stewardess to point out the secret weapons storage facility, as she commonly did, for you could hardly miss the dozen or so heavily built concrete entrances distributed around the base of the mountain and ringed by a high barbed wire fence. Once your tour bus unloaded you inside, you were escorted throughout by guards, their elbows bent at right angles, carrying loaded pistols — pointing upwards, you noted with relief. Everywhere, security was ostentatious, with armed MPs at the ready at every door and in every room. Yet once when I was visiting Sandia, the Albuquerque newspaper carried a front page account of the robbery of the mess hall cash register at the weapons storage site, noting that the thief escaped without a trace.

In high echelons, there were obviously mixed feelings about the study. Many among the top brass of the Army wanted the study because they believed that wider awareness of the devastation fallout would cause in a nuclear war would lead to reduced reliance on nuclear weaponry and correspondingly greater emphasis on conventional arms, and would thereby enhance the Army's place within the total defense structure. A certain number of Army officers were gung ho over nuclear warheads delivered by artillery, and their interests did not stand to be furthered by greatly increased awareness of the perils of fallout. But within the Army they were a minority. The Chairman of the Joint Chiefs of Staff, Admiral Arthur W. Radford, an ardent advocate of the massive retaliation strategy, was believed by everyone I knew to be fearful that any publicity about fallout would impair the credibility of that strategy. Many were honestly curious to learn just how great the peril might be. The AEC, RAND, the Sandia Corporation and the National Weather Service were studying various aspects of fallout. But no single study had yet been undertaken bringing together into one comprehensive package what was being learned, little by little, piece by piece, in various agencies and research institutions.

One thing I was given to understand at the very outset was that the study should not be undertaken in such a way as to emphasize the hazards of fallout to Americans and American society. It seemed logical enough to me that if we were interested in the way fallout might affect military capabilities, we had to appraise, among other things, what it might do to our civilian society, for civil society is the basis for the existence of the military. But when first I proposed, tentatively, to make a detailed study of the likely effects upon a real American city of a hypothetical nuclear attack, I was told that in no case should we study possible damage to this country. What we should study was the damage to the other guy. At that time, on the Pentagon side of the Potomac, they wanted no undue attention to what a nuclear war might do to the American landscape.

Inasmuch as the directive emphasized that the study was to be of the "military implications" of radioactive fallout, my own logic would have required that we give major effort to examining what the facts of fallout might imply concerning our national policies and military strategies with respect to nuclear weapons. Several individuals, most of them outside the government, had been trying to think analytically about this problem, and I was acquainted with most of them and their thinking. The earliest one to address the question had been Bernard Brodie, then with RAND, who had moved into the subject from studies of the Italian air war theorist, Emile Douhet. Brodie's thinking was as sound as any of those who were to theorize on the subject throughout the fifties. Those who followed included Bill Kaufman, also of RAND, then Tom Schelling, then Herman Kahn, Paul Nitze and Henry Kissinger. Subsequently the fashion spread within the defense community to speculate about deterrence and strategic theory in a world of nuclear weaponry.

The difficulty was that there was no experience and comparatively little fact to go on, and it all amounted — *as it still does* — to theorizing in a vacuum. One of the most frequent analogies in those days involved likening deterrence — or call it nuclear blackmail if you wish — to what was called the "game of chicken". This attempt to find some parallel with real life posited a situation in which there were two automobiles, driven at top speed on a collision course, with each driver intent on scaring the other into being the one to turn aside to avoid certain death for both. This contrived, artificial analogy left aside basic questions of purpose, of values, of *why play such a game.*

However logical it might have been for us to address this problem, we never tried. It was not desired that we should. Raising the question gets into values that are necessarily subjective. It should at least be possible to try to understand the nature of the problem and point out clearly the values at stake to those with responsibility for making grave decisions. Unfortunately, this is not the area where intellectual effort has been concentrated.

Lacking either the wisdom or the encouragement to attempt anything more, we decided to concentrate on estimating as best we could what the physical effects of fallout would be in Russia in case of a full scale nuclear war waged with current weapons systems and following current strategic concepts and existing war plans. With this much as a point of departure, we hoped, in view of our commitment to study the "implications", to be able to say a few useful things about how those effects would affect Soviet military capabilities, both directly and indirectly, by impairing the ability of Soviet society to support continuing military operations. We were not proposing to say anything about how the prospect of such damage should influence our strategies.

On a wall in a Top Secret, high-ceilinged basement room directly below the entrance to the JCS area near the River Entrance to the Pentagon, we put up a Mercator projection map, about 36 feet long and 12 feet high, of the USSR and immediately adjacent areas. Our first task was to enter the population of the Soviet Union on that map. The U.S. Census Bureau had recently completed a Soviet population study in cooperation with Princeton University and the Scripps Foundation, and this provided us with what was very probably the best information available outside Russia itself. Because of enormous population losses during World War II (generally estimated at over twenty million), extensive relocation and general disruption, both the total population and its geographical distribution were under dispute among students of Soviet demography. The figures we had provided estimates of population for all cities over 100,000, and elsewhere down to the oblast level. Population not credited to cities we distributed over the map in the form of dots, each dot representing 10,000 people, with each such dot placed where we guessed the center of gravity of that population would most likely be. Our whole map of Russia was spotted with these dots.

For big cities we had separate, large scale maps on which we followed the same practice of entering population as 10,000 person dots.

Here we ran into a typical problem. Even assuming our data accurately reflected people's residential location, which of course was too much to expect — where would they be when the bomb went off and when the fallout arrived? That would depend on the time of day, the day of the week, the season of the year. It would be different in peace time from war time, before or after a bombing alert, the second day or the second week of the war. It would depend on evacuation policies, mobilization practices, and official determination either to keep essential industries and services in operation or to hold casualties to a minimum.

Our first impression was that these uncertainties might invalidate our estimates, because shelter could be an important factor, and shelter could vary from one location to another. But eventually these uncertainties appeared to have less consequence. Within urban target areas, where most potentially effective fallout shelters might be found, immediate blast and thermal effects spread so widely that protection against residual gamma radiation from fallout was often of only marginal utility. Either the shelter would be destroyed, or the residual radiation would be so intense that emergence from the shelter within any reasonably short interval would be prohibitively hazardous. The imponderables surrounding almost every factor we would have liked to take into account contrasted with those stark measurements of the destructive force of bombs that had been tested, and growing knowledge of the unseen but deadly perils of radiation.

We dug up the best information we could find on housing and other architectural patterns throughout Russia, and learned that in most rural areas neither basements nor masonry structures were common. As a result, shielding from gamma radiation would very generally be minimal, except in special cases where there were mines or tunnels, or else suitable industrial or communal structures. Eventually we settled on arbitrarily assuming that everyone was at home for the first 24 hours. This overlooked those who were out in the open, completely unshielded, and those who on the contrary enjoyed more substantial shelter. Our guess in the end was that such differences were not critically significant, partly because when we sought to imagine in greater detail the consequences of such unprecedented and massive devastation, we found almost innumerable problems and hazards facing the survivors that we had no way to measure.

As a means of envisioning at least some of the local peculiarities that might modify the overall situation, I had two graduate students in sociology study two Russian cities in the greatest possible detail — the people, the buildings, the roads, transportation of all kinds, residential and work places, hospitals, industries, economic functions, diurnal and seasonal movements of people, location and character of possible shelter, the demographic and ethnic makeup of the permanent residents as well as their political subordination, and indeed everything that might conceivably affect behavior in a nuclear war situation. The two were cities about which considerable information was available: Smolensk, in western Russia, and Irkutsk, far to the east in Siberia. After several months of immersion in study of their respective cities, the two graduate students were asked to speculate on the courses of behavior open to the residents in the face of the particular attack, with physical damage and fallout, spaced over two weeks, assumed by our study.

If a lighter level of attack and general damage had been assumed, the particularities we were attempting to envision in Smolensk and Irkutsk might have had highly significant effects on results. But with the level of attack we did assume (which incidentally was but a very small fraction of the level of a war in the 1980s), those particularities did not greatly affect the outcome. For instance, Pio Uliassi, who studied the

Siberian city of Irkutsk, discovered extensive nearby mines that in an emergency *could* have provided excellent short-term shelter for many thousands of the third of a million people in that city. But that refuge would have meant little unless people got there before the bombs reached the area, and unless the mines were previously stocked with water and food. A decision to evacuate would have entailed a decision to close down not only the industries and the political control center for that area of eastern Siberia, but also the trans-Siberian railroad and land communications between eastern Siberia and all of Russia to the West. (We did not appreciate the significance of this at the time because we were still imbued with the official doctrine that the Sino-Russian world was a monolithic state controlled from Moscow and that therefore major transportation between east and west was not of immediate vital importance to the Soviets.) But the attack left the city of Irkutsk utterly devastated, and the surrounding area was a radioactive wasteland.

Smolensk was a smaller city, of about a quarter million, strategically important as a rail center in a war engaging Russian forces in Europe. As our hypothetical attack turned out, the early bombs intended for Smolensk in the first wave of attacks did not arrive on target, and Smolensk enjoyed a brief reprieve. For something like 36 or 48 hours there were no blasts in the vicinity, nor any fallout in measurable quantities. Then, suddenly, a rain dumped a very heavy dose of fallout over the entire area, and not too long afterwards the place was clobbered by one of a series of attacks intended to erase high priority targets missed during the earliest sorties. Lou Schatz, who was assigned the study of Smolensk under these particular assumptions, was honestly baffled as to how the people might behave. The interval following the first round of bombing was long enough so that evacuation would have been feasible for most of the population, even on a highly individualistic rather than organized basis. And Lou reasoned that because most of the population originated in rural areas not too far away, they would feel they had places to flee to in time of peril in the city. But would they try, and if so would they start in time? Would the authorities let them desert posts presumably considered vital to the continuing war effort? What would be the reaction to the initial absence of either blast or fallout in the face of knowledge of attacks and fallout elsewhere, some even visible on far horizons? We thought of countless questions we could not pretend to answer.

For our hypothetical attack, we got an attack program from the Strategic Air Command that they described as plausible in terms of their current capabilities and intentions in event of all-out war. Never, of course, would SAC have provided us with an actual war plan, nor would we have had the innocence or temerity to ask for one. Quite understandably, SAC operational plans were about the most closely guarded of all military secrets. I believe it is no exaggeration to say that there were elements of SAC operational plans that Curt Lemay, then chief of SAC, would not have disclosed even to the President.

Keeping outsiders — "outsiders" including even high civilian defense officials — ignorant of what went on within high echelon military circles was standard procedure in both the Pentagon and high service commands then, and, I suspect, remains so to this day. I know of a few occasions when it was relaxed slightly, but never for long nor enough to allow even those with most of the high clearances to appreciate the fact that critically important information was being withheld. That closely held monopoly on vital information was often exploited. There were times when neither Secretaries of Defense and their emissaries, nor even the President, were dealt with in full candor.

This was illustrated a few years later, in the spring of 1961, early in the Kennedy presidency, when Robert McNamara was in his first year as Secretary of Defense. This was a period when most of us civilians in WSEG enjoyed the greatest confidence, I believe, that the inner military clique ever accorded to the civilians who worked closely with them. Secretary McNamara in his first weeks developed a long list of questions he wanted answered as a means of informing himself sufficiently to make major policy decisions. It was rumored there were a hundred such questions all told. Supplying the information to answer most of them required considerable work. The questions were parceled out to the services, to a few in-house research groups, and especially to a group of operations analysts McNamara had recruited (many of them from RAND, with the aid of Charlie Hitch, who had come from his post as head of the Economics Division of RAND to become Comptroller of the Defense Department, and later was to become President of the University of California).

There was widespread unhappiness within the services at the demands for information put upon them in this way by the Secretary of Defense. The reaction was common that this amounted to sticking his nose into service affairs that were really none of his business. This resentment was combined with the idea that his ignorance of military matters was so complete that the whole effort to educate him was a waste of time. One of his questions did in some way involve SAC operational plans and capabilities, and was assigned to three ex-RAND analysts. Armed with a special letter from the Secretary of Defense, they spent several weeks in the JCS area gathering what they were led to believe was the full story concerning the questions they wanted answers to. But several JCS officers I had worked with who apparently did not consider me as much of an interloper as McNamara's men, dismissed their searches for information with smirks, saying those agents of the SecDef *thought* they were getting the full story but were just too ignorant to realize that the truly important stuff was being withheld. And I remember General Tic Bonesteel, with whom I was on especially friendly terms, and who was widely reputed to be a leading intellectual among the Army brass, asking as we walked down the hall after some meeting, "Have you been called in yet for the latest TV quiz show? It's the one called 'Youth Wants to Know'."

To what extent the attack program provided us was really representative of what SAC might have done in an all-out war, I could not tell. But the negotiations with SAC to secure it were conducted by our WSEG chief, Lieutenant General Sam Anderson of SAC, very close to Curt Lemay, and he very clearly accepted it as realistic. The data included not only targets, but details such as anticipated abort and attrition rates, timing of attack phases, re-attack priorities, and so on. For incorporation into our study, the material was turned over to Colonel Ola P. Thorne, an officer I came to know well and to respect for his intellectual honesty. Ole war-gamed it. That is, using appropriate randomized tables, he produced a record of what the SAC force levels and their weapons would do in carrying out that program. The result was a two week series of ground zeros in which hits and misses were recorded according to the anticipated CEP's supplied by SAC, along with timing of detonations. All of these were duly entered on our maps, both large and small.

The next step was to chart the nationwide fallout pattern on our big map. On the maps of major cities, we charted both radiation fallout patterns and the concentric rings of blast and thermal effects. Those "cookie cutters" for blast and thermal effects could be used only for those cities for which we had large scale maps. From the U.S. Weather Bureau, we had received a characteristic mid-summer weather and wind pattern for Russia and for as much adjacent territory as might sustain seriously damaging fallout in our hypothetical war. This extended not only into much of Eastern Europe but also over much of China and over the two major northern islands of Japan, Hokkaido and Honshu. Development of hypothetical fallout patterns under various assumptions of weather and upper atmospheric conditions was a problem that the Weather Bureau, the AEC, RAND, and the Sandia Corporation had been working on ever since awareness of the downwind hazards of nuclear blasts had begun to dawn following the mid-Pacific tests begun in the late forties. For our fallout patterns we used the materials developed by these groups, and John Magee brought in consultants from them to help develop the specific patterns we finally plotted on our huge map. For our cookie cutter measurements we used the criteria worked out by the Physical Vulnerability Branch of the Air Targets Division of Air Force Intelligence.

The fallout patterns depended for their configuration on wind strength and direction at various altitudes. But radiation intensity within those patterns would vary according to distance from point of detonation, the type and size of weapon, and the chemical environment in which the blast occurred. Even if airburst there would be some fallout, but massive fallout would come only from surface bursts, and in this case the intensity and duration of radiation hazard would vary according to the chemical makeup of the earth's crust (and other materials within the fireball) where the detonation occurred. As these varied, so would the combination of isotopes that comprised the radioactive cloud. This was entirely John's bailiwick and my memory is mainly confined to the impression that although the range of possibilities was considerable, John and his consultants reached agreement on assumptions that no one was to challenge, even though many uncertainties were resolved by compromise, that is, by accepting whatever variables appeared most probable. My impression was that in marginal cases where levels of fallout remained relatively low, different assumptions might have made significant differences in final calculations, but in cases where fallout levels were high, it didn't matter much which variables were used — the devastation would have been great in any event.

There was one exception I remember. That was the possibility of thunderstorms with heavy downpours, a highly localized phenomenon that can greatly increase fallout in the immediate area while somewhat reducing the amount of radioactive debris otherwise carried downwind. What this might mean showed up in one of the local situations we attempted to envisage when a thunderstorm and downpour descended upon our hypothetical refugees, exposing them to vastly greater danger. It was all entirely hypothetical, but illustrative of the countless real life complications overlooked by abstract generalized treatment of such phenomena. In reality, years before, a Japanese fishing trawler, remote from the Pacific tests, had been a purely chance victim of just such a radioactive downpour.

Upon the quagmire of all these debatable assumptions as to what the physical facts might be, we had to proceed to the main questions. What were the implications of these physical facts? How many people would be killed? Disabled? Immobilized?

How would the survivors behave? How much industrial capacity would be destroyed or rendered inoperative and how would that affect immediate logistic requirements? What would be the effect on people's ability and will to act coherently and efficiently as a united society? To obey and support constituted authority? To support the continuance of the war? What would be the effect of all this upon that sacred cow, "economic war potential"?

There was really no end to the questions, and probably there was not one of them for which there was really any honest answer. Many of us sensed that the questions we were trying to ask ourselves might be relevant to strategies of wars waged with other weapons, but not to whatever might result if indeed a nuclear war broke out. I am convinced that many of us felt that even in the best of circumstances the awful holocaust of nuclear war was utterly out of proportion to anything that might be either gained or lost by engaging in such madness. But the right kind of questions had not yet been seriously addressed, so far as I know, to anyone in authority by anyone whose credentials demanded serious response. So far as I was ever concerned, the good people labeled pacifists were right except for the completely disqualifying factor that as doctrinaire idealists they focused so exclusively on their goal that they neglected the problems of how to get there.

It was clearly impossible to prove anything specific and numerical, yet this was a world of inquiry dominated by physical science concepts where numerical specificity is the rule and failure to quantify is commonly regarded as a confession of woolly headedness.

One could of course make persuasive calculations of the range of probable deaths and disabling injuries likely to result immediately from the hypothetical attack. One could say with some confidence what the upper and lower boundaries of reasonable probability might be, and explain the variables that could lead to either higher or lower levels within that wide range. And one could cite at least a few of the incalculable uncertainties that would probably affect the final outcome of such an unprecedented holocaust. But even though based on the broadest possible base of social experience and knowledge, such statements would amount in the final analysis to speculation, and as such could be either accepted or rejected, depending upon how they appealed to previously established attitudes, regardless of the rationality and factual underpinning of those attitudes. It was indeed an intellectual problem within a political environment, which meant that perspective determined everything.

We obviously had to bring to bear whatever available recorded knowledge of human experience seemed in any way similar and therefore presumably relevant to the sort of holocaust we were hypothetically designing. This drew on three major areas of experience. The most obvious was World War II, not just Hiroshima and Nagasaki, but the Tokyo and Hamburg and Leipzig firestorms, each of which resulted in more immediate casualties than either of the atomic bombings, with overall national effects on the countries involved. There was also the bombing of Britain, first in 1939-40, then the buzz-bombing toward the end of the war. The Strategic Bombing Studies immediately after the war had studied the effects of these bombings extensively and intensively, including monographic inquiries into the apparent psychological effects and the political reactions of survivors, with emphasis on people's willingness and ability to carry on the war, as well as the survivors' attitudes toward the enemy that was bombing them and toward the leadership responsible for defending them. These studies were done by a whole range of sociologists and psychologists, most of them of considerable academic repute. I had been familiar with the studies for years, and I considered them a mixed bag, some shallow, others cautious but with insights. This material had to be used. It was the one source everyone in the business knew about (although very few had plowed through it), the one source that seemed relevant. RAND had a junior analyst, Fred C. Ikle, assigned to study this area. Fred had been working for years on a book on the social effects of wartime bombing, and RAND was trying hard to get some publisher to publish it. I had never been much impressed by Fred, but he was strongly recommended to me by Hans Speier, an amiable and often brilliant refugee from Nazi Germany who was an unswerving Cold Warrior. Out of deference to Hans, I brought in Fred for a temporary tour of duty, lasting several months, as a consultant to do a piece on what World War II experience could tell us to expect concerning the effect of extensive nuclear bombing on Russia. This was a mistake. Fred was a Swiss immigrant, and was punctual, proper, cautious to a fault. The study he did for me was like the book that RAND finally succeeded in getting someone to publish. It was a tired, unimaginative rehash of previous studies of the subject, mostly the USSBS material.

Along with Ikle's regurgitation of USSBS, I dug into what I could find out from well-known histories and monographs of the immediate effects of the Black Death of the 14th century. The plague had devastated much of Asia before spreading in 1347 to Mediterranean Europe, and the following year spread northward over most of Western Europe and the British Isles. According to the most scholarly estimates, it brought agonizing death to about one third of the total population, and some small cities were almost entirely wiped out, whereas some isolated areas escaped almost entirely. Its first wave lasted for weeks, even months, and it was mysterious — no one at the time understood the cause although it gradually dawned on many that somehow it was contagious. The factors of mystery and duration struck me as more pertinent to high level radiation than either sudden natural disasters or conventional bombing with high explosives or incendiaries. That, of course, was only an assumption.

The many accounts of the Black Death I consulted described a wide variety of human and social responses. You could find examples of almost every conceivable sort of behavior, from mob madness and wild orgy to coldly rational, richly generous, and heroic conduct. If you sought to generalize, it was next to impossible not to emphasize whatever aspects appealed to your predilections.

Two major judgments were hard to avoid, however First, there could be little doubt that the Black Death (which struck Europe first and worst in the two or three years beginning with the winter of 1347-48, but recurred spasmodically but less severely and in more limited areas for the next half century) was probably the most traumatic affliction visited upon whole continents of people at one time within recorded history. But on the other hand, the vast depopulation is credited by almost every historian I know with hastening the first major breakthrough in the emancipation of serfs in much of Western Europe, by making labor so scarce that peasants who had previously been the mere chattels of the lords of the manor were able to bargain commutation of their bounden duties to wages or payment in kind, and even to escape from the chains that bound them to the manor. Moreover, the intellectual movements that mark what we call the Renaissance, while probably not helped along by the Black Death, were certainly not destroyed by it.

Another conceivably relevant source was research then being conducted in what was called "disaster behavior", mainly for the Office of Civil Defense, notably by a team consisting of sociologist Charles E. Fritz and social psychologist Harry Williams. I enlisted their services as consultants and came to know both of them, and their work, very well. As a team they had made on-the-spot studies of the behavior of survivors of tornados, hurricanes, floods, major fires, and earthquakes here in America. On the basis of carefully disciplined research they had developed findings that suggested convincingly that in such minor disasters, there was a reasonably predictable pattern of survivor behavior, and that this pattern was in many respects significantly different from popular impressions and even from the notions prevailing among officials in agencies called upon to police and provide relief to disaster areas. Although relevance to the nuclear war situation was questionable in some ways, the Fritz and Williams studies seemed to offer the best insights of any available materials concerning what to look for in the bewildering conjecture we were dealing with.

It was evident when we completed charting the fallout patterns that casualty figures would be very high. How high was of course a question we could not evade even though we might have great reservations about any numbers. We had four young research assistants whose first task was to tabulate the population within the various fallout contours, recording, of course, the hypothetical doses they would be subjected to in accordance with the shielding assumptions we had worked out. In addition, they tabulated the population within the cookie cutter outlines representing degrees of blast and thermal damage. Knowledge about human toleration of gamma radiation was considerably less then than now. It was never simple. Effects are cumulative although the body is capable of some repair, at least to the extent that immediate effects of a given dosage will be less if it is spread out over a long period of time rather than received over a very short period. In consultation with the AEG Division of Medicine, John settled on 450 roentgens as L/D 50, meaning a dose of 450 r would be lethal to 50% of all people, while 1000 r would be 100% fatal very soon if sustained within a short time. Below 450 r the proportion of deaths would decline and fewer would be disabled. Presumably those who were physically strongest, in their physical prime, would be least affected. Those who did not die might have their life expectancy shortened significantly, and many would be ill and incapacitated for the period when they might have contributed to helping others, to restoring damage or to supporting the economy or the war effort.

We never fully completed the tabulation of expected casualties in the detailed way I had undertaken. The two bright young men fresh from graduate school brought into the project, George Pugh, a nuclear physicist, and Hugh Everett, a mathematician, were convinced that I was going into needless detail. For my part, I felt we were already over-simplifying to a degree that could result in missing truly significant realities. But deadlines were approaching, and we accepted their proposal to adopt statistical short cuts. First they wanted to put the whole thing in a big computer, but it took only a back-of-the-envelope bit of arithmetic to find that it would cost far more in both time and money to do the programming alone, not to mention computer time, even with further simplifications, than to proceed with my own laborious, manual tabulations. Instead, to hurry it along even more, we took a random sampling of areas where we had completed tabulations, and extrapolated this to all of Russia. This amounted in fact to a potentially gross over-simplification of even my own over-simplified model, because there were indeed local differences that this did not take into account. Above all, there were highly critical local interrelationships that it ignored. Such interrelationships were apt to be important, because, in most of the recorded experience we were drawing upon for insights into the likely improvisations resorted to by people and governments following local disasters, what was done involved depending upon adjacent but undamaged areas for relief and rehabilitation. In our hypothetical case, disaster was almost everywhere. For these reasons I was far from happy with it.

But I went along with the calculations nonetheless, and there were reasons for not objecting strenuously. We had ended up with figures of over half the total population of the Soviet Union either dead, dying, or incapacitated, with damage heaviest in European Russia but extending all the way from the Polish border to Vladivostok. From what I knew, I concluded that while our figures were no better than educated guesses, probably no estimates could be more useful. Everything I knew pointed to the probability that going into greater detail would have resulted in an even greater and more graphic picture of devastation. But if the prospect of killing and maiming over half the population of a huge nation within two weeks was insufficient to excite the imagination and stimulate fresh thought about the monster we had spawned, was there any chance that raising the estimate to, say, two thirds or three quarters, would make any difference? The problem was not to improve the numbers, but rather to make the numbers mean something real.

There were factors of considerable potential importance that we mentioned, but made no attempt either to emphasize or calculate. The prospect of forest fires over millions of square miles, especially if the war occurred in a comparatively dry period, was one. Contamination of food and water supplies, and wholesale death and contamination of livestock, poultry and domestic animals was another. Rendering very large areas so radioactive that they would be uninhabitable for extended periods of time (*permanently* so far as present generations were concerned) was another. Long-term genetic and carcinogenetic effects we did not mention, although with today's greater awareness they would seem important. And although we had assumed that the attack occurred in mid-summer, the situation would probably have been vastly more difficult for those under attack or for survivors if, instead, it all took place during the coldest part of a Russian winter.

However questionable some details might be, there was never any serious objection to the picture we painted of what might be expected to happen to the Soviet Union if SAC were turned loose in an all-out attack. But the problem of the implications remained. Of course it was clear that, since the Soviets already had a stockpile of nuclear weapons, albeit much smaller than ours, and some delivery capabilities, again much smaller than ours, despite the disparity we would at least be seriously hurt in an exchange. But for our study that subject was taboo, even though it was a heavy concern that could scarcely be ignored. During the period when most of our work was done — from late 1955 to early 1957 — the fear of war with the Soviets in the near future was somewhat less than it had been a few years before when first we learned that the Russians had developed the H-bomb, and considerably less than it became after the startling advent of Sputnik in October 1957. (I remember, however, that within days after the Soviets tested megaton weapons at high altitudes over the arctic island of Novaya Zemlya, there was much concern among our physicists and electronics experts about the resulting worldwide disturbance of radio communications. This suggested that we really had no idea what previously undreamed-of hazards the detonation of hundreds of megaton weapons might bring about.)

Whatever the taboos, it seemed obvious that more serious thought should be given to seeking stronger active defense against airborne attack on this country, and also to the feasibility of an accelerated program of passive defense (civil defense was the common expression). Equally clear, perhaps, was the implication that we should put greater emphasis on the conventional forces that might be utilized in situations where the issues did not warrant recourse to nuclear war and where the threat of nuclear war would not be credible. This last consideration, of course, was widely believed to be the reason why the Army had instigated the study.

Any notions of arms control, or of mutual reduction of nuclear weapons, or of outlawing their production or use, were completely foreign at that time and were never seriously discussed within the defense community, even among defense intellectuals of my acquaintance, despite the fact that Harold Stassen, the perennial Presidential candidate, was beginning to talk about arms reduction, and a few civilians with no government connections were beginning to sponsor forums of interested individuals to brainstorm their way towards a solution for the terrible dilemma that mankind was creating for itself. There was an Iowa businessman who, with Mary K. Lasser, sponsored several such gatherings to which I was invited, and I remember attending one at the Harriman estate in the Catskills, another at Princeton University, still another at the Fairlie Foundation near Warrenton, Virginia. Nothing ever came of them so far as I am aware. They were assemblages looked upon by many as relaxing three or four day vacations, with an interesting interchange of ideas, and also frequent clashes of ideologies, among a few of the near great willing to participate, along with many defense intellectuals, and others who were merely confirmed hawks, or confirmed pacifists, or who loved the sound of their own perorations, or who loved to be seen in what they considered an intellectually distinguished gathering.

Because almost any statement of what the "implications" might be would inevitably be controversial, and at least to some extent reflect the preoccupations and perspectives of those considering what the "factual" basis was, I had decided early in the exercise that we needed to bring in, as consultants, individuals of prestige within the defense community, whose combination of intellectual attainment, impartiality between the competing services, and general background in national policies, commanded respect. I managed to obtain as consultants Paul H. Nitze, Lincoln Gordon, Max Millikan, and, to a lesser degree, I managed to get Henry Kissinger for a couple of sessions. Although at that time he was less renowned than the others, he was already consulting at the White House, and never contributed more than a few grunts over the papers I asked him to comment on. Paul Nitze, whom I came to know quite well over the next several years, was by far the most impressive of the lot. I found him a man of brilliant intellect and high integrity. A man of considerable wealth, he had entered government work during World War II, helped direct the United States Strategic Bombing Survey and was one of the authors of the Marshall Plan for Europe. He became a close disciple and advisor of Secretary of State Acheson, under whom he succeeded George Kennan as Chief of Policy Planning and had a principal part in drafting NSC-68, the policy paper approved under Truman that established the Cold War hard line that was to prevail through the fifties. In later years he was to become Assistant Secretary of Defense for International Security Affairs, Secretary of the Navy, and perennial second man in the American team negotiating SALT with the Russians.

I respected and admired Paul immensely, and later, in the winter of 1960-61, I joined a policy discussion group he sponsored that included such diverse personalities as Reinhold Niebuhr (whom I considered a kindred soul), Roger Hilsman, Arnold Wolfers, Hal Sonnenfeldt, Jim King, and sundry others, mostly Cold Warriors. Despite my admiration for Paul, I always had big questions about him. He seemed utterly incapable of considering the Soviets as anything but unmitigated evil in absolutely every respect in a way that to me was inconsistent with the unmistakable intellectual urbanity he displayed in every other respect. So far as U.S.-USSR relations were concerned, it was a matter of us good guys and those bad guys. Every Soviet military move was preparation for conquest, never merely defense, while every US. military move was exclusively for purposes of defense against this Soviet threat. He used to remark how he and Acheson agreed that George Kennan had been taken in by Soviet deceptions, and had acted in some matter in a way he and Acheson found less than completely above board. I read into his words about Kennan a reaction to Kennan's more moderate views of the Russians and their Soviet masters. Anyway, I could never believe in the black and white world Paul believed in when it came to U.S.-Soviet affairs. I could never understand how a man so clear-headed, so widely informed, so fair-minded in all other matters, could have what I regarded as an extremely simplistic view of the Soviets.

I never questioned the fact that the USSR was a cruel, despotic police state. I judged Stalin, always, as a ruthless tyrant determined to consolidate the Communist revolution regardless of the millions of innocents who had to be done away with in the process. And not only Stalin, but most of the Soviet leadership, appeared to me to be clearly paranoid in their attitude toward the surrounding capitalist world, and clearly capable of considerable cynicism in dealing with it. I was fully aware of their ideology that called for eventual worldwide overturn of capitalism in favor of a Utopian dictatorship of the Proletariat, and also of their frequent use of Communist Parties in other lands to serve the interests and purposes of Soviet foreign policy. But it has always seemed to me that a sense of history required judging Soviet policies in the light of Russia's long inheritance of despotism under the Tsars, the repeated invasions of Russia from all sides, continued in modern times by Napoleonic armies, by the British, Turks and French in the mid-nineteenth century, by the Germans twice in this century as well as by Western Allied Forces (including U.S, troops in Vladivostok) to aid the White Russians at the end of World War I. This, to me, seemed a root cause of Soviet belligerence, and as a long-term matter the problem was to contain the Soviets without war until their psychotic fears of the outside world might abate. And the only chance of this occurring was to avoid provocative measures that seemed threatening to the Soviets, even as we made sure to keep our guard up.

I never argued with Paul on the matter. I believed he was sensitive enough to know I did not fully share his views. I tried to tell myself at times that my experience with Paul was a lesson in how honorable, well-informed, and even brilliant individuals can hold views on a particular subject that from my perspective seem compatible only with ignorance and vulgar prejudice. And perhaps he had similar thoughts about me. But one could also reflect that it is men of the same brilliance (and obsession) who can lead crusades against the infidel, start world wars, or, in this age, turn the whole northern hemisphere into a lifeless crater.

Lincoln Gordon, a professor from the Harvard Graduate School of Business, had been, along with Paul, one of the behind -the-scenes authors of the Marshall Plan, for a long time was consultant to the White House and the State Department, and later was to become President Kennedy's Ambassador to Brazil. Max Millikan was professor of political economy at Massachusetts Institute of Technology and head of its Center For International Studies, a highly respected outfit I had done business with before. Wild Bill Elliott, professor of political science (international affairs), was a highly colorful, very voluble man who had been occasional advisor to presidents for a generation. He was famous at Harvard for his evening seminars on current international affairs, and his hawkish views were highly predictable and warmly picturesque. Henry Kissinger was at work first on his book on *Nuclear Weapons and Foreign Policy* and then was teaching at Harvard, but short of tenure. I think both Elliott and Kissinger received consultancy checks for modest amounts from IDA, but neither ever did more than say a few words that contributed nothing other than to support my claim that I had consulted them.

Formal reports on our studies were submitted to the JCS over a period from the late spring of 1956 to the summer of 1957. Throughout this period, and indeed from the very start, the direction and progress of our studies were being reported to the three services by the officers assigned to the project, and by the research director of WSEG to DDR&E. Sometime before all the reports were in, word of the project somehow leaked to the General Staff School and the Industrial War College at Fort McNair, and authorities there addressed a request to Gen. Anderson, head of WSEG, for me to give them a 50 minute briefing on the study.

Anderson told me about the request but said he might have to refuse it because Admiral Radford, Chairman of the JCS, had forbidden anyone to discuss the project or give briefings on it. Anderson succeeded however in getting an injunction, and I was permitted to give the briefing at a Top Secret, Restricted Data level to the assembled class of flag officer candidates at Fort McNair. I necessarily confined myself to describing what we had decided was the likely range of devastation in Russia in case of a full scale SAC attack, and to what we thought we knew about the behavior of civil populations in historic cases of sudden disaster or broad catastrophe. I recall that there was a lively and friendly question and answer period following my presentation. But at a similar briefing in the same place a year or two later, when I had been invited to discuss further developments in research and thinking on the problems of mass devastation in a possible nuclear war, emphasis had shifted to lively concern over civil defense in the U.S., and to possible restraint upon use of nuclear weapons because of their awesome and unpredictable destructiveness, which indeed were the truly *military* implications of our study, the reception seemed to me considerably less enthusiastic!

Beyond developing what were by far the best informed and most carefully considered overall appraisals yet made of the likely devastation in a nuclear war, we had little to say that should have been a surprise to anyone who had been following closely the broadening knowledge of nuclear war prospects, either through classified Government reports or by reading everything on the subject that appeared in open publications, from the *Bulletin of the Atomic Scientists* to *The New York Times*. But there was something new in the fact that this was not only an official Government study, but a Joint Chiefs of Staff study. As such it included data and judgments provided by federal agencies considered final authorities (to whatever extent there were such things as authorities) on the crucial areas involved: numbers, sizes and types of weapons; radiation, blast and thermal effects of nuclear detonations; likely attack patterns including consideration of plan aberrations through aborts, miscalculation, attrition from enemy action, weather and other variables that could not be predicted. Although there was little that was really new, these factors assured major impact.

Most of what we said about human response to the attack was hardly new to specialized students, but much seemed new to those for whom the study was intended. From the numerous studies of response to bombing during World War II in USSBS, we generalized concerning initial responses to bombing. The studies suggested that lesser degrees of damage and casualties tend to unite survivors, to heighten their antipathy to the enemy doing the bombing. But if the period of damage, death and danger is extended over time, if casualties and damage begin to exceed the ability of governing authority to provide expected relief and protection, resentment against that authority tends to grow until it equals the resentment against the attackers. The suffering and deprivation and anguish caused by the bombing replaces whatever issues were previously presumably at stake in the war, and a new world is created, so to speak, wherein whatever issue was previously considered the cause of the war evaporates, temporarily at least, and the problems confronting the survivors in this completely changed world become, for the time being, all that matters.

Again, there was really nothing new about this. But to my mind the implication, which we never made explicit, was that there is no such thing as winning a nuclear war. Any cause for which a nuclear war is fought will disappear from view and be lost forever because there will be new problems and difficulties facing whoever survives that will be infinitely worse than any sacrifice endured had they chosen, instead, *not* to contest the original issue by force. One might imply such a conclusion to the JCS, but not quite out loud, at least not when Admiral Radford was Chief of Staff. It is not inconceivable that the good Admiral knew it (though I doubt it) because I knew many officers whom I believe did. But you did not clearly articulate the obvious, though even SAC suggested it with its mottos "Peace is Our Business" and "We win the wars that are never fought." The dependence upon nuclear weapons had forced us into a horrible dilemma we feared, but saw no way to escape from, and found it easiest to deal with, for the present, by simply ignoring the ultimate consequences.

Our project did have the effect of leading to the JCS directive of February 28, 1958 for a study of "The Effect of Civilian Morale on Military Capabilities in a Nuclear War Environment" which was explicitly intended to apply to the United States and for which I became Project Leader.

The format of WSEG studies, following Pentagon precedent, consisted of "Reports", which were quite brief formal summaries, on top of "Enclosures", which might be extensively detailed and served as supporting monographs, and at the next level below there would be "Annexes", ordinarily containing even more detailed compilations of supporting information. The Chiefs themselves generally read the Reports, rarely anything else, and depended on project leaders or more junior officers on their staffs to inform them of the content of the Enclosures in briefings in which there would be much graphic material, and main points could be absorbed quickly - often not too thoroughly — through the ears, and, so far as the eyes were concerned, by graphs and charts. The method was undoubtedly efficient but led to over-simplification. As for the Annexes, they were all too often mere collections of graphs and statistics of dubious relevance put in to give bulk and impressiveness to the complete report, much like superfluous footnotes in doctoral dissertations.

There was one report we issued that was received with great enthusiasm by our JCS sponsors, although I never considered it worth more than a footnote in an enclosure. This report merely expanded slightly on the fact that the particular weather and attack pattern and resulting fallout we had assumed for our study led to rather heavy hypothetical fallout over Hokkaido and Honshu, the two northern most and largest Japanese islands. The report went on from this to recommend that, assuming Japan would be a friendly power, SAC might consider either airbursting its bombs in eastern Siberia in event of war instead of surface bursts, or consult weather and wind patterns prevailing at the time of the attack before deciding upon surface bursts. There was also the added thought that similar precautions might be considered around the whole eastern and southern perimeter of the USSR. My own feeling was that this was dream world balderdash, but it was widely looked upon as a really practical, down-to-earth operational suggestion of real merit.

I believe the fallout study was among the most influential, in the long run, of such undertakings. But of course it would be naive to expect high-level decisions to be taken immediately on the basis of its results. Conclusions are almost never so black and white that plausible objections cannot be raised. Almost always it is possible to argue that the sponsors or the perspective of a study are less than 100% neutral. So the response to a study that sets forth conclusions implying policy changes is commonly to initiate another study, generally by some other group. That had in fact been the way our fallout project began; previous studies raised the questions we tried to answer, and ours was merely the most ambitious and most prestigious of such studies up to that date. Others would follow, and although I am no longer privy to such matters, I am confident they continue to this day. This procedure applies especially whenever a study suggests changes of policy that highest authority will not or cannot carry through. Action seems impossible, for political or other reasons, yet the problem cannot be denied, and so as a sop to those who keep raising the unwelcome problem, another study is authorized.

It is partly for that reason, and partly for the everlasting reason of lack of corporate memory within the institution itself, due to the constant turnover of personnel within military organizations, that, as those of us more permanently in the business used to say, "Every three years we have to re-invent the wheel."

Chapter Two

THE "HUMANE ALTERNATIVE"

Another example of this phenomenon concerned chemical and bacteriological warfare weapons. As early as 1950, a study had been made of toxic chemical warfare agents with conclusions that were generally negative. The following year a directive was issued for "An Evaluation of Offensive Biological Warfare Weapons Systems Employing Manned Aircraft", and a less than enthusiastic report was completed in July of 1952. In 1954 a directive was issued for a study of "The Status of Biological Warfare Systems" and a generally negative report was again turned in, in mid-1955. The Army Chemical Corps was deterred neither then nor later, and a directive for "A Reappraisal of Biological Warfare" was issued July 9, 1957, and another for a study of "Toxic Chemical Warfare: 1959" almost exactly a year later, on July 25, 1958. I had a minor role in both the latter studies, in each case providing an enclosure on the likely political and social problems involved in resorting to such weapons. I rapidly learned what little I could about the chemical and bacteriological weapons then stockpiled or being developed, receiving the standard briefings from the various specialists, mainly at Camp Dietrich near Frederick, Maryland. The newer nerve agents were coming in, along with what were represented to be (and I believe indeed were) incredibly lethal chemical agents. It was standard procedure for a briefer to hold a tiny vial high before you and declare it contained enough Agent X or Y or Z to wipe out the entire population of European Russia. The difficulty was merely to divide it up and deliver it to each of those doomed people. That was a problem they were "working on".

The Chemical Corps was small, but they were ardent believers in their research (it was the lifetime career of many of them), and their self-interest made it easy for them to have almost complete faith in the weapons they were working on. Often they represented them to be the humane alternative to nuclear weapons. Some chemicals would merely disable people temporarily, *providing* they received just the right dosage. A smaller dose would be ineffective, while a dose twice as large would be fatal. Of course there were problems in distributing the cloud of vapor sufficiently evenly in the face of vagrant air currents to disable people without killing them, but the vagaries of such factors as air currents, weather, and human error were easily ignored by those who had the faith.

The report we turned in on biological warfare in August 1958 was strongly negative, primarily because it seemed clear that the proposed agents were essentially uncontrollable and could result in as great a hazard to ourselves, if we used them, as to the enemy they were directed against. They posed insuperable problems of delivery, as well as of delay and uncertainty of effectiveness. We were informed the JCS approved the report. But it clearly had no significant effect on the Chemical Corps, which went right on with its research and even experiments in delivering incapacitating germ agents. Utah sheep later became inadvertent victims of one experiment. More recently there was news of Chemical Corps experiments with airborne disabling contaminants in San Francisco, and in the subway system of New York.

On the chemical side our reports were very negative, with the single exception, due to the personal judgment of one analyst who studied possible use of defoliants, that the use of such agents as a weapon *to reduce crops and food supply, in event of conflict with either Russia or China*, was judged a feasible possibility *in a long drawn out war*. At that time, the use of defoliants in Vietnam, and the consequences, were not even dreamed of. Otherwise, detailed studies made the use of nerve gases, which were the gases both most favored and most feared, appear undesirable in the extreme. A Marine colonel with wide ground combat experience made a study of all the practicalities of conducting day-to-day operations when troops had to be protected both from spillover of their own nerve gas and possible retaliation in kind, and it was abundantly clear that the conduct of military operations in the airtight garments and shelter needed would be, as a practical matter, so impossible that seriously considering it was ludicrous. Again a study with significant and strong documented conclusions, and again no action taken.

We used to wonder how it was that the Chemical Corps continued merrily on its way. It was small, and had no political clout we knew of, no special friends in Congress, no outside lobby of industrial groups. The only argument that made any sense at all for continuing their research and for stockpiling these unusable weapons was that the Russians were doing so, and we had to have ready a response in kind. To me this was never persuasive at all. Likely it was the same argument the Russian chemical warfare enthusiasts used. It was possible also that the intelligence concerning great Russian activity in this field was, at best, grossly exaggerated, because it was that same Chemical Corps that was responsible for the intelligence about what the Russians were doing in this field. My best judgment is that the inertias of a huge, not very responsive bureaucracy were the reason for the persistence of Chemical Corps programs. It was a comparatively small matter, there was no public outcry, so why do anything to rock the boat?

Chapter Three

THE CIVILIAN
MORALE PROJECT

The study I directed from the end of February 1958 to October 1959 on "The Effect of Civilian Morale on Military Capabilities in a Nuclear War Environment" was in many ways a repeat of the Fallout project. The main differences were that we considered the case of the United States this time, instead of Russia, and did not go through the tedious business of trying to make estimates of damage and casualties. We simply assumed extensive damage and casualties, and concentrated on trying to anticipate how the civilian population would react, how the extensive devastation and casualties would affect military operations, and what measures might be taken to minimize such detrimental effects. I brought back most of the consultants we had used for the social and political aspects of the Fallout Project, and had a retired Army General, Maddrey Solomon, try to develop estimates (based on raw data obtained from the Army) of immediate requirements for logistic support and civilian labor in a nuclear war situation, and, on the other hand, of the capacity of the military, including both Reserves and State militia, to assist in relief efforts in distressed areas. That part never amounted to much more than a bundle of ifs, ands and buts, partly because of the complexity of the problem and partly because we had made no effort to specify, in our hypothetical way, the location or volume of damage and casualties, or which military installations remained intact and which were either heavily damaged or destroyed. Nevertheless, the impression was projected that in general the military would be in as much need of civilian aid to continue operating as the civilian sector would be in need of aid beyond its own capacities if it were to continue as an organized social order functioning through previously established institutions. Not knowing any better word for it, we coined the term "privatize", which I suppose one could dismiss as jargon, to describe the most common sort of behavior that should be expected when constituted authorities and institutions failed to provide for the most basic human needs. People, both as individuals and as groups, would almost surely fend for themselves. Conduct would range from something like anarchy to the other extreme of improvised cooperation of comparatively high efficiency (considering the circumstances). It would be both "good" and "bad". The point was that as institutions failed, they would be replaced by on-the-spot improvisations, and respect for previous authority and institutions and leadership would be largely lost unless it recovered fairly soon and began to function according to expectation. Some new leadership and some new social arrangements would probably evolve. The devastation and suffering would be the issue, and whatever issue brought on the debacle would be, for a time at least, lost from view. If the level of devastation were low enough to enable established institutions and authorities and leaders to recover sufficiently before much time had passed, enough to restore order and services, many expediencies adopted in the crisis might be abandoned and the old order could resume, although certainly not without changes. If damage were great and effects lasting, the changes would be that much greater. Such were the rather obvious conclusions we sought to suggest.

We did have one major new ingredient, however, in the Civilian Morale project. Toward the end of the Fallout Project, I had brought in Charlie Fritz and Harry Williams to make a minor contribution concerning probable behavior of bomb damage survivors based on their studies of disaster behavior in recent floods, fires, hurricanes and such. For our Civilian Morale Project, they wrote a paper that sought to relate what had been learned from such studies to the problem we might face in dealing with the casualties of a nuclear war. They also tried to assemble data on popular responses to warnings of impending disasters in those cases where there had been warning. Here was material that related directly to contemporary America and our own institutions and that was based on systematic observation by trained scientists. They had not studied the events from afar or long after, but right at the scene, as soon as they were aware of the disaster and could get there. They had interviewed survivors, local leaders, government officials and relief administrators both public and private, systematically and in a disciplined way. Their quite persuasive findings contradicted many popular notions and mythologies concerning the way people behaved in such situations. Indeed, they found that much media reporting of events tended to perpetuate such myths, conforming to stereotypes rather than observing accurately and in detail. And all too often, they found, officials in charge of bringing relief to survivors approached the task from the perspective of those stereotypes. In reality, looting and anti-social behavior were far less common than widely assumed, and there were strong tendencies in precisely the opposite direction. Disaster tended to bring survivors together, to induce friendly cooperation among people who previously were strangers, to unite those not united initially against whatever was perceived as the common threat or source of danger. Not only were looting and rioting unusual, such behavior when it did occur was usually the action of individuals or groups from outside the disaster area, and was often greatly exaggerated by the media. Policing following disasters was usually needed to control the traffic of people who came either as sightseers or to help the relief effort, rather than to protect property. At least for short periods immediately after disaster — which was all that was studied — people most commonly responded courageously to injury, coped cheerfully with shortage and hardship, improvised imaginatively to deal with difficulties, and shared with strangers where, in a normal situation, they would have resented inconvenience and told others to go their way.

This study by Fritz and Williams was very warmly received. Not only was it a well documented study so far as data permitted; it told people what they wanted to believe. There was, however, a real question as to whether behavior in the situations they had studied had any relevance to the situation we were trying to envision. Today at least, I think not, although at that time I did not pursue the serious questions that lurked in the back of my mind. The levels of casualties and devastation in any nuclear war would have been greater by several orders of magnitude. Duration of danger and deprivation would have been greater. And scapegoating in wartime disaster situations had possibilities far greater than in comparatively small, natural disasters whose causes were not so readily controversial. But in that period there was a prevailing apprehension that dread of nuclear war would convert people to pacifism, and that pacifism would disarm us before our enemies.

I believe that the Fallout Project and the Civilian Morale Project contributed to heightening official concern about civil defense and to a period of greater emphasis on the role of conventional ground forces within our total military establishment.

Civil defense never really got anywhere beyond putting signs on bridges and highways that they would be closed in event of enemy attack (a most ludicrous gesture because the only thing people could have done, in such an event, was to try to evacuate by those very routes marked to be closed). This was later changed into the program to inventory suitable fallout shelter areas, put markings on them, and in a few cases stock them with water and canned goods. Sirens were installed in many urban areas without giving people any clear idea how to respond to them in case of a real emergency. They were tested so often that their familiar wail was unlikely to alarm anyone, except perhaps in the midst of a highly publicized crisis. Annual Civil Defense exercises continued, with Executive Reserve Officers going through the motions, atop Mount Weather, along with local Civil Defense directors throughout the country, pretending they were appraising, communicating, giving orders, just as they would at the beginning of a war.

My personal judgment about civilian defense was ambivalent, and I believe this reflected the mood of many who were knowledgeable. A broad program of protection from blast effects always seemed out of the question, and only a program of fallout protection seemed at all feasible. I constructed, with my own hands, a lean-to fallout shelter in my own basement. Although for years I associated daily with people who talked and advocated civil defense, none I knew ever did likewise. Most talked as if they believed war would come, eventually, but for reasons I can only try to guess they took no action to protect themselves and their families even though most of them felt others should do so. I knew enough about the mood in the Joint Staff to feel convinced that if the almost constant confrontation spilled over into armed conflict, it would very rapidly escalate into nuclear war if their plans and advice were followed. Few whom I knew questioned this. Yet there was a strange gap between what they said they believed and what they actually did.

The Army, meanwhile, although much of the time arguing that the big need was to develop conventional arms which could be used in limited conflicts, or to deter limited conflicts under protection of the nuclear umbrella, was placing much hope in the development of Nike Zeus, the antiballistic missile intended to shoot down incoming missiles with its own comparatively small nuclear warhead. In later years, at least a few of these were set up in the outskirts of Washington, including one I visited near Lorton prison. I remember a discussion of Nike Zeus with two physicists, one from Bell Telephone laboratories and the other from the Johns Hopkins applied physics laboratory, who had worked on the design of the system, in which I questioned the reliability of such weapons. I confess I was just generally skeptical of devising instrumentation that could be depended on to intercept one missile traveling several times the speed of sound with another missile traveling equally fast. But more than that, I was aware, in a layman's way, of the phenomenon known as electromagnetic pulse, which is an electromagnetic wave produced by nuclear detonations and said to travel faster than the speed of light, and which, although very imperfectly understood, was known to be capable of instantaneously short-circuiting and generally disrupting all manner of electric and electronic instruments and equipment. How would the Nike Zeus instrumentation stand up and function in the presence of multiple nuclear blasts? Moreover, there was talk at the time, in research and development circles, of the development of missiles that could be programmed to change trajectory and speed in the course of flight, specifically to overcome the tracking that would be necessary to aim a counter missile. And it would apparently not be difficult, in an era of electronic countermeasures, and counter-countermeasures, and even counter-counter-countermeasures, if not to jam the acquisition radar completely, at least to make it uncertain, without complete knowledge of the opposing equipment, to know whether one's acquisition system was functioning or not. At one juncture I asked the major advocate of the system how happy he'd be to sit under a mid-Pacific target, protected by a Nike Zeus, while a simple little half megaton weapon was lobbed at him from a couple of thousand miles away. The gentleman acknowledged he would not think of such a thing, even though, theoretically, the anti-missile missile ought to work in actual usage just as the tests of various components, tried out separately, had indicated they should function when assembled and put into operation as a single functioning whole.

Chapter Four

THE STRATEGIC
WEAPONS STUDY

The Tenor of the Times

In 1960, a third to a half of the entire staff of WSEG was assigned to work on WSEG 50, which was a study of the comparative strengths of the strategic forces of the U.S. and the USSR. This was a period of the greatest fear yet of Soviet intentions and Soviet strategic striking power. In the immediate aftermath of the shooting down of Gary Powers in his U-2 over the Russian heartland, Khrushchev ranted and humiliated an embarrassed and flustered Eisenhower, and followed this up by boasting of 100-megaton bombs in the Soviet arsenal while unquestionably massive weapons were being air-burst over Novaya Zemlya. Tension was growing over the status of West Berlin, with frequent harassment of Autobahn convoys, occasional buzzing of flights into Tempelhof airport in West Berlin. There was growing friction over escape of East Germans into West Berlin, accusations of Western use of West Berlin as a base of espionage, and a rising crescendo of Soviet threats to sign its separate peace treaty with East Germany.

Soviet detonation of a few monster megaton bombs combined with Sputnik and subsequent space flights suggested strategic capabilities for rocket attack on the continental United States, against which we evidently had no means of defense. Our means of countering, with apparently outdated delivery by manned aircraft, was perhaps inadequate. Our own lagging development of long range rocketry gave rise to general excitement over the "missile gap", which Kennedy made a key issue of his 1960 campaign for the presidency, blaming it, as well as the loss of Cuba, on international Communism, on the Republican administration, just as the Republicans throughout the previous decade had blamed the Democrats for the loss of China. It was in this deeply apprehensive atmosphere that WSEG 50 was undertaken. Most of us were truly fearful, even though a coldly rational analysis of available facts would indicate that for the present and immediate future our strategic strength was vastly greater than that of the Soviets. I do not believe any of us really needed an ambitious study to prove this. But this is an area in which, although one may on one occasion boast of overwhelming strength, on another one may as readily feel almost cravenly fearful.

All of our intelligence indicated we were far ahead of the Soviets in numbers of weapons. The Soviets had gone in for much higher yield weapons than ours. Our choice of smaller yields had been based on the judgment that the extremely large yield weapons were an inefficient use of resources. And we saw no reason to revise that decision. One reason for preferring medium strength strategic weapons was that the destructive radius (blast and thermal effects) of nuclear weapons increases only by the cube root as yield of weapons is increased. At the center of the blast the heat and over-pressure are in proportion to the yield — they *are* the yield. But as the effects extend outward they diminish by the cube root. Thus, three one-megaton weapons, for instance, would have a far greater area of destructive effect than one three-megaton weapon. The main advantage of the larger weapons was that they would be more effective against heavily hardened installations near the epicenter of the blast. And as for efficiency of delivery vehicles, there was no evidence then that ICBM's could be delivered with anything like the accuracy they were credited with a decade later. In fact, it was common talk in those days that our best geophysical knowledge was insufficient to enable us to tell with confidence precisely how far it was, for example, from Mandan, North Dakota to Sverdlovsk, or from Tyuratam to Omaha. Satellite observation is believed to have corrected this in recent years. Obviously enough, the Soviets had stressed missiles because their situation put them at a disadvantage with bombers. We had perfected refueling techniques for our B-52's, and there was convincing evidence that the discipline and morale of SAC were of very high order. We also had forward bases ringing much of the Soviet Union that could be used by medium range bombers, and much forward deployment was nuclear armed. In addition, there was our very strong naval presence, Atlantic and Pacific, and above all in the Mediterranean. Moreover, the fifties had been a decade of rapid advance in electronic warfare, including a long series of innovations in radar applications. There was development after development, and study after study in WSEG, of electronic countermeasures, electronic counter-countermeasures, and electronic counter-counter-countermeasures. And our experts appeared unanimously convinced that we were far ahead of the Russians and that the equipment aboard our attack planes would in most cases effectively disrupt Soviet target acquisition capabilities, and this, when combined with the various operational tactics SAC was continuously working on, would assure penetration to targets.

Unquestionably, there was ambivalence in prevailing attitudes about all this just as there was about civil defense. But much of the time, in most of our thinking, there was deep apprehension. Today it seems that Khrushchev had, up to then, effected one of the most bold and successful bluffs recorded in modern history. Not only were people fearful of growing Soviet military power, but most were as convinced as ever that the peril we faced was a Communist conspiracy, centered in Moscow to conquer the entire world, and that, above all, the Communist enemy threatening us was a monolithic empire in which every part and every event was directed by Moscow. Despite Yugoslavia, despite recurrent unrest in Hungary, East Germany, Poland, Czechoslovakia, the glib notion prevailed that there were no real divergences, no variously contending parties, no groups of socialists calling themselves Communists who might deviate significantly from Kremlin communism. If, in a different context, you argued that in any business organization, any "Free World" political organization, any religious organization, any labor union, any tribal group, any fraternal brotherhood, any college faculty, indeed any organized group of people anywhere, there would inevitably be contending parties seeking at least slightly different objectives and that sooner or later some would splinter off, nobody would disagree. So much was common wisdom. No one would dispute, either, that there were factions within the Soviet Communist Party when it came to discussing certain issues such as the succession to Stalin, and furthermore, it was customary to refer to non-Russian Communist states as Satellites that remained Communist only because of the presence of Russian occupation forces. But despite all that, it was still prevailing dogma that the Communist world was a sort of monolithic theocracy, and the men and groups who controlled it were really not bound by any of the otherwise universally applicable laws of human behavior.

An illustration of this came in mid-summer of 1960, when we were all heavily involved in WSEG 50. I learned that Don Zagoria, the CIA's expert on Sino-Soviet relations, had been called in to give presidential nominee Jack Kennedy a briefing on the recently confirmed split between Maoist China and the Soviet Union. There had been increasing reports of friction between the two for some time, so the word that a break had come and was really serious was hardly a great surprise to those who followed current international developments. In those days we had occasional seminars for senior staff members, both military and professional, intended to help them stay abreast of major matters relevant to our work. I brought in Don Zagoria to this group to repeat the briefing that the White House had had him give the Democratic presidential nominee. It was an excellent briefing, well-attended. After the question and answer period which indicated that many or most of the audience simply did not believe what they were hearing, I was cornered by several of my colleagues who wanted to address tougher questions to me than they had directed at our guest. Most of the questions suggested one or the other of two reactions. Either Zagoria and the CIA (or I for bringing him in to give his spiel) were guilty of being "soft on Communism" and misreading marginal evidence of minor disagreements into something far greater than what was actually happening, or the Chinese and Russians were putting on an act to convince us that they were breaking up, in order to further some sinister plot. Not everyone reacted in this way, of course. There were others who, like me, believed some sort of break would come sooner or later because of the enormous difference in cultural heritage between the two nations, their longstanding antagonisms and border differences, and simply because centrifugal forces are inevitable in far-flung empires. And we took heart at new signs of fissures in the Communist bloc. But there remained that large group, including a lot of bright and well-meaning men, who simply would not believe it.

WSEG 50, the Strategic Weapons Systems study, was such a comprehensive study that it was divided into several sub-projects. The project leader was a second generation Greek, George Contos, from the New York area, trained academically as a chemist, but whose career had been exclusively in operations research, a field in which he was very much a True Believer. I never had any reason to question his credentials as a journeyman chemist, but rightly or wrongly I considered that beyond the field of his training and most immediate professional responsibilities, he was myopic. He included me as one subproject leader, I assumed, because at that time my prestige was reasonably high within the organization, and there had to be someone with at least some reputation in the field to direct the studies that centered on the strategic aspects of what seemed to emerge from examination of purely physical factors. The main part of the study was basically a statistical exercise in which estimates and assumptions supplied by the responsible agencies were analyzed in almost infinite combinations.

From CIA, NSA, and the three services' intelligence agencies, we received estimates of Soviet strategic weapons systems for the immediate future, numbers, characteristics, deployments, and guesses of strategic intentions. From SAC and TAC and the Navy, we got comparable information concerning our own strengths. To these were added a range of estimates of such factors as abort and attrition rates, and CEP's under varied conditions. A series of situations were posited and explored concerning circumstances of the assumed strategic strikes, ranging from a Soviet surprise first strike to a U.S. surprise first strike, and including simultaneous initial strikes. Variant defense postures and warning times were taken into account. This part was a sort of geometrical exercise, with all conceivable angles examined statistically, always assuming each side continued to fire its strategic weapons so long as any remained to be fired. Both ground bursts and airbursts were considered, and both counterforce and urban-industrial targeting were included for examination, as well as at least some targeting of ground force concentrations.

To estimate the damage effects of these hypothetical nuclear attacks, damage and casualty factors that had been developed in previous studies, including our fallout study, were used. This ended up in the form of a series of factors for damage and casualties per megaton of weapons delivered under each of several assumed conditions. Even with this vast simplification, the calculations required not just hours, but days, of computer time. This led of course to many volumes of computer printouts.

The underlying theory of this analysis was that, in view of acknowledged imponderables, the best one could do was to lay out the entire range of conceivable possibilities and explore the likely outcome of each. There would be "a best case" and "a worst case". Then there would be one step beyond. One would try to determine under which set of assumed circumstances, if any, the losses incurred (losses meaning damage and casualties) would be "acceptable", and under which other circumstances the losses would be "unacceptable". "Acceptable" was the key word. I remember no serious attempt to define acceptability. Tacitly, it was widely understood that there could be no really acceptable definition of "acceptable" losses. But if you were going to talk about the prospect of waging nuclear war, you could not totally ignore the likelihood of sustaining losses yourself, and so you had to have some word that would signal the circumstances under which you would or would not use them, and it had to be a word that begged the question.

In the parlance of the Pentagon, the question of "acceptability" was a can of worms. I was happy not to be asked to suggest some definition. Had I been asked, I might have suggested that if losses could be held low enough so that the precipitating issues would not be overwhelmed by the issues created by the conflict itself (an extremely unlikely possibility), they might perhaps be judged "acceptable". But this would have amounted to answering one question with another question.

Fortunately, so far as my prejudices were concerned, the two young men who were in charge of the computations produced a series of calculations that said the losses on both sides would be "unacceptable" even under the most favorable circumstances. If the USSR launched a preemptive strike against the U.S. under the most favorable circumstances, the U.S. could still counterattack with sufficient force to inflict "unacceptable" losses. On the other hand, a comparable U.S. preemptive strike on the USSR would still leave the Soviets with sufficient striking power to inflict "unacceptable" damage on the U.S.

I forget what the numbers were, but I'm reasonably sure that the lower levels ran to something like one quarter of the population either killed or seriously wounded, with even greater proportions of devastation in urban-industrial areas, not to mention the long term contamination of basic resources (about which we know more today than then).

The two young men responsible for all this, theoretical physicist George Pugh and mathematician Hugh Everett,[1] struck me as from extremely bright to brilliant in their fields, but very naive about the world of man and society and politics, and hopelessly unaware of how much there was to be known about mankind and about the values for which mankind and nations went to war — or failed to. But I had no quarrel with the conclusions of their elaborate mathematical calculations.

The Command and Control Dilemma

The most exciting part of the Strategic Weapons study, and probably its most important segment, was its enclosure on Command and Control. There was little or nothing about it that was entirely new. But it brought together ideas and considerations, previously dispersed or neglected, in a way that gave them a dramatic new impact. For several years there had been a growing and uneasy awareness that the control of military forces in nuclear war would be enormously difficult and complicated and that we were critically unprepared to exercise that control with the largely traditional organization, procedures and equipment that we had inherited from the established practices of World War II.

Everyone recognized that events could occur with unprecedented rapidity in a nuclear war, and that decisions of national life or death might have to be made on an almost split-second basis, especially at the beginning of the crisis. It was understood that the crucial elements of what we did or did not do were military, but that the authority and responsibility for decisions were political. And it was believed that, as things stood, it would be possible, swiftly and with comparative ease, to decapitate both our national political authority and our national military command.

It was recognition of the vulnerability of the White House, Pentagon and Capitol that, years before, had led to the groping establishment of alternate military and civilian command centers, one in a hole in the ground in the Catoctins, another atop Mount Weather, initially in the old Weather Bureau building, and later in another hole in the ground. We had our annual exercises rehearsing what it was imagined we would be doing in case of a real crisis, but only a handful of us underlings participated. Few of us took them seriously, and the absence of high-ranking officials suggested they did not take them seriously, either.

Following these gestures at recognition of the problem, a National Military Command and Control Center was established in the JCS area on the second floor of the E Ring just inside the River

Entrance of the Pentagon. The NMCC was a close copy of the war rooms that senior officers had become accustomed to in World War II and the Korean War. There were maps on the walls, a big table to accommodate the officers, always a Brigadier General on duty as Duty Officer, a comprehensive encrypted communications system, and a secure telephone for communication with the White House and all major commands. Special clearance was of course required for access. There were situation charts displaying disposition of friendly and other forces. Routinely the service chiefs or their deputies gathered daily for briefings on all developments of importance, worldwide. If at any time there were actions or developments deemed especially important, the briefing would be presented by the senior officer of the J-3 task force that had been assigned to follow that action. Theoretically, there would then be a discussion of decisions or actions to be recommended, and when agreement was reached, a recommendation would go forward to the Chairman of the Joint Chiefs, the Secretary of Defense, or the theater or field commander, depending on the nature of the case. Of course nothing of consequence ever happened that way, nor did anyone I know really expect it to, although the charade was played out in all apparent seriousness.

Everyone's major concern, and the occasion for the strategic weapons study, was the possibility of general war with the USSR. If such a war occurred, it was widely believed it would be initiated by a Soviet attempt at a preemptive strike against our strategic forces. In any event, it seemed clear that much might depend upon extremely rapid decisions, instantaneous worldwide communications, and coordination of our vast military defense complex deployed from Korea and Japan and the Philippines through Middle East installations to all of the NATO areas even as far north and west as Norway and England. There were major naval commands in the Pacific, the Mediterranean and the North Atlantic, headquartered in Pearl Harbor, Naples and London, and in Norfolk. We had operational understandings with our NATO allies to whom certain responsibilities were delegated in event of war. Perhaps most important of all were the underground headquarters of the North American Air Defense Command (NORAD) near Colorado Springs, from which warning would presumably come if that most dreaded event, a surprise attack, were detected; and of SAC at Offutt Air Force Base outside Omaha, which would issue operational orders when authorized by the President.

Even a very general acquaintance with the facts was sufficient to indicate that we faced an enormously difficult, extraordinarily touchy, and potentially tragic problem. And the more you learned about it, the more difficult, touchy and dangerous it seemed. In an intercontinental missile age, there might conceivably be no more than half an hour between the first detection of a surprise attack and the arrival of nuclear warheads on target. In that interval, the first radar readings would have to be confirmed, and everyone knew that in the past there had been several false alarms, recognized as such only after delays. After the first blips on a radar screen, there would probably have to be a decision first to pass the information up the line, with some indication of what level of attack it appeared to be and how firm the judgment was — no easy matter as anyone who had read radar screens could affirm. In those days when our full dependence was on airplane deliveries, those of our bombers on alert could scramble at first warning within minutes, and under our Fail-Safe procedures could proceed without irrevocable commitment long enough to provide considerably more time for confirmation and presidential decision. But the center of the command system that controlled our forces worldwide, that would make the decisions and issue the orders, whether to attack or hold back, to execute current contingency plans or amend them, might easily have been eliminated by the time the B-52's were well off the ground and moving in flight formation.

But suppose, just suppose, that all of the high military and civilian political authorities were eliminated, at the very beginning, before command authority was properly, and to the knowledge of all, delegated to successor authority. Who would know for sure what to do, what was going on, what had happened, what other service arms were doing, what our allies were doing, how much of our own forces and indeed of the United States itself was still intact, what, amid vast alarms and confusion, including reports intended to mislead, could be believed?

The NMCC was on the side of the Pentagon nearest the White House, only a bit over a mile away, and the Capitol, half again as distant. Three megaton weapons would instantly eliminate all three. Two would take care of the first two, even if delivery accuracy was mediocre. Their communications, easily damaged, would cease to exist. Alternate underground command posts could be similarly taken care of. All with no more than five weapons delivered within the CEPs we credited the Soviets with having attained.

There were many within the defense establishment concerned with such things who shared a growing feeling that something should be done. The question was what. Inertia had to be overcome to settle on some course of action. There were a few proponents of greater hardening of existing command posts, adding others, and doing something more about emergency evacuations. But what was most discussed was the creation of some sort of mobile command posts to take over in time of emergency. Some favored command posts on wheels — special railroad train setups. Others advocated special ships, surface or submarine, and still others championed the idea of airborne command posts. No need to specify which service proposed which solution.

Among those who had become deeply interested in this situation was Joe Lewis, a downeast Yankee trained as an electrical engineer who had been one of WSEG's more senior operations analysts ever since its establishment. It was he, as I recall, who proposed that the Strategic Weapons study include a special study of the command and control problem, and he was assigned to direct the study. The study was comparatively short and simple. It was compiled by assembling the data available from the best sources concerning physical vulnerability of the current command posts, repeating what intelligence had been telling us about Soviet progress in weapons development, and presenting what appeared to be the advantages and disadvantages of the various alternatives to fixed command posts that had been informally and rather loosely talked about. The study was capably done. Its strength, however, resided less in what it said than in the fact that it presented the problem graphically and dramatically in a high-level paper which could hardly be ignored by those with responsibility to act in a matter of such undeniable importance. It was this paper, more than any other minor specific factor, that led to the establishment of a system of airborne command posts. The system involved keeping a plane with an emergency commander-in-chief aboard in the air and in communication with the NMCC at all times, code-named "Looking Glass" in later configurations. There would always be an effort to get the President aboard such a plane, but even in the worst case the idea was to have a general officer aboard, provided with contingency plans and residual authority to direct a war if and when the regular high command failed to answer.

Exploring "Implications"

My own part in the Strategic Weapons Systems study was close to being cut and dried. As in the fallout project, my assignment was to explore the implications of what was learned from examination of the physical facts. And these implications seemed, for the most part, obvious enough. With strategic weapons systems so destructive that in effect the use of them was self-defeating, the one sure implication seemed to be that the only military forces that might be profitably employed would be conventional forces that might be used without great danger of their use escalating into nuclear war. By 1960, there was nothing new in this notion. Many defense intellectuals were propounding this view, and most Army strategists and spokesmen were advocating a beefing up of limited war capabilities as the one area that should be accorded greatly increased emphasis in defense spending.

Such was the majority view in the Army, but there were a few Army officers who over the years had been so anxious to get a share of the nuclear arms pork barrel that they had become enthusiastic champions of tactical nuclear weapons. Also, within the AEC there were weapons designers interested in exploring the possibilities of smaller yield nuclears, even as small as fractional kiloton weapons. Combined as a lobby for tactical nukes, they were so influential that various small and shorter range nuclear weapons were being developed to replace conventional artillery. This of course prompted a controversy that has lasted even until the time I write this. Is there much chance that lower yield nuclear weapons could ever be used as artillery against an adversary that possessed large nuclears without almost certain escalation into unlimited nuclear war? My own conviction, then as now, was that in any area such as the European theater there was no chance worth preparing for that such weapons could ever be used without precipitating, almost immediately, full-scale nuclear war. Granted, the presence of nuclear artillery might inhibit enemy actions out of fear that counteraction might involve use of nuclear weapons and therefore escalation. But how confidently might we assume the Soviets would submit to our use of nuclears without responding in kind? And at that time we believed they had large yield weapons only.

In the fog of war and the atmosphere of distrust bound to permeate a conflict situation, how well could limited use be either perceived or trusted as such? And so on.

There was indeed an almost endless area of speculation in this as in other areas of nuclear warfare strategy. So much could happen so fast, so much would be irreversible and incomprehensible and totally unforeseen, so much would depend on how unknown human beings might react to an unprecedented situation, that the field was wide open to speculation. Theorizing about nuclear war was a sort of virtuoso exercise in creating an imaginary world wherein all statements must be consistent with each other, but nothing need be consistent with reality because there was no reality to be checked against.

Speculating about all aspects of nuclear war and strategy had become a game played by a score to a hundred generally bright young men with active imaginations. Jim King, Tom Schelling, Herman Kahn and Bob Komer were among the most facile and least inhibited. But many others, Paul Nitze, Bernard Brodie, and Bill Kauffman, were among the more cautious. Often there was supposedly serious discussion of nuclear strategies by analogy with domestic problems, sporting events, playground quarrels — anything. It was all like painting cloud castles.

Tom Schelling, who years later left RAND for an economics professorship at Harvard, seemed to me the most brilliant and the most sincere. He generally talked without notes, and with his eyes half closed, like an inspired pianist improvising infinite variations on a simple theme, would elaborate endlessly on theories of deterrence by drawing analogies to children's behavior in the community playground or people playing penny-ante poker.

Herman Kahn became the most widely known of all, especially after the success of his book *On Thermonuclear War* (1960). Trained as a physicist, Herman had worked in that capacity at RAND until bitten by the bug of nuclear war theorizing. He was of sufficient girth to be called fat without exaggeration, and invariably wore a wide and completely impervious grin. My friend Charley Fritz called him the Top Banana of the Nuclear Warfare Circuit. I once introduced him to an audience of JCS officers as a man who could make the prospect of nuclear war sound like a picnic, and he was obviously pleased. His manner was always jovial, even when he began by saying, "Let's think about the unthinkable", quickly followed by a topical joke. Herman could talk about Doomsday bombs, big enough to destroy continents or alter the earth's orbit, or 200 million dead in 200 minutes, assuring his audience of the reality of the prospect with a rather amused attitude toward the whole business. Sometime during the mid-sixties Herman left RAND to found his Hudson Institute, a think tank that specialized in everything, solved any problem anyone asked them to solve, for an adequate consideration, of course. For a while Herman then became a foremost futurologist, predicting "scientifically" what the year 2000 and even the 21st century would hold in store for us.

Bob Komer was a man the CIA let loose at times to attend various conferences dealing with nuclear weapons and Cold War strategies. He was perhaps the readiest to talk and most versatile of all three. On an impromptu basis he could become a plausible expert on almost any Cold War or nuclear war subject you might name. Later, during the LBJ administration, with the rank of Ambassador, he became the man who ran the non-military portion of our Vietnam effort while General Westmoreland commanded the military operations.

Henry Kissinger had of course been the first to break into print with an entire book on the subject, *Nuclear Weapons and Foreign Policy*, in 1956. It created quite a stir. I was happy to see a book appear on the subject because I believed the issue should be widely aired. But I was not too pleased with the book itself, nor were others I knew who had been following nuclear developments closely. Both Paul Nitze and Bernard Brodie were quite critical of the book, both in conversations with me and in published reviews. Among many there was the feeling that Kissinger had opportunistically seized upon the subject that others had been patiently grappling with for years, and with some support from the Foreign Policy Association had rushed into print, using and misusing the speculations of others who for their part had held back from such an ambitious venture until they felt on more solid ground.

I remember pushing a copy of the book at General Sammy Anderson during the days of the Fallout Project. Sammy looked at it suspiciously in his best SAG manner, which suggested that nuclear weapons and deterrence were affairs for Curt Lemay to handle, and were not the concern of foreign policy specialists or Harvard academics. He did, however, have the book "staffed" by the Air Force, later showing me their critique of it, which was moderately favorable, and he even read at least some parts of the book himself. Kissinger continued over the years to issue pronouncements on nuclear war theories, and especially on the vexing problem of the utility of tactical nuclears. But he never joined the nuclear warfare lecture circuit. I suspect he knew that keeping his foot in the door as a consultant at State and the White House (and only occasionally WSEG), while keeping his post at Harvard and finally getting academic tenure there, offered the best gamble for becoming, at some later date, an American Metternich.

There were, of course, many who were seriously concerned who did not indulge in strategic theorizing of this sort. But it was an area impossible to ignore, and many of the more cautious minds tended to dwell on the politics of confrontation and alliances. Where national existence itself might be at stake in a war, the effect of that threat upon political behavior in time of crisis seemed as worthwhile a field of inquiry as the invention of nuclear war scenarios in which emphasis was on physical factors rather than eventual political realities. It should have been automatic to turn for help on this question to the State Department or to the office of the Assistant Secretary of Defense for International Security Affairs (ISA). But on several counts this was out of the question. There was at that time no office of political-military affairs at State as there is now. I had lunch a couple of times with ambassador-level foreign service officers I knew to see if they thought I could get State to contribute to the study. They thought my idea was appropriate enough, but advised that any request for a study would have to go to the Secretary of State from the Office of the Secretary of Defense and then be referred down through several echelons to country desks that simply were not prepared to handle such business. And if by chance any work was done, it would have to return up the ladder in State, with the prospect of policy review at every echelon before, in whatever condition it remained, it could be delivered to the Secretary of Defense. It would of course be very nice for us to keep informally in touch. But none of us had any authority whatever to talk about such matters. As for ISA, although it had nominal responsibilities in this area, it very plainly lacked the staff.

The best I could do in the end was to bring in, as a consultant, Arnold Wolfers, Professor Emeritus of International Relations from Yale, and at the time with the Washington Center for Foreign Policy Research of the Johns Hopkins School of International Affairs. Wolfers was the most widely respected academic specialist in this area except perhaps Hans Morgenthau of the University of Chicago. Arnold had specialized, moreover, in the political problems of NATO and the Warsaw Pact nations and the year before had edited a well-received book on *Alliance Policy in the Cold War*. What Wolfers produced for me was an excellent background paper that suggested the range of political strains on the opposing alliances that might significantly influence national behavior in a crisis in which nuclear war appeared imminent. In my mind it realistically raised the possibility of many contingencies that in an emergency would make it wise to depart significantly from the assumptions underlying existing planning. But I question that it made much impression upon anyone who had any power to influence anything. Top level decisions would be made, or influenced, by officials too busy to participate in, or even read, such a study.

It is perhaps impossible to put over more than one or two points at a time on any important subject in such a framework. In addition to presenting dramatically the command and control vulnerability that spurred creation of an airborne command post, the point that the Strategic Weapons System study got across, perhaps as well as possible, was that even in the best circumstances imaginable, the losses the U.S. would sustain in a nuclear war would be "unacceptable". Therefore, improvement in our active military capabilities should come mainly in the area of increased capacity to fight a limited war (limited war being construed to mean war waged without nuclear weapons). Mine was the part of this study that dwelt on that very obvious conclusion — obvious, perhaps, without any such study, except to the remaining few who believed the threat of massive retaliation should be the answer to almost every provocation, great or small.

The study was completed and went through the process of being approved by our review board near the end of 1960, after that year's elections but before the new President and new Secretary of Defense took office. Very probably because of the interregnum, nothing further happened to the study until, not more than a week after Kennedy's inauguration, I received a call at seven o'clock one snowy morning that Secretary of Defense McNamara wanted a briefing on the project at 9:30, leaving little time to get organized. The Director of WSEG and the four or five of us who had major pieces of the study were shown into

McNamara's office where Charlie Hitch, whom I had known for years while he was at RAND, was the only other person there besides McNamara himself. The briefing began with listings of all the strategic weapons in the inventory, their characteristics and capabilities, identifications of those being phased out and specifications of those coming into the arsenal or in the research and development phase.

Almost immediately it became apparent that we had a different type of audience than we were used to. Instead of sitting back and listening passively, McNamara almost immediately began to take notes on every significant point that was made, and soon was directing questions, sometimes to Charlie Hitch, sometimes to the briefer, to make sure he understood what was being said. Many of his early questions revealed his lack of familiarity with the weapons systems that were the subject of our study. But it quickly became evident that when he did not understand something fully, he asked questions until he got answers that made things clear. And he often questioned briefers to the full extent of their knowledge. I was frankly amazed at how fast he seemed to learn. Except for a short break for lunch, the briefing went on all day. My own part of it was reserved for the last, and I was very late getting home for dinner. We had not presented a tidy formal briefing of the customary kind, nor as we had intended. But by the end of the day, always taking notes, the Secretary of Defense had heard, and had seemed to absorb, almost everything we had to say.

Within no more than two or three days we had another call for a briefing, this time for McGeorge and Bill Bundy. The former was there as the eyes and ears of the President. This time we managed to present the material in the customary form in a briefing that lasted, probably, two to three hours. The Bundy brothers listened closely and complimented us on the study, but there was none of that intense, querying interest that McNamara had shown. And a few days later it came turn for the Joint Chiefs. The briefing proceeded without a hitch. But when it was concluded, at which juncture there would usually be questions, perfunctory or otherwise, just one question was asked: "Who else is getting this briefing?"

PART III

THE CRITICAL
INCIDENT
STUDIES

The Command and Control enclosure of the Strategic Weapons study was probably the immediate precipitating agent for a broad directive to WSEG early in 1961 to study almost all aspects of command and control. Command and control amounts to vastly more than the mere military jargon makes it appear to be. Development of a dependably survivable communication and command system (to this day, twenty years later, several agencies are working on it) is by no means all that is involved.

Even if the physical and technological means of communication and command are unimpaired, everything may still depend on human factors. High command decisions are usually the culmination of a process involving literally countless inputs, almost any one of which may be critical to the outcome. They entail such factors as the choice, in every stage of the process, from the lowest to the highest levels, made by individual human beings, of the few critically important bits of information out of what is literally an infinitude of bits of information. They depend on human judgment to determine what to look for — a very uncertain factor, because humans rarely recognize the significance of the unexpected.

Within the Operations Directorate (J-3) of the JCS there was keen awareness of the critical importance of these human factors, as there was, also, among many of those in the defense community not addicted exclusively to technology. There had begun to be studies of how we tried to manage matters in such affairs as the Quemoy-Matsu crisis in the Formosa Straits a couple of years before. It had occurred to me that if we could undertake and intensify studies of crisis management not just as conventional historical studies based on surviving documentary materials, but on the *complete* flow of information through the command center — most of which never got into permanent files — and even observe the command operation contemporaneously, *as it occurred*, we might improve our understanding of the process. Most of those with whom I had discussed the idea dismissed it as a noble pipe dream. Responsible operators would never tolerate analysts looking over their shoulder to find out how things might be done better. That would amount to nothing but irresponsible kibitzing.

Nevertheless, in the spring of 1961, J-3 indicated orally that they would probably have us make such studies, and in the early summer they made this official with a signed memorandum. In the absence of Joe Lewis, who had been put in charge of all Command and Control studies in WSEG, I was handed the memorandum by the general officer then in command of J-3: "I think it may be good for you to study our operations and suggest how they might be improved," he remarked. "But you are to tell *us* about the mistakes we make — not advertise them to the whole world." And to safeguard this close confidentiality, it was specified that our studies should be in the form of memoranda delivered directly from our project to J-3, bypassing both the regular WSEG review board process and standard JCS distribution.

Thus began what, for me, turned into seven years of intensive study of how and where command decisions were made, and what factors determined the direction they took. In those years there were studies of some sixteen incidents, or crises, during the sixties, in which military actions were taken. These included the Laos crisis of 1960-1961, two crises in the Dominican Republic, one under the Kennedy administration and one under the Johnson administration, the Cuban missile crisis, the Congo crisis centering around the assassination of Patrice Lumumba, the Tonkin Gulf crisis of 1964, and the Berlin Wall crisis and surrounding incidents precipitated by Soviet harassment of Allied access to West Berlin. There were other studies of the handling of critical situations caused by disorders in the Panama Canal Zone, the Watts riot in Los Angeles, and the Northeast Power Blackout.

Although I was the initiator of these studies, I had close working knowledge of only two of them, the Laos affair and the protracted problem of Communist threats against West Berlin. At the very beginning I was joined by Ed Janicik, Len Wainstein and John Ponturo, who worked full time on the other incidents. The four of us were helped considerably by others who worked on detachable aspects of particular problems. But it was largely like basic historical research, which meant laborious, almost endless grubbing through mountains of detail that needed to be integrated by a single mind aware of all details as it appraised a single problem.

From the beginning, we were granted access to documentation never granted, so far as I know, to any other individuals or study groups for the purpose of historical record. But the degree of access varied considerably. Unrestricted access came only as confidence in us grew.

Tight control was the necessary price for access to the material used in many of the studies. To anyone familiar with the workings of organizations engaged in operations that cannot be publicized, this should be understandable. To get the picture as fully as possible, it was regularly necessary to have privileged material. Material from CIA and State came into JCS that was clearly intended to be revealed to no one who did not have actual operational responsibility. For J-3, or any agency, to have lived strictly by the rules of the game would have meant asking permission of the agencies from which these materials came before releasing it to us. The effect would have been to delegate to the security officers of the originating agency the responsibility for determining whether or not we got the material, and security officers are notoriously inclined to concentrate on preventing leaks and wholly unconcerned about the necessity of sharing essential information.

Probably the extreme example of the sensitivity of the material that, at least at times, was made available and used, was that of President Johnson's recorded conversations with the NMCC Duty Officer. For very good operational reasons, all conversations over that classified command link were recorded. This provided an indisputable record of oral reports and commands, inquiries, requests, replies — all sorts of things of which it was good to have an undeniable record rather than a hazy memory. During some periods of tension over events in Vietnam, President Johnson would call the NMCC Duty Officer in the middle of the night ("when he got up to pee," was the saying around NMCC) to ask if there was anything new, and to find out how "our boys" were doing. I remember at least one brief period when we kept two highly trusted typists busy transcribing tapes of these calls. How many heads would have rolled had LBJ learned of this is hard to tell, but surely those in positions of responsibility would have felt his wrath, and I'm sure they were well aware of it.

It was apparently the fear of major breach of security that finally brought an end to the Critical Incident Studies. Sometime in 1968 there was a leak to Senator Fulbright of the Tonkin Gulf study. When he publicized the matter, a progressive tightening of security began. All copies of the studies were taken from the safes of those of us who had worked on them and placed in a special area to which only a selected few had access. Within about a year a point was reached when those of us who had made the studies were no longer permitted to see what we had written. Some of my colleagues of those days attribute the final phases of restrictions on the studies to a general tightening of security in response to Dan Ellsberg's delivery of copies of the Pentagon Papers to *The New York Times*. There was a time after my retirement in 1969 when I was told all of the reports had been destroyed. More recently I have been informed that copies of all the studies are still in existence under control of the NMCC, but access to them is severely restricted. I see little reason why they should still be held so closely. They amount, essentially, to little but historical monographs, based on privileged information rarely available to historians dealing with incidents that occurred fifteen to twenty years ago. Nothing in them could be of any practical use to an enemy. Some details would no doubt be embarrassing to some participants, but most of those are dead now, and most of what would be embarrassing has long since been leaked to newsmen or made public by the Pentagon Papers or by congressional investigating committees.

Chapter One

THE LAOS CRISIS: 1960-1961

The first study undertaken, and one that I did entirely by myself, was on the Laos Crisis of 1960-61. Laos had been a hot spot of diplomatic maneuvering, undercover operations, and some overt military operations, as well as politically motivated economic aid, ever since 1954, and it remained a critically contested area for another fifteen years until it resolved itself into an incontestably Communist state.

However, the period from August 9, 1960, when an obscure Lao paratrooper Captain named Kong Le staged a coup to overthrow the government installed the previous spring by a faction sponsored by the CIA, until June 1961, when President Kennedy and Chairman Khrushchev, in Vienna, agreed to support a local cease-fire and settle for a neutralist Laos, was the period when immediate dangers were greatest and pressures upon those making operational and policy decisions were most intense.

Whereas some later studies of other crises were undertaken as actions unfolded, and with more nearly complete access to the facts, I did not begin this study until the summer of 1961, two or three months after the tension had relaxed. My principal source was the file of material that had been in the hands of the JCS action officers throughout the crisis. This consisted mainly of military message traffic, intelligence reports, special studies and reports, pertinent contingency plans and appraisals, and copies of State Department and CIA message traffic and reports that these agencies saw fit to supply to the JCS. These were voluminous, but obviously not complete. There were White House and NCS materials, informative but less voluminous, and again incomplete. It was reasonably clear, nevertheless, that the available material provided the basis for understanding pretty well what information was at hand when most decisions were made, even though it did not disclose clearly everything that was going on.

One major lacuna was a record of the working papers of the special White House task force on Laos set up by Kennedy in February 1961. Concerning Laos, Kennedy evidently lacked confidence in the judgment of those in State, CIA and Defense who until then had been making decisions (uncoordinated, and often at odds) regarding that country, and who had been the authors of "the mess" he had inherited from Eisenhower. That task force, with Kennedy himself playing a major and constant role, became the action office from early March on, when the little Laos affair had grown into a major superpower confrontation. From then on, the Pentagon was called upon for information, appraisals and recommendations, but with the White House task force and Kennedy himself taking direct control, the materials in the JCS action officer files became an obviously incomplete record of how and why decisions were made. It had become a superpower confrontation at the highest level, with Kennedy dealing directly and even face to face on occasion with Gromyko, Prime Minister Macmillan, President de Gaulle, Nehru and Khrushchev. Whatever information the JCS supplied I believe I knew about, but whatever the White House knew but did not deign to tell the JCS I could only guess. (Some of it would be later confirmed or revealed in such memoirs as those of Ted Sorenson and Arthur Schlesinger.)

I had one minor advantage. Major General John A. Heintges, who had been the senior U.S. military man in Laos in the year preceding the crisis, was assigned to the JCS in an office not far from mine and graciously helped me by recalling the background and personalities involved in the events I was trying to understand. His reminiscences not only added color to the cold documentary materials — the message traffic, intelligence reports and formal appraisals — but helped me interpret references and innuendos that were otherwise obscure.

Laos was a little landlocked country of about three million people just beginning to emerge into the modern world. It was not and never had been a nation as we understand the term. It had no railroad, its single French-built north-south highway about half its length was impassable during monsoons, east-west roads were trails, a few recently constructed airports accommodated only smaller planes. Its boundaries and ethnic makeup had shifted over the centuries as different dynasties had divided it up and as it had endured invasions, and sometimes rule, by Thais, Vietnamese, Khmers and Chinese. It had been the last area brought under control by the French in their step-by-step colonial conquest, in the late 19th century, of what came to be known as French Indochina. But the French never exploited it as much as they did Annam, Tonkin and Cochinchina, nor did they exercise so tight a control. It was largely illiterate, and wholly Buddhist, except for minorities of preliterate, animist, aboriginal tribes in more remote mountainous areas. From the time of their conquest in the 1890s, the French ruled Laos largely through the agency of the royal family and a princely and hereditary elite estimated at no more than 20,000. Many of them were educated in France and took on many French cultural traits. The masses remained largely unchanged from their dreamy past.

In the early stages of World War II, the Japanese occupied French Indochina intent on making it a part of their "Greater East Asia Co-Prosperity Sphere." The war kept them too busy elsewhere to give Laos even as much attention as had the French. With defeat looming, the Japanese in March 1945 declared Laos an independent kingdom. This left the land free of any foreign suzerain for the first time in several centuries. But Ho Chi Minh and his Vietminh guerrillas were already active and growing in strength in the forests and countryside of adjoining Tonkin, and occasionally infiltrated the mountainous Lao border. In those Lao borderlands they began to recruit Laotian guerrillas who absorbed at least much of the anti-colonialist, nationalist ideology of Ho and generally were taught to share, however they understood them, the Marxist notions advocated by the Vietminh. Politically, these guerrillas were the beginning of what became the Lao Patriotic Front (Neo Lao Hak Sat), later more commonly known as the Pathet Lao, which was really the name of their military organization.

Soon after the Japanese surrender in August 1945, the British transported Free French Forces to South Vietnam, and soon thereafter French paratroopers were dropped into key areas of western Laos to restore French colonial rule. Some of the old ruling elite welcomed the return of the French, others were opposed, and a few joined the Pathet Lao in their guerrilla opposition. This tripartite division became the basis of the three political groups that for two decades would struggle to gain control of the country. There was a desultory, inconclusive, back and forth struggle in Laos from the time the French colonialists returned until the Vietminh's defeat of the French at Dienbienphu. This was followed by the 1954 Geneva Accords which confirmed the independence of Laos.

By this time the Pathet Lao had established themselves as the party of the left. They were generally strongest along the border with North Vietnam, whence came ideology and material support of various kinds. Centrist and rightist political groupings developed among the older ruling elite. The centrists tended generally to be neutralist, nationalist, and to advocate coalition government including all political groups within the country. The rightists drew much strength and most leaders from the military, wanted to exclude the Pathet Lao from any coalition government and sought support from anti-Communist foreign governments.

In 1947 a constitution was promulgated making Laos a constitutional Monarchy with an elected National Assembly. In practice elections were generally meaningless. With a largely illiterate population, they were commonly rigged, and coups d'état were found to be a more expeditious means of changing governments. In the years preceding August 1960, there were ten changes of government, most of them either outright coups or changes brought about by the threat of force. There was some occasional violence in this period but, generally speaking, there were more alarms than excursions, more deployments than battles, and political upheavals resembled games of musical chairs, neither really democratic nor very violent. Prince Souvanna Phouma, a centrist, was Prime Minister three times during this period, as he was three times during and after 1960. His half-brother, Prince Souphannouvong was throughout this period the leader of the Pathet Lao and as such in jail when the rightists were in power, and a Cabinet member when the centrists tried to govern. Phoui Sananikone was Prime Minister twice, both times deposed abruptly but without major violence. Prince Boun Oum, a rightist, had been Prime Minister briefly back in 1950, and was Prime Minister of the right wing faction that emerged from the confusions of the 1960-61 crisis.

If until the crisis of 1960-61 the struggles in Laos had many comic opera aspects, and if until then most Americans had never even heard of the place, all this was to change in the eight months beginning August 9, 1960. As the French gradually withdrew after 1954, the country evolved into a client state of the United States, and the struggle for control of the country gradually turned from a largely local conflict of parties into a confrontation between the U.S. and the Soviets. By 1957, the U.S. had two major but uncoordinated programs in Laos, one operated by the CIA, and the other a program of foreign economic aid. In 1960 there were an acknowledged 700 Americans in the country, mainly in the administrative capital of Vientiane. They were either U.S. civil servants or contract personnel paid for by the American aid program. Initiated on a small scale in 1953, by 1960 that program had cost the U.S. $300 million, and on an annual basis amounted to about three fourths of the Lao national budget. The 700 Americans included some but not all of an organization called the Programs Evaluation Office (PEO). The PEO consisted of temporarily decommissioned ("sheep-dipped") regular Army officers. They were in Laos, really, as a Military Assistance Advisory Group (MAAG), but could not be identified as such because the 1954 Geneva Accords forbade the stationing of any foreign military personnel in Laos except the French. Many of the Americans there, both civilian and military, gave the impression that they had come to Laos for a lark or a fast buck. The French were there to help develop and train the Royal Lao Army. The Accords, undersigned by all the great powers except the U.S., declared Laos neutral. But U.S. policy since some time before 1958, as developed by Secretary of State Dulles, sought to make Laos into a bastion of democracy, democracy to him meaning anti-communism. To help bring this about, we had brought in a sizeable CIA contingent, supposedly secret, but that was at times blatant enough to be written up in the French and American metropolitan press. The CIA had its own airline, including both cargo planes and trainer aircraft suitable for light combat if not opposed by modern fighters. The CIA had instigated the formation in 1957 of a right wing group called the Committee for the Defense of National Interests (CDNI), which had surfaced in 1958 and had largely dominated Lao politics since then. CIA operations were covert, controlled out of Bangkok, and often not revealed to the American Ambassador.

It is out of the question here to provide a detailed chronicle of the events that comprised the Laos Crisis of 1960-61. As I write this it is 18 years since I completed the study, many details have dimmed. I am denied access to what I wrote. There were so many backings and fillings that no narrative could possibly provide a full account of the vicissitudes of those eight months without going into such detail it would fill a very large book.

Yet I can remember clearly several things that the study revealed about how decisions were made concerning our policies and actions. We were not making decisions and policies, much of the time, the way we thought we were or the way we professed that such decisions should be made. Sometimes actions were taken or decisions were made in one place or by one agency that committed us in a direction that clearly would have been decided otherwise if the presumably responsible echelon of command had decided what course to pursue in the light of information that was, incontestably, in the hands of other agencies or echelons presumably serving the U.S. Sometimes information that was crucial to high policy decisions was present at low echelons but was filtered out and lost as it was forwarded to higher echelons. This appears to have occurred occasionally for reasons of maintaining operational secrecy. Often the slip occurred because somewhere along the way the relevance and importance of the item was not grasped by an intermediary. More often the difficulties arose from the fact that different American agencies, and factions within these agencies, had conflicting ideas of what actions would best serve our interests, and much of the time, lacking coordination, they worked at cross purposes.

We had four agencies involved in Laos: the Embassy, the Economic Cooperation Administration (ECA, but known by different names in different years), the PEO and the CIA. Each had its mission, and all were, theoretically but by no means in fact, coordinated through the Embassy. As a result, much of what one agency did came as a surprise to other agencies, and frequently the policies and actions of our agencies were in open conflict.

In Washington, where all issues of undeniable and obvious importance were referred for decisions, the level of ignorance of the significant details was considerably greater than in the field, and the levels of surprise and consternation were even greater. Sometimes this led to decisions at top levels in almost complete ignorance of what, at the local level, were crucial considerations. At other times it led to deferring decisions and either losing fleeting opportunities, or providing what seemed to be tacit approval to one agency to pursue one policy while another agency pursued a different and actually conflicting policy. In simplest terms, much of this resulted from the fact that there were basic differences in the policies of the different agencies — differences that only the

President had power to resolve — and for as long as Eisenhower was President he avoided making that resolution, partly, perhaps, because the contradictions and conflicts were never made clear to him.

Let me recall some illustrative details. The 1960-61 crisis was precipitated by a coup engineered by a Lao Army paratrooper Captain named Kong Le. On August 9, 1960, Kong Le marched a thin battalion of troops into the administrative capital city of Vientiane, seized government buildings, patrolled the streets and declared a curfew, called for the resignation of the existing government, pledged allegiance to the monarchy, promised to expel all foreign military personnel and announced that a new government would be formed to include all factions and be neutralist so far as the contending great powers were concerned. Both our Embassy in Vientiane and our State Department and White House in Washington were taken by surprise and reacted with unmistakable bewilderment that was evident both in such public statements as were issued and in the secret message traffic between Washington and Vientiane.

But Kong Le was our boy. He was an obscure young officer who had been hand-picked by our clandestine special forces people as someone to whom we should give tactical military training. None of our policy-making people either in the Embassy or in Washington, however, were in on the secret, nor had they ever even heard of Kong Le. Under the 1954 Geneva Accords, such training was forbidden, so it had to be done secretly. Kong Le and his battalion had been set up in a secret camp not far from Vientiane and supplied and trained by our clandestine operators. They had kept the operation strictly secret among themselves, partly to prevent security leaks, and partly no doubt because there were policy differences among American officials and agencies, and some would have disapproved of the operation because it violated international agreements we had promised to comply with. Among the factors contributing to this compartmentalization was the fact that Ambassador Winthrop Brown, then nominally in charge in Vientiane, was less convinced that a neutralist Laos would be so tragic to American policy than was the then Assistant Secretary of State for Southeast Asian Affairs, Graham Parsons. Moreover, in that era there were many American ambassadors who preferred to remain aloof from clandestine operations. The message traffic in both directions between Vientiane and State in the period immediately following the coup indicates clearly that there was no high-level knowledge of who Kong Le was nor of what political faction he represented. Inasmuch as the overthrown government was a right wing government we had helped install the previous spring, it was assumed, however, that he was not militantly anti-communist, but rather, either secretly a communist sympathizer or an irresponsible adventurer following the established tradition of military coups as a way to power and fortune.

The coup had been accomplished with utmost ease because practically all the government leaders were at the time in Luang Prabang, the ceremonial capital of the realm, attending memorial services for the king who had died the previous year. The strong man of that government was one General Phoumi Nosavan, leader of the CDNI, supported by, and indeed the agent of, the CIA. That the CIA was at the time very active in Laos was an open secret in Vientiane, in Bangkok, in the French press, in the *New York Times*, and to the Soviets. But exactly what they were doing, or what their connections were with Nosavan, had never been reflected in Embassy reports to Washington, nor in Washington queries or instructions to the Vientiane Embassy. This was clear in CIA message traffic but unmentioned in State and Defense Department communications.

It had indeed been clear from Kong Le's first proclamation that he sounded like a neutralist, which must have been confusing to the few who knew that he was the creation of our undercover operators, whose agency policies were to support the government he had overthrown. Someone, in selecting Kong Le, had evidently goofed, but this never, to my knowledge, became an issue. The most plausible explanation for the miscalculation is that it is extremely difficult for Americans to judge the ultimate aspirations and values of people who are the product of a completely different culture.

It was a matter of days, however, before Kong Le made it unmistakably clear that he wanted a neutralist government along the lines of his initial proclamation. He managed to have a successor government formed in Vientiane, headed by the internationally respected Souvanna Phouma, who returned from his exile in Paris. The new cabinet included a few ministers from the deposed government, and both Pathet Lao and CDNI participation was invited. This action was given sanction by a formal royal request to form such a government.

The new government controlled Vientiane and the immediate area, and housed those Lao agencies that administered our various aid programs (which in many cases were riddled with highly publicized graft). We refused to accord diplomatic recognition, but, apparently to prevent collapse of all government functions, we continued to provide it with non-military aid administered through our foreign aid program. At the same time, we diverted the flow of military supplies to General Nosavan, who was rallying some of the Lao Army forces loyal to him at Savannakhet, a downriver town, in preparation for an advance on Vientiane.

There was parlaying back and forth between Souvanna Phouma and Nosavan for about two months, during which Nosavan was invited to join the government and did not flatly refuse, before serious hostilities began. This interval permitted the Nosavan forces to organize and receive substantial military supplies while the CIA recruited a small mercenary force in Thailand to help in the final assault on Vientiane.

On the other side Souvanna Phouma obtained Pathet Lao participation in his unrecognized neutralist government, and as Nosavan's military buildup grew, the Pathet Lao resumed guerrilla operations against his forces in the north and east. Assistant Secretary of State Parsons flew to Vientiane but despite strong language failed to persuade Souvanna that inclusion of the Pathet Lao in his government would mean the inevitable triumph of Communism. Souvanna failed equally to persuade Parsons to terminate U.S. military support of Nosavan and accept a neutralist Laos. These events led to the arrival of a Soviet Ambassador, who denounced American aid to Nosavan, and declared that the USSR would support the neutralist government. Very soon after, the Nosavan forces began their advance, which was only feebly opposed. After a somewhat abortive and indecisive cannonade of Vientiane from across the Mekong by the Thai group gathered by the CIA, Vientiane was taken by the Nosavan forces. Souvanna and his closest followers took refuge in Thailand, while Kong Le's small band took to the countryside where they were joined by some remnants of the Pathet Lao for continuing struggle against Nosavan.

This much was only the beginning of a long seesaw, obscure, never decisive struggle. The ever-complacent king now reversed himself and recognized a new government, headed by Prince Boun Oum, which had been the provisional government Nosavan set up in Savannakhet right after the coup. The U.S. immediately extended diplomatic recognition. But the Pathet Lao were growing stronger along the Vietnam border, whence came increasing supplies, and Soviet planes, which began providing logistic support, openly, to the Kong Le and Pathet Lao forces. Rejoicing over the recapture of Vientiane had hardly died down before ominous signs began to appear of a formidable Pathet Lao buildup to add to Kong Le's forces. Soviet logistic support and possible Vietminh reinforcement, it was feared, might sweep all before it. The most disturbing early alarms came on New Year's Eve, and resulted in Admiral Harry Felt, then CINCPAC, ordering all U.S. forces in the western Pacific to go on Defense Condition Two (DEFCON 2), which is the last state of readiness preparatory to actual combat.

As a result, in the wee hours of New Year's Day 1961, American officers and men throughout the theater were roused from their post-celebrant slumbers to report for immediate duty. How much that DEFCON order owed to celebrations at HQ, I can only guess. It was rescinded a couple of days later as it became clear that the Vietminh had not invaded Laos in massive numbers as first rumors had been interpreted to indicate. Later intelligence indicated nothing more than usual border crossings, and indeed there was a bit of a lull for a time.

But that a Pathet Lao buildup was continuing was undeniable, and Soviet aid was increasing.

What may be considered the comic opera phase of the Laos crisis came gradually to an end during the final weeks of the Eisenhower presidency. The comedy, if it can be so designated, arose largely out of the spectacle of the different American agencies involved in Laos working at cross purposes, and the failure of the lame duck administration to take the decisive steps necessary to ensure consistency. Secretary of State Christian Herter was far from the dominant personality that Dulles had been, nor was he apparently as single-mindedly certain that any government not ostentatiously anti-communist was evil. The documents I saw indicated that Under Secretary of State Livingston Merchant was aware of the confusion in at least a general way and would have preferred to end it, but apparently he lacked the necessary clout.

Affairs were at times handled in peculiar ways. There was one occasion when a cable from Vientiane almost literally begged for a Washington decision to resolve a head-on clash between agency directives, and in an effort to resolve it, Eisenhower's Military Aide, General Andrew Goodpaster, caught up with the President on a Georgia golf course but failed to get Eisenhower to order strong action either way. Evidently not wishing to accept responsibility for a decision the President himself could not be induced to make, the good general authorized a reply that evaded the issue.

On another occasion of a different sort, forces in the field backed by the U.S. against the government then in Vientiane were desperately short of rice. When delays occurred in delivering rice to the hostile forces, Ambassador Brown was instructed by Washington to deliver a 24-hour ultimatum threatening immediate termination of all U.S. aid unless rice supplies were delivered. The Ambassador delivered the ultimatum, and then, when he visited the airport at seven the next morning to check, he found the Prime Minister not only on the scene, but personally helping load the small cargo plane with the bags of rice to be parachuted to the hostile forces. The Ambassador ended his report on the matter with the comment, "I hardly knew whether to laugh or cry."

One of the noteworthy features of researching this period was that most of the story was nearly as complete from what one could glean from close reading of the *New York Times* and *Le Monde* as from Secret and Top Secret reports and message traffic in the files of those handling the problems for the Pentagon Command Center. Not only did these papers have reporters on the spot, who described, for instance, such matters as the comings and goings and flamboyant manner of the CIA Station Chief, whose actions and identity in official communications were invariably extremely hush-hush, but *Soviet* press accounts and radio broadcasts reported American clandestine activities that always were Top Secret and Eyes Only in American message traffic. Of course one had to see the American documents to judge whether or how much of these open accounts were accurate. But most of the story was there and about all that was missing was the confirmation that in many cases only official documentation could supply.

In the face of the growing threat that developed right after New Year's Eve, hurried studies were undertaken of various forms and levels of military intervention. Phoumi Nosavan's forces were superior in numbers and equipment as well as being coached by American military advisers supplied by the PEO, but when faced in the field by the Pathet Lao they showed little inclination to fight. Both France and Great Britain strongly favored a neutralist Laos under such a government and leadership as that represented by Souvanna Phouma. The oriental members of the Southeast Asia Treaty Organization (SEATO) — Thailand, the Philippines and Pakistan — which Secretary of State Dulles had hastily brought into being in response to the Vietminh victory in Indochina, were not sufficiently alarmed at the prospect of Communist victory in Laos to promise more than use of bases and the merest token forces if the U.S. intervened openly and militarily. There were military missions from CINCPAC, and from Washington, to check up on the information both distant headquarters were routinely receiving from the field. It is hard not to suspect that the visiting firemen selected those field officers to talk to whose views they knew would agree with their own. Indeed some dispatches clearly indicate they were very selective in whom they sought out. Invariably these visitations were widely regarded in the field as superficial, often as mere boondoggles. The feeling was that they were too brief and sketchy to provide the basis for anything more than a most superficial judgment, whereas their own regular reporting was more comprehensive, more attentive to crucial complexities, and therefore a better basis for policy determination. This often led to resentment because regular reporting commonly went to no higher echelon than some desk officer where it frequently was buried, whereas the junketeers went back and reported directly, with all the flourish of penultimate authority, to echelons high enough to have real influence on national policy and command decisions.

The various proposed contingency plans for undisguised military intervention drawn up during the early weeks of 1961 revealed many difficulties. There were, first of all, enormous if not plainly insurmountable logistic difficulties in case significant ground force actions were considered. Laos was a land that afforded no supplies and absolutely everything would have to be brought in. But Laos was landlocked, could be reached only by air, and only one airport could accommodate anything larger than very light aircraft. There were no railroads, and the one north-south highway was often impassable during monsoons while east-west roads were mere trails, many through jungle or mountain terrain. Our only big nearby airbase was the ostentatiously secret establishment we had built at Udorn in Thailand. Many older heads in the Army, which of course would be the service bearing the brunt of any major intervention, were strongly opposed to plans that would lead to our getting bogged down in a land war in Asian jungles, and Laos was the very epitome of all the dangers they envisioned as an unfavorable place in which to deploy American combat forces. Another major difficulty was the reluctance of our allies in SEATO to become involved, a reluctance that became stronger and more evident the closer we seemed to come to any binding decision to intervene openly.

The reigning judgment was, nevertheless, that we had already committed our prestige to keeping Laos from going communist, that if Laos went Communist all of the rest of southeast Asia would follow suit (the domino theory) and that, therefore, our own American national security interests were (somehow) immediately involved. And neutralism was equated with Communism because it was the prelude to Communism. Therefore, regardless of difficulties, we *must* intervene, and because of the difficulties, in the background of every plan was the presumption that if necessary we would go it alone, as the saying was. Above all, it was assumed, because of these difficulties, that if lesser measures failed, we would resort to nuclears. We would bomb whatever the source was of support for the Pathet Lao. This would of course include North Vietnam, China and Russia. But plans stopped with this *presumption*, with no further consideration of the specific deployments or operational tactics to be used in various situations. That was that, and that was as far as planning and consideration of alternatives went for the first month of 1961.

On January 19, 1961, the day before his inauguration, Kennedy spent most of the day with Eisenhower, and according to the accounts of his intimate advisors, much of their time was spent on the impending showdown with Russia over the fate of Laos. And within weeks, if not days, policy and decision-making on Laos shifted to the White House, where a small Laos task force was set up that included Ted Sorenson, McGeorge Bundy, and Arthur Schlesinger, and to which President Kennedy himself gave enough time and attention to warrant his being considered the working head of the group. There was thus finally a single point of ultimate responsibility for our policy and actions in Laos instead of responsibility delegated to various agencies that were seldom coordinated and often in open conflict. This did not, however, mean that there was suddenly a smooth coordination of everything. Far from it. Operations were much too diffuse, too complex in detail, and in many cases secreted behind multiple layers of security precautions.

No one knew all of the crucial actions and interactions that our varied agencies and programs were engaged in, let alone the background or ties with Lao and Thai forces they were associated with. In the best of circumstances it would take time to gain effective control. None on the task force was an expert on that country or on the events leading up to the crisis. Moreover, to learn about it, they had no place to turn except to those whose acts and policies had led them into the mess in which they found themselves. (According to Schlesinger, "mess" was the word Kennedy used in referring to the situation.)

But Kennedy and his task force approached the problem not only with the idea of establishing executive machinery to coordinate our actions, but had in mind a major change of our national objectives in Laos. Kennedy was ready to settle for a neutralist Laos. Now, having replaced the last neutralist government with the Nosavan government that was clearly about to fall before the Pathet Lao, the problem was to find a way of preventing a complete Communist victory and inducing the left wing in Laos, and their supporters in Vietnam, China, and above all Russia, to settle for a truly neutral Laos. But there were many obstacles. The Pathet Lao, the Vietminh and their backers in China sensed that the tide was now running in their favor and could hardly be counted on to abandon readily a complete victory that seemed almost in their grasp. And on our side, although there was no unanimity within the military and foreign policy establishment, there was widely pervading reluctance to accept in Laos anything other than an openly anti-Communist government. But such an outcome seemed unobtainable without resort to nuclears because the location favored the Pathet Lao. They and their nearby Vietnamese, Chinese and Soviet allies could readily assemble guerrilla and conventional forces that the CDNI could not hope to match.

Kennedy and his immediate advisers gradually evolved a

strategy that borrowed from former Secretary of States Dulles's massive retaliation strategy while repudiating Dulles's doctrine that neutralism in Third World countries was a mere prelude to Communism. Precisely how fast this strategy crystalized, or even how fully Kennedy was converted to all features of it, is not clear. Kennedy and his inner group were in a learning process. Obviously they were very unhappy with the situation confronting them and dissatisfied with the proposals suggested to them for dealing with it. But they could neither simply abandon Laos, nor accept the obvious risks of the plans suggested to them. So they flooded the JCS with questions, especially on such thorny matters as what measures were available in the event of large-scale Chinese intervention in response to such small ground forces as our contingency plans called for (which were in fact all we could possibly deploy and supply within any time less than several months). The only answer, of course, was nuclears, and the question then was where the conflict might spread. The nature of the queries to the JCS certainly suggest that there was no satisfaction with the only answers the military seemed able to provide. But although Kennedy was obviously greatly concerned about this, no evidence I ever came upon revealed any hesitation to proceed on a course of direct confrontation with the Kremlin. The latest testimony of White House intimates suggests Kennedy was confident Khrushchev was no more eager than he was himself for nuclear war over Laos.

If so, this was the game of "chicken" the armchair nuclear strategists had been theorizing about for years.

The CIA, which all along had been recruiting mercenaries from various sources for various tasks, stepped up such efforts. Filipinos were brought in, some Nationalist Chinese were recruited from Taiwan as technicians, while from the highlands of northern Laos Hmong tribesmen, called "Meo" by the Laotians, were recruited as foot soldiers, and the agency even reached into northernmost Burma for a few hundred Kuomintang troops who, years before, had taken refuge in those jungle fastnesses after being driven out of Yunnan by Chinese Communist troops. The tribesmen especially were reputedly good fighters and actively hostile to intrusions into their territory by more modern troops, or signs of distant authority, be they Pathet Lao or royal Lao. But they lacked modern arms, and there is no record of their having had any significant effect upon operations in this period. (In later years in renewed conflicts and in greater numbers, some tribes were destined to be first cannon fodder and then refugees from their homeland.)

Although the CDNI had controlled Vientiane since mid-December, had had their boy, Boun Oum, formally installed as Prime Minister, and had become the sole recipients of U.S. aid both economic and military, the situation continued to deteriorate through January and February, and by March had become deeply ominous. Most combat was indecisive and desultory, but the Pathet Lao were obviously intent on building up for decisive actions later. They were concentrating in a large plateau area in northeast Laos called the Plaine des Jarres. There they were receiving ever-increasing Soviet materiel, including more modern arms, by means of what was later described by a Russian official as the biggest supply airlift the Soviets had ever undertaken. Soviet and Vietminh advisory and technical assistance not only increased but became more open. Several minor incidents occurred of minor brushes between Soviet planes and aircraft from the American Embassy and Air America (a CIA airline). Most important of all, Nosavan's army showed little taste for combat with the Pathet Lao, and there was never, throughout this period, an American report that suggested it would be a match for the Pathet Lao whenever the Pathet Lao chose to take the offensive. Nothing could save Nosavan's army, or the Boun Oum government it had installed except intervention by an outside, friendly force. This judgment was never argued or questioned. It was considered so obvious it was simply assumed in all the situation papers of this period.

It was not until mid-March that the Pathet Lao began their long anticipated major offensive, and this had the effect of accelerating decisions and actions. Phoumi Nosavan's inability to muster any effective resistance became so evident that whatever hope Kennedy had ever had of seeing him or any other CDNI personality emerge as an effective leader was abandoned. Gradually it dawned that neutralism was the only alternative to communism. This impression was reinforced by out-of-channels advice directly to Kennedy from David Ormsby Gore, a longtime personal friend and at the time Under Secretary of State in the British Foreign Office, and also from Averell Harriman, whom Kennedy respected highly. The latter influenced Kennedy to give credence to the views of Ambassador Brown, whose on-the-spot appraisals of personalities in Laos were customarily filtered through the contrary ideology of the Southeast Asia Office of the State Department headed by Graham Parsons. Harriman, although acting as Ambassador-at-Large at the time, interviewed Souvanna Phouma without authorization while in New Delhi on other business. It was mainly on the basis of the impressions he developed on that occasion that he joined Ormsby Gore and Brown in recommending to Kennedy that Souvanna Phouma was a genuine neutralist-nationalist, rather than a crypto-communist, as most regular American official sources had been reporting him to be. It was evidently on the basis of these, and perhaps other impressions from outside the properly channeled sources of information, that the President would make his decisions. State, Defense and CIA were largely by-passed, although requests to them for information continued. Clearly, however, the credibility quotient with which their reports were received was falling. A neutral Laos was fully accepted as the best hope for American policy.

It took a little longer to settle on Souvanna Phouma, partly perhaps because, as he spent his exile touring foreign capitals seeking support for a neutral Laos, in his first visit to Washington he was snubbed by Secretary of State Rusk, who, inadvertently or otherwise, chose to make a speech in his native Georgia rather than give an audience to Souvanna. Souvanna then went to Moscow, where he was welcomed.

We had encouraged the reactivation of the International Control Commission (ICC), composed of representatives of the governments of Canada, India and Poland. The ICC had been established to supervise the neutrality provisions of the Geneva Accords of 1954. This was scarcely more than a gesture. The Commission had been abandoned some time before as the ultimate in futility, as was recognized by everyone and as indeed it had probably been intended to be. It was guaranteed to be powerless not only because it lacked means of enforcement, but also because its charter required unanimity of all parties, like the *liberum veto* of ancient Poland, before decision could be reached on any infringement of neutrality. It had never served as more than a forum for charges and countercharges. But support for reactivation of the ICC was consistent with a policy favoring a truly neutral Laos, and now that Soviet assistance to contending factions in Laos had become as evident as our own, we had nothing to lose by the gesture.

As the Pathet Lao offensive began, the Seventh Fleet was moved in force into the South China Sea, a few hundred Marines were flown into Thailand to positions across the Mekong from Laos. Our sheep-dipped PEO officers put on uniforms and moved openly with the Royal Laotian Army that they had previously been advising and training in a civilian guise that fooled no one (except possibly Americans back home). In the course of time, I know not exactly when, around a dozen of them were killed. And a force of 30,000 was raised on Okinawa for rapid deployment while buildup began of a larger expeditionary force of 60,000. These latter moves were not advertised, but it had to be assumed the Soviets would know about them. Very possibly the principal intent was as a signal to the Soviets. Exactly what Kennedy's ultimate intentions were, if worse came to worst, I never knew. His intimates of those days have since indicated that even they were not sure. The questions that the White House directed to the Pentagon suggest quite clearly that Kennedy was skeptical in the extreme of the military plans that were proposed. Where would the troops be landed without being sitting ducks as they landed for the hostile forces already there? How could they possibly be supplied? How greatly would deployment of forces there weaken us in other hot spots? In Berlin? In Korea? Even in South Vietnam, which was becoming troublesome? And above all what would we do if we had not just the Pathet Lao and Vietminh to deal with, but the Communist Chinese, whose border adjoined, and who had not tens of thousands, but hundreds of thousands of ground troops close at hand? It may seem strange, but it was a fact that it was not until such searching and highly specific questions came from the White House that those developing the various contingency plans made a stab at addressing the problems of dealing with adversary reactions to their contingency plans. Otherwise, the nearest approach was the expressed reluctance of many Army officers to "get bogged down" in Asian jungles. (A month or so later, sometime in April, General Douglas MacArthur added his voice, in direct counsel to the President, to the growing opposition to getting American ground troops involved in Asia.)

The only answer the Pentagon, or anyone else, could give to that ultimate question of what we could do if we did intervene on the ground and met superior ground force, and worse came to worst, was to resort to The Bomb. Bomb Hanoi, Peking, ultimately Moscow and all the rest.

The idea was plainly abhorrent to Kennedy. Through Bundy he had been briefed, although how fully I do not know, on our WSEG 50 study of comparative strategic nuclear strengths of the U.S. and the USSR. It is evident he was already deeply worried, faced by crises over both Southeast Asia and Germany, by the prospect of nuclear war, and within three months was to direct still further highly specific questions about the amount of damage to us, to our allies, and to the Communist countries, in the event of nuclear war. And he was soon to direct that studies be made to determine what meaningful civil defense measures were in fact feasible. Yet everything of record on the Laos crisis indicates that, however reluctantly, he was seeking to at least appear determined to go that last fateful mile rather than simply turn Laos over completely to the Pathet Lao and their Communist supporters. The later memoirs of his intimates in the affair suggest they believe he was convinced Khrushchev was no more ready than he was to push matters to such an extreme. In this it later turned out that he was right.

But at the time no one knew. And the problem was more complicated than a simple game of chicken with Khrushchev. Khrushchev could not by any means fully control the actions of the Pathet Lao and the Vietminh, nor could he easily renounce them. As for China, which was at least equally opposed to our influence in Laos, the Sino-Soviet breakup was already under way, and although those two greatest Communist powers both opposed us in Southeast Asia, neither was dependably ready to serve the bidding of the other, and neither would hesitate to complicate the maneuvers of the other if it could gain by doing so.

In a dramatic telecast on March 23, replete with maps of Communist advances in Laos and details of Communist subversions and aggressions elsewhere, Kennedy declared strongly that the U.S. would under no circumstances permit the Communists to take over Laos, but at the same time he emphasized that the U.S. would be happy with a truly neutral Laos. This amounted to a retreat from the inherited policy of settling for no less than an actively anti-Communist government, but its greatest force was as a commitment of American prestige not to permit Laos to be conquered militarily by the Communists. It could readily be interpreted as preparation of the American public for open, large scale intervention. Kennedy had Secretary of State Dean Rusk repeat the terms to Gromyko a few days later, then followed this by giving the same message to Gromyko in the White House Rose Garden, hoping thereby to convey the impression that he really meant what he said.

As the management of the crisis shifted to the White House, the record of events in the files of the small group in J-3 in charge of the matter for the Pentagon diminished. By the end of March it was obviously very incomplete. I could tell, in general, what was going on, as much almost from reading the papers as from the material that found its way into the J-3 files. But increasingly the details of how decisions were reached, and why, were no longer fully revealed in the flow of information to which the J-3 action officers were privy.

Kennedy conferred with Prime Minister Harold Macmillan on Laos at Key West in mid-March and in Washington in early April. Other heads of state, notably Nehru, were brought into the discussions, especially those that were signatories of the 1954 Geneva Accords. All were intent on resolving the issue without military conflict between the major powers. All favored an immediate cease-fire and a neutralist Laos. Precise details of how a neutral Laos would be governed, its boundaries delineated, and its neutrality assured, were to be determined by later negotiation. Macmillan emerged as the major intermediary and soon after his second meeting with Kennedy, in April, a cease-fire was proclaimed. Not long after that, negotiating teams were dispatched to Geneva to settle the details.

With this, the tension eased in the sense that confidence grew that full scale war between the U.S. and the USSR would be avoided. But the fighting on the Plaine des Jarres did not immediately end. Each side wanted to control as much of the country as possible before any binding agreements were reached. In consequence, military actions continued, on a somewhat reduced scale, with both American and Soviet logistic and advisory support going to the contending parties. Neither we nor our Soviet or Chinese adversaries fully controlled the local forces we supported.

Pathet Lao aggressions led to fears on our side that by the time a formal agreement was reached, they would have nibbled away so much that the understanding to settle affairs by negotiation would end up as meaningless. Nevertheless the Boun Oum government, though generally outfought, managed to hang on to the western half of the country, including the two capitals and most of the valley lands along the Mekong. Very possibly the Pathet Lao did not push farther into this area because of the presence of token American troops just across the river. But this is only speculation based on the fact that wherever the Pathet Lao attacked in force, they attained their evident objectives. They may have feared that if they pushed too far, U.S. troops would become involved.

The 1960-61 crisis may be said to have ended with the April ceasefire, which was more ignored than heeded, or by a somewhat more effective truce in May but which still was never fully observed, or with a more formal agreement between Kennedy and Khrushchev a month later, on their June 3 summit meeting in Vienna. From a longer perspective, however, the crisis did not really end then, just as it did not really begin on August 9, 1960. That period from August 1960 to June 1961 may be reasonably seen as an almost arbitrarily delineated segment of a continuum that had neither a clearly defined beginning, even if one goes back as far as 1954 or even 1945, or moves forward in time to 1975, when a Communist government took over control of that still half primitive land still trying to find its way into the modern world. There have been changes and reversals and awakenings all along the way, and it would be arbitrary to say that in a turbulent world in which the underlying causes of change are as great as ever, the pattern of the future has now been permanently established in Laos.

There were continuing squabbles in Geneva, not only between the main adversaries, but among participating allies, on both sides, and even within our own delegation. (Several American delegates who remained committed to the repudiated policy of opposing a truly neutralist Laos had to be sent home lest they undercut the efforts of Ambassador Harriman, who headed the mission.) And in Laos itself the ceasefire was frequently broken by minor, guerrilla-type actions. There was indeed never an end to cheating and double-dealing. Again in 1962 the Seventh Fleet put in an appearance in the South China Sea and again there had to be a gesture suggesting Marine deployment to persuade the Pathet Lao to restrain themselves. But negotiations continued, finally leading to another Geneva agreement that was destined to endure, fitfully, and subject to about as many transgressions, as the first one.

The worst violence, however, was to be reserved for the latter stages of our Vietnam War. It was then that our heavy air attacks on the Ho Chi Minh Trail, a mere sideshow of that greater tragedy, wreaked such violence on Laos that it vastly accelerated further political disruption of a little land that, like Cambodia, suffered devastation for no other reason than proximity to the quarrels of others.

Somewhat to my surprise, my study of how our command and policy decisions were made during those eight months of American involvement in Laos was well received by all of those within the WSEG establishment who reviewed it, including military men whom I considered to be hawkish toward such matters. I was surprised because although I had begun the study without any very strong leanings in any direction, except that I was not of a mind to be frightened by the notion of a neutralist or socialist Laos, in the course of the study I became pretty well convinced that, as a nation, we did not understand the situation we were trying to deal with in Laos, and for that reason we would have been far better off not to become so deeply involved. And I am sure this was evident in what I wrote, although I cannot remember exactly any opinions I expressed except a statement somewhere to the general effect that we were dealing with social developments that even the wisest of humans might not understand nor know how to influence or control. There was no regular Review Board review, because our charter for these studies called for none, and the study was sent as a memorandum from the Director of WSEG directly to J-3, which under existing procedures did not require file copies to be sent elsewhere or require retention somewhere in the DOD files until formal decision was made either for destruction or transfer to Archives. This was the dodge to be employed in all of the sixteen Critical Incident Studies, several of which were to be vastly more sensitive, sensitive not on national security grounds, but rather because they were potentially embarrassing to some person or group in positions of responsibility.

I did come to the conclusion during my study that, in addition to the major problems posed by our different agencies working at cross purposes, we were critically handicapped by doctrinal rigidities and logical inconsistencies. So far as doctrinal rigidity is concerned, the difficulty is exemplified by the failure of so many at policy levels to understand that far more was involved than a simple difference between "Communism" and "Freedom". Although at one moment officials might refer graphically to the immense cultural distance between the primitive world of Laos and our own modern world, there was almost never a distinction between a Pathet Lao or a Vietminh on the one hand and an Apparatchik in Moscow or a Comrade in Leipzig or Peking or Bucharest. A Communist was a Communist, wherever or whenever he was, undifferentiated by cultural inheritance or nationalistic influence, and immune to the forces of environment and circumstance that shape the lives and thoughts, and eventually even the social organization, of the rest of mankind. Communists were simply considered not subject to the laws of behavior that dominated the conduct of all other human beings.

We knew it was a different world. But our appraisal of it remained uncompromisingly ethnocentric. We judged events in Laos in terms of the prevailing mythology of the United States circa 1960. The basic difficulty was that we did not understand then, and most of us do not understand now, that neither capitalism as we currently understand it, nor communism as Moscow understood it, was relevant to the situation in Laos. Yet, like 13th century crusaders, or 16th or 17th century religious zealots, we were set on imposing our faith on the heathens.

As part of the doctrinal package, we ignored what we really knew about the inescapable slowness and delays and detours involved in lasting social change. We therefore tended to react to every new political vicissitude as if whatever immediate arrangement might result was final and forever binding, rather than just another phase in the long unwinding of revolutionary change that any society emerging from a tribal feudal age was bound to undergo as it entered a world increasingly dominated by electronics, jet propulsion, atomic energy, and competing social ideologies which were themselves evolving and adapting, however much their most ardent advocates insisted that they represented unchanging principles. Because we assigned so much importance to the immediate, we repeatedly committed ourselves to individuals and groups whose interest was in restoring the past rather than adjusting to the future, and who therefore were bound to succumb to the inexorable forces of change. Our Communist adversaries, on the other hand, had the philosophy and the patience to associate themselves with those committed irrevocably to change, who sought almost anything as better than the past, and looked for modern models to emulate. These, they hoped, they might ultimately shape to their own taste. We made it easy for them by turning away any who were not as doctrinally opposed to "Communism" as we were, and by supporting those who were opposing any change at all from the older social order.

The Communists were by no means all wise. They were on occasion even more rigid doctrinally. But they did have the great advantage of assuming that movement away from past arrangements was inevitable. What we took so long to grasp — and in many quarters still do not seem to understand — is that the Moscow model cannot be long imposed on any significantly different society or situation, and that societies calling themselves communist or socialist may become as different, even as antagonistic to each other, as capitalist or feudal societies.

THE BERLIN CRISIS
OF 1961

My next study was of the Berlin Crisis of 1961, which I undertook because it seemed to me so overwhelmingly important, and because Europe was much more familiar ground than the Far East.

In retrospect it seems reasonably clear that we were not as close to worldwide conflagration over Berlin in 1961 as most of us feared at that time, or for some time afterward believed we had been. I shared those fears and those I worked with were, most of them, equally fearful. Indeed, I believe that, in this country, with but few exceptions, the more one knew about our diplomatic exchanges with the Soviets and above all about our contingency planning and intramural studies of tactics to be employed, the more convinced he was that we were operating on the brink of nuclear war. I do not believe that our NATO allies fully shared this fear. At times they seemed apprehensive that we might act precipitously and thereby bring on an otherwise avoidable cataclysm. Our Soviet and East German adversaries seemed least fearful of all.

It was the Soviets and the East German Communist regime that were pressing the issue. They wanted to force us to recognize the legitimacy of the Soviet-imposed Communist regime in East Germany. They wanted to squeeze the U.S., Britain and France out of West Berlin so that city might become the capital of a Communist Germany. They wanted to stop the flow of intellectuals, skilled and professional workers, liberals and others from East Germany into Berlin and West Germany. They had been trying to accomplish as much of these objectives as possible ever since we accepted the division of conquered Nazi Germany into the Russian and three western occupation zones, along with the administration of the capital city of Berlin by means of a comparable quadripartite zonal arrangement. They had tried to gain their ends by varied harassments, threats, bluster, indeed every conceivable means short of open warfare. The American, British and French zones became West Berlin, the Soviet zone East Berlin, because from the beginning the Soviets exercised unilateral control over their eastern half of the city and the four-power Kommandatura, supposed to exercise centralized control, survived only as a vestigial, merely nominal authority.

Annoyances began immediately, with the earliest occupation, but it was not until 1948 that Stalin, by his Berlin blockade, made the first dramatic move to drive the West out of Berlin. Only after our 341-day airlift defeated this move was the blockade lifted. After a lull, harassments were resumed in other ways to keep us mindful of our precarious position.

By the end of the fifties, harassment of air, rail, and Autobahn traffic into West Berlin had increased, but never assumed the proportions of a blockade. Meanwhile Khrushchev, no doubt emboldened by Soviet developments in rocketry and fission-fusion weaponry, grew increasingly clamorous for his kind of settlement of the issues of Berlin and East Germany. No doubt partly as a result of the fears inspired by Khrushchev's inflammatory rhetoric as well as by the failures and repressions of Ulbricht's regime, the exodus from that Communist state increased despite strong measures to stop it. By mid-1960, it was evident to those closely following the scene that another crisis over Germany and Berlin was building.

The major element that was new in the 1961 Berlin crisis was the intensity provided by the Soviet attainment of a large and growing nuclear capability. The Berlin Blockade Crisis of 13 years before had involved more intense military activities, including loss of allied lives in the airlift. But this time the threat of nuclear war, made dramatic by the beginning buildup of Soviet missilery and megaton warheads, brought a new and frightening dimension to any consideration of the possibility of war breaking out over the issue of Berlin.

Preoccupation with the development of Soviet ICBMs, with the missile gap, and with their effect on our deterrence strategy with respect to Berlin (among other things) became a growing concern immediately after the first Sputnik. By 1960 there was a flood of studies and intelligence estimates relating to the threat of Soviet ICBMs and their effect on the possibility of a Soviet pre-emptive strike against SAC.

On January 11, 1960, DDR&E published a Top Secret "Analysis of the U.S. Strategic Posture, 1960-61, With Particular Emphasis on 'The Missile Gap'" which concluded that the missile gap predicted by a 1959 National Intelligence Estimate (NIE) would not, during this period, comprise a "deterrence gap." But soon thereafter a new NIE replaced the earlier appraisal, to which DDR&E responded on February 29 with a re-evaluation suggesting that in the period 1960-63 the Soviets would acquire the capability "to destroy our SAC bomber and missile bases in a single all-out attack by Soviet ICBMs." There were complications in the predictions, however. One was that our Ballistic Missile Early Warning Station (BMEWS) at Thule in Greenland would become operational in June 1961, and would at least theoretically reduce the effectiveness of any attempted surprise attack. On April 4, 1960, still another study estimated that with the 15 minutes warning BMEWS would provide, one third of SAC could be airborne before missiles reached target.

Another sort of complication arose, however, out of speculation, which greatly affected estimates of Soviet missile capabilities, over whether the Soviet ICBMs had what was called a "reprogramming capability." "Reprogramming capability" meant that an ICBM could be quickly reprogrammed to direct it to a different target from the one it was previously programmed to hit. Such a capability, if it existed, could make any given number of missiles vastly more efficient in destroying a given number of targets. It was assumed that no missiles yet developed had better than, say, a 50% chance of landing close enough to the point it was targeted to hit to destroy it. To have 75% chance of destroying the target would then require 2 missiles, to have 87.5% chance of destroying it, 3 missiles would be required, and so on. Presumably a surprise attacker would want high assurance that most of the most important counterforce targets would be destroyed. Without reprogramming, several missiles would have to be fired simultaneously, therefore, to attain high confidence of destroying a given target.

But with a reprogramming capability, it might be possible to attain the desired level of assurance by holding back duplicating strikes until after it was ascertained whether or not the missile launched first would strike the target.

So far as probability calculations might be concerned, there were additional factors to consider. There were several stages at which a missile might go wrong, and its likelihood of reaching the target increased as it succeeded in passing each successive stage. These stages began with the original lift-off, then proceeded as height was attained and first stage boosters dropped off; once the cruising arc was established, the major variables were a function of the firing mechanism (did it work as calculated?) and the CEP. These last two might not become known immediately by any means then available, but they were a comparatively small fraction of the factors that could result in a miss. The major sources of inaccuracy (at least it was so considered) concerned the initial phases, and these could be monitored by radar from the firing point. Therefore it could be known within a very few minutes, even seconds, whether there was no chance at all of the missile reaching its target, or whether the chances of hitting it were raised to the much higher level of probability depending only on the lesser variables at the terminal end of the flight.

The cold facts were that our intelligence concerning the qualities and capacities of Soviet missiles was unquestionably debatable, even at best, on almost all counts. And as for measuring reliability and accuracy of ICBMs or other long range missilery, we possessed no really dependable knowledge of what we could count on even with our own missiles, even in peacetime practice, let alone under the pressures and confusions of first wartime use of weapons never employed before.

But there were abundant guesses — indeed there had to be — of the probabilities of every factor involved. All this provided a field day for probability-minded mathematicians more committed to complicated computations than to rigorous examination of the basic data going into the computations. In WSEG we had two brilliant young operations analysts, George Pugh, a physicist, and Hugh Everett, a mathematician. They had raced through rapid casualty estimates for the Fallout Project, and were soon to turn out volumes of printouts of devastation and casualties, Russian and American, under both "optimum" and "minimum" assumptions, for WSEG 50. When word came from somewhere, early in 1960, that it was possible that the Soviets might have, or might be developing, a reprogramming capability for their ICBMs, amid considerable excitement within our restricted area they proposed and gained immediate acceptance of a proposal to make it the subject of an urgent study. Thus, on March 11, 1960, WSEG approved and sent to the JCS their study of "Implications of Soviet Possession of a Reprogrammable Ballistic Missile System." The central conclusion of that study was that if the Soviets possessed a reprogramming capability for their ICBMs, as *available in 1960* according to the last NIE, they "would be in a position to launch an attack with a high degree of confidence that almost all retaliatory systems then on the ground would be destroyed." The report was made a bit more scary by a suggestion at the end of the study that a Soviet decision to launch would probably not be detected by political intelligence because a necessary preparation for surprise attack would be to reduce our state of alert and lull us into confidence that no attack would occur. They cited an NIE of three years before (NIE 100-2-57) as authority for this speculation, and then noted that, at the moment, Khrushchev was cultivating an air of detente along with giving evidence of high confidence in Soviet missile capabilities. In other words, the more pacific Khrushchev seemed to be, the more frightened we should be. It seems obvious now that there should have been much skepticism about that report, but I remember none within WSEG.

The WSEG study was discussed by the CFCS with the Secretary of Defense three days later and thereafter studied by the staffs of the three services. By June 1 there was a considered JCS appraisal of U.S. and Soviet nuclear capabilities which concluded that although both the U.S. and the USSR were vulnerable to attack with nuclear weapons, the Soviet capabilities suggested by the WSEG and DDR&E studies were not very likely. In response to Defense Secretary inquiries during these first months of 1960, when the missile gap scare was a major national issue, the JCS repeatedly assured the Secretary that for the present and near future our nuclear deterrent remained effective as a deterrent, although always there were Air Force objections that argued estimates of the Soviet nuclear threat were too low, and always there were recommendations, concurred in by all services, that to maintain our position we needed to strengthen it considerably to keep up with the growing Soviet threat.

During all of 1960 there was a continuing flow of studies. Except for the reprogramming studies, none was on an urgent or almost frantic basis, as those of 1961 relating to contingency plans for Berlin came to be. These 1960 studies reflected apprehension in many quarters that contingency plans approved two years before might not work, had not been sufficiently examined in the light of secondary problems that might arise in an attempt to carry them out. Above all, it was argued, they might be inadequate in the light of Khrushchev's growing confidence in Soviet Missilery, and his increasing bluster over West Berlin and the absence of a peace treaty formally ending World War II were interpreted to mean they would soon be put to the ultimate test.

Because of the tripartite occupation of West Berlin, an

American-British-French center for developing contingency plans on Berlin — code name LIVE OAK — had been established in NATO headquarters just west of Paris. Although its original mandate was for planning responsibilities only, all communications relating to the joint occupation of West Berlin filtered through it. It was not until July 1961, at the height of the Berlin crisis, that it was proposed to make LIVE OAK a command as well as planning center. Until then it was just one more group engaged in contingency planning for Berlin. The officers assigned to LIVE OAK were responsible to their own national commands, and represented them in the development of plans and policies which presumably had the approval of all three occupying powers. U.S. Army forces in Europe were directly under the command of the Commander in Chief of U.S. Army Forces in Europe (CINCUSAREUR), located in Heidelberg, while all American Air Force elements in Europe were under the command of the Commander in Chief of U.S, Air Forces in Europe (CINCUSAFE), headquartered in Wiesbaden, not to mention that the American Commander of all NATO naval forces was in London while the most powerful concentration of American naval forces was in the Mediterranean with headquarters in Naples. LIVE OAK was supposed to develop agreed tripartite plans for actions to be taken in a Berlin emergency. But there were growing differences among those three powers concerning how major crises should be handled. France was developing her own nuclear capability, and showing increasing restiveness over the rather large rear echelon presence of American military on French territory.

As American doubts of the efficacy of older contingency plans for dealing with a stoppage of access to Berlin increased, the most prominent recurrent American notion was that if a battalion-size probe failed to reopen the way, we should proceed to attempt a probe with some larger force before resorting to nuclear weapons. The British and French were opposed to this from the start, ostensibly on the ground that preparation for larger conventional military action would weaken the credibility of the nuclear deterrent. There was the further complication that whereas it was only the U.S., Britain and France that were immediately involved in Berlin, any war that might be precipitated over West Berlin would invariably involve the other NATO members, from Turkey, Greece, Italy and Portugal in the South to Belgium, the Netherlands and Norway in the North, and these allied nations had no direct voice in our policies for Berlin. Finally, the main Autobahn from the west into Berlin was within the British NATO defense zone. Although American military traffic regularly travelled that route, a genuine military probe would be at enormous disadvantage if confined to the narrow strip of the Autobahn. To operate effectively against roadblocks — which could be set up quickly and easily — a probing force would have to take to the enveloping countryside to outflank them.

While studies of larger and more elaborate probes were proceeding in the Pentagon, beginning no later than early January of 1960, the level of plans actually approved at the operational level in the field early that year is indicated by the March 22 Letter of Instruction sent by U.S. Commander in Chief General Lauris Norstad to the British Commander in Chief who in an emergency would have been in direct command of a probe. The instructions also suggest the complications revealed by detailed consideration of actual operations.

> A 3-part military force of approximately battalion combat size will be given the mission of proceeding from Helmstedt toward Berlin along the axis of the Autobahn, surmounting en route such obstacles as the force can cope with and maintain contact, if opposed.
>
> The decision to move such a force on the Autobahn is one which can be made only by the three governments; it is possible that the governments may decide to confine the force to the surface of the Autobahn and its verges. A force operating off the Autobahn would have to be more extensively organized than one held to the Autobahn.

The key factors which will be considered in the planning are the composition, organization and assembly of the force, its training requirements, and logistic support and a general concept of the tactical operation.

Apart from air reconnaissance flown in the air corridors, no consideration will be given to the employment of combat air in support of the ground force in its movement from Helmstedt toward Berlin. However, if the Soviets or East Germans attack the ground force, it may be necessary to support its disengagement by use of combat air. Therefore, the capability for combat air support should be readily available and apparent to the Soviets.

Likewise, atomic weapons will not be placed initially in support of the ground force, although they should be readily available.

Although he continued to advise the Pentagon that our Berlin partners, especially the British, were opposed to any enlargement of our probe plans, Norstad throughout 1960 repeatedly sought to have LIVE OAK develop plans for a probe larger than battalion size before accepting a choice of alternatives between defeat and recourse to nuclears. He appealed by letter directly to Mountbatten on August 22 for approval or consideration of some force larger than battalion size. On September 19 Mountbatten replied, repeating that the U.K. was of the opinion that a probe by a battalion-size combat team, backed by the ultimate nuclear threat, was all the force that was needed. Norstad repeated his request twice that December and again on January 3, 1961. It was only after this early 1961 urging that Norstad was able to persuade the British to participate, through their LIVE OAK representation, in any consideration at all of a division-size probe.

The story of how the 1961 crisis unfolded has been much written about. Both Ted Sorenson and Arthur Schlesinger, who were intimate advisors of President Kennedy throughout the crisis, have written accounts that throw light on the subject I was not aware of at the time. What I knew was what went on in the Pentagon, which supplied the information on which the President and his advisors depended in large part for the decisions they made. What I mainly lacked, as best I can see the matter now, were insights into how Kennedy reacted to events in ways not revealed in public or in the classified material to which I had access. So far as I can judge now, the intimate accounts indicate that Kennedy was a little more skeptical of both the estimates and the military proposals supplied by the Pentagon, and by former Secretary of State Dean Acheson, than I had documented reason to believe at the time. Likewise, he was credited by those who worked closely with him during those crucial days with being more confident than I had reason to believe that Khrushchev was running a bluff, even though he was as deeply concerned as he could possibly be to avoid actions that might inadvertently touch off a nuclear war no one wanted.

There is no doubt that the President, aided by his comparatively few intimate advisors in the White House, was calling the shots throughout the period when tension was high. That was from the time of the summit in Vienna in early June 1961 through the height of the crisis in mid-summer until the winding down of the sense of immediate threat as that year ended.

I had no inside knowledge of how Kennedy, in the privacy of the White House, made his decisions. What I did know concerned the long and sometimes tortuous process of supplying the information and proposals on which those high level decisions were presumably based. I do not know how much of all that actually reached him except in certain cases. This points to one of the most crucial aspects of all high-level decision making. In most cases no one anywhere knows how much, or what aspects, of the information and recommendations developed for the White House was summarized, filtered out, watered down, given additional emphasis, or possibly eliminated as needless detail, by those inevitable intermediaries who decided what the President should see and consider. A large fraction of the material simply had to be "massaged", as they called the process in the Pentagon, because the sheer bulk of paper that was turned out was enormous. That process of selection, elimination, emphasis, condensation occurred all along the line, from the lowliest desk officer or intelligence operative or analyst through the many echelons in the Pentagon, State and CIA, until finally in the White House they decided what the President should or should not bother with.

Almost immediately after the 1960 election, plans were initiated by a small inner group to have former Secretary of State Dean Acheson undertake a comprehensive re-evaluation of U.S.-NATO strategy. The prime mover was Paul Nitze, who in the new administration was to become Assistant Secretary of Defense for International Security Affairs. Others in the original group were Ambassador David Bruce, Roswell Gilpatrick, soon to become Under Secretary of Defense, and Dean Rusk, destined to be Secretary of State. The major governing expression of our national strategy on the subject was the outdated NSC 5803 of February 7, 1958, which implied the U.S. would go immediately to genuine war if only limited military forces could not re-open access to Berlin. It was entirely natural, almost predictable, that Paul Nitze would push Dean Acheson for the task. They were close friends and their approaches to such a subject were almost identical. Neither was a military man, but both considered that in dealing with the Soviets it was necessary to think in predominantly military terms. And both were deeply convinced that the problem was urgent and critically important.

No sooner was the new administration in office than a working group was formed, headed by Acheson but comprised of those named above plus Ambassador Finletter (who was then from NATO), with a working staff drawn from Defense, State, CIA, the White House, and Al Wohlstetter from RAND. An organizational meeting was held on January 31, at which time it was decided officially that Acheson would head up the study group, that Under Secretary of State George Ball and Ambassador George McGhee would represent State while Nitze would represent Defense.

An Army Colonel heading the European Division of ISA was made Executive Secretary. A large part of his job was to channel requests for staff studies and monitor their execution. These provided the factual material, or more accurately, the *estimates* of facts then currently accepted by responsible organizations. These were to serve as answers to questions posed by Acheson and his colleagues and thus provide the base material with which to build the policy paper. Acheson immediately propounded his questions, soon followed by a great flurry of reports. The sources of these were mainly various elements of the JCS and of our Supreme Allied Commander in Europe (SACEUR) — Norstad. The preliminary drafts, prepared generally by staff officers of the colonel level with special responsibility, were then reviewed and occasionally revised at the highest military echelon (either SACEUR or the CJCS) before submission to the Acheson Committee. It should be noted that both CJCS and SACEUR were assisted in their reviews by their own immediate and specially chosen staff assistants.

Acheson's report to the President, dated March 29, 1961, entitled "A Review of North Atlantic Problems For the Future", although nominally a committee report, amounted essentially to a comprehensive expression of Acheson's personal views on the subject. The report was first reviewed at the 477th NSC meeting of the same date, March 29, and a slightly revised version with the new title of "Proposed Policy Directive Regarding NATO and the Atlantic Community" was given high level distribution on April 3. It was called "proposed" because it was understood there would be further NSC discussion. But without such further discussion and despite some express reservations, especially from Norstad who reflected concerns of his West European colleagues, the Acheson paper amounted to a broad policy directive for many months to come.

The paper covered many points, but the most important provision of all came in the words from sub-paragraph 6(b) of Part II, "A Pragmatic Military Doctrine":

> The U.S. should propose that the objective of
> improving NATO's non-nuclear forces should
> be to create a capability of halting Soviet forces
> now in or readily deployable to Central Europe
> for a sufficient period to allow the Soviets to
> appreciate the wider risks of the course on which
> they are embarked...

Such was the gist of our idea of what our deterrence policy best should be, for the rest of that year, to be effective without too great a risk of inadvertent nuclear war.

At the same 477th NSC meeting that provided preliminary approval of the Acheson NATO paper, the President asked Acheson to undertake a comparable study on the specific subject of West Berlin, which was rapidly emerging, along with the issue of a peace treaty formally ending the war, as the immediate issue over which crucial confrontation with the Soviets would most likely occur. This was to be completed by the time the President returned from his planned meetings in late May and early June with de Gaulle, Khrushchev and Macmillan. That request resulted in another great flurry of staff studies from early April until late June. This time, most studies concentrated on the problem of the tactics and forces required for keeping avenues open to the hostage city of West Berlin in the face of either East German or Soviet harassment, or their full scale opposition, for an interval long enough to allow the Soviets to become impressed with the imminence of all-out nuclear war should they persist in blocking transit. The studies all conceded Soviet superiority in conventional ground forces, and the questions posed for these input studies centered on ways to impress the Soviets that we would use military force, even including nuclear weapons if necessary to maintain free access to Berlin. This involved convincing our reluctant NATO allies that they should accept the risks of such a strategy. This in turn raised the question of possible unilateral U.S. action in the event the allies disagreed on the strategy. What echelon of command should have the power to initiate tactical nuclear response in a fast developing crisis? How far forward should our tactical nuclears be deployed and how safe were they from either seizure or unauthorized use? How could we share determination of strategy without in fact giving our allies veto power over use of the weapon? How could we convince Khrushchev we would resort to nuclears, if he blockaded Berlin, without making our Allies fearful we were trigger-happy? How feasible would it be, as a practical matter, to "go-it-alone" on European territory, from European bases so far from home? And so on.

New Appraisals of the Soviet Missile Threat

When Kennedy returned from his European trip, the Acheson Berlin study was still unfinished, but there was a Top Secret National Intelligence Estimate awaiting. It was NIE 11-8-61, "Soviet Capabilities For Long Range Attack", dated June 7. Its main conclusions were:

> The Soviet leaders, particularly Khrushchev, have been deeply impressed by what they regard as a major improvement of their strategic position resulting from their achievements with long range missiles.
>
> We have reviewed the direct and indirect evidence pertaining to the development of the Soviet ICBM system. We are still unable to confirm the location of any ICBM launching facilities other than those at the test range. We are able, however, to support on reasonably good evidence a minimum number of two to four operational ICBM site-complexes.

At this point there were footnotes. One said Army Intelligence called the evidence "tenuous" rather than "reasonably good". Another said Air Force Intelligence believed "reasonably good evidence supports existence of ten to fifteen operational

ICBM site complexes" while "tenuous evidence" suggested existence of a number of other deployment locations. (It should be noted this was considerably before we had developed the satellite monitoring system. We had radar observation around the Soviet perimeter, but our estimates at that time had to be based mainly on communications intelligence plus the other time-honored sources, and these, in such a matter as the *number* of missiles and launchers, provided no better than a basis for *inferences* which could vary widely according to the perspective and the interest of those making the estimate.)

The NIE continued:

> ...we believe that...evidence supports the view that: (a) the USSR has been conducting a generally successful ICBM program, at a deliberate rather than an extremely urgent pace; (b) the USSR is building toward a force of several hundred operational ICBM launchers, to be acquired in the next few years.
>
> 3. We estimate that the probable Soviet force in mid-61 is in the range of 50 to 100 operational ICBM launchers, together with necessary operational missile inventories and trained crews. This would probably involve the present existence of 10 to 15 ICBM operational site complexes. This estimate should be regarded as a general approximation. The major bases for it are our sense of the tempo of the program and our judgment of the relationship between what we have detected and what we are likely to have missed. We estimate that they will continue to be deliberately paced and will result in force levels about as follows: 100 to 200 operational launchers in mid-62, 150 to 300 in mid-63, 200 to 400 in mid-64. Some of the launchers activated in 63-64 will probably be for a new and improved ICBM system.

At this point a footnote indicated that State Department intelligence favored somewhat lower estimates, Army intelligence considerably lower estimates — "no more than a few" — in 1961, while Air Force Intelligence believed Soviet strength was much greater currently and would reach far greater numbers in the future — "about 850 operational launchers in mid-64, 1150 in mid-66."

No great analytical powers were required to see that the intelligence estimates of Soviet missile strength were not very firm and that they coincided remarkably with the points of view of those contributing to them. The White House was certainly wary of Pentagon estimates and judgments as a result of its very recent experiences in the Laos crisis and the Bay of Pigs fiasco. But information of some sort was needed to help reach decisions concerning courses of action to be followed in the impending Berlin confrontation. Within less than a week (on June 12), McGeorge Bundy, acting no doubt on instructions from Kennedy, sent a memo to the Secretary of Defense asking these specific questions:

> If general war plans were implemented within the next year:
> - How much of the Soviet nuclear striking force would be destroyed?
> - What would be the probable resultant damage to U.S., European, and Soviet civil societies?
> - What are the major uncertainties underlying these judgments, e.g., regarding size and disposition of Soviet missile force?
> - How crucial to outcome would be the matter of who struck first?
> - If present U.S. plans were changed to increase the proportion of offensive force brought to bear exclusively on military targets, how would it affect answers to questions above?

Answers were requested by June 26.

The following day (June 13), the JCS referred the request to J-3 (Operations). The J-3 staff worked overtime for a week and on June 21 submitted a draft reply to CJCS. With minor amendments and a covering memo signed by the Chairman, the reply was forwarded on June 23 to the Secretary of Defense as JCSM-430-6l. The basic replies to questions as written by J-3 were provided by a working group of officers currently assigned on short tours of duty to J-3, and the amendments provided by the JCS itself were made by officers assigned, similarly on short tours of duty, to work directly for the Chiefs of Staff of the four services.

The JCS response was forwarded the next day (June 24) to the Secretary of Defense and on June 26, ISA sent it to Bundy in the White House. The JCS memo consisted of a very short covering memo plus an Appendix and two Annexes. It was the Appendix and Annexes that provided the substantive response. The memo itself said nothing except that general war plans were not keyed to specific situations and in the case of nuclear war arising from the Berlin crisis no particularities would obtain except that, being a crisis, there would be a better alert status and deployment and hence improved prospects (for *our* strike forces, no mention being made here of effect upon Soviet status of a crisis situation). It was stated that latter phases of a general war could "not be predicted in detail," but that the information provided in the Appendix and Annexes was adequate to answer the questions that had been asked. It noted that the answers were based on recent studies of the expected outcome of a U.S.-Soviet war in which our initial strategic attack was based on the current general war plan (SIOP-62)[1], which had become effective on April 1, 1961.

In summary, the memo concluded that "the U.S. possesses the ready and effective power to face the possibility of a major crisis with confidence. Our strengths are adequate to deter enemy rational and deliberate resort to general war, and, if general war eventuates, to permit the U.S. to survive as a viable nation despite serious losses, and ultimately to prevail and resume progress toward its national objectives."

Following this summary reassurance, the appended material sought to answer questions with startling precision. To the question, "How much of the Soviet nuclear strike force could be destroyed?" the response was: Of 148 targets constituting a nuclear threat to the U.S., 136 would be destroyed by the U.S. Alert Force, and all 148 by the Full Force. Of 254 targets constituting a Soviet nuclear threat to our forward area (outside the continental U.S.), 121 would be destroyed by our Alert Force and 247 by our Full Force. Of 93 targets comprising the satellite *air* threat, 29 would be destroyed by our Alert Force and 88 by our Full Force. Of 983 targets comprising Residual Air and Surface Capability (non-nuclear), 415 would be destroyed by our Alert Force and 852 by our Full Force.

Following these surprisingly precise estimates it was acknowledged that results would vary depending on status of both forces, and which struck first, these factors to be discussed in later annexes.

The second question was "What would be the probable resulting damage to American, European, and Soviet societies?" and it evoked these answers: Of 103 Government Control Centers in the USSR and China, 83 would be destroyed by the Alert Force and all 103 by the Full Force; 23 "lesser control centers" might be destroyed as "bonus effects" of Full Force attacks on other targets: 199 cities in the USSR would be struck by the Alert Force with resultant casualties of 56% of Soviet urban population and 37% of total population; 295 Soviet cities would be struck by the Full Force with 72% casualties to the urban population and 54% casualties among the total population. In China, Alert Force would strike 49 cities inflicting 41% casualties on urban population and 10% of total population, rural and urban. Full Force would strike 78 cities incurring 53% casualties among total urban population and 16% of total Chinese. In satellite states in Europe, all targets were military installations, but incidental to striking these the Alert Force would inflict 1,378,000 civilian casualties and the Full Force 4,004,000. For the Western Europe of our allies, no figures were given because, it was stated, numbers of casualties would depend on Soviet strategy. (There was no mention of incidental civilian casualties in allied territory that might result from *our* possible use of either nuclear artillery or airborne nuclear weapons against Soviet forces in Europe.) As for the U.S., again the question was evaded, and no figures given. It was acknowledged that several studies had been made, and of these it was stated that the best was that made by the Net Evaluation Subcommittee (NESC)[2] in 1959, but that "the results of that study are not available to the JCS for this purpose"(!). Nevertheless, it was stated that a "synthesis of results of all known studies" was that "the general consensus has been that while a nuclear exchange would leave the U.S. in a seriously damaged condition, with many millions of casualties and little immediate war supporting capability, the U.S, would continue to exist as an organized and viable nation, and ultimately would prevail, whereas the USSR would not." Reassuring words, unless you speculated on what motivated them, or on the intellectual competence of those who made such confident judgments on this very special and difficult matter.

The third question was "What are the major uncertainties, e.g., regarding the size and distribution of the Soviet missile force, which underlie these judgments?" To this the response was that the major uncertainties concerned the size, location, posture and operational readiness of the Soviet missile force, their early warning capability, and their ability to achieve spontaneity of attack upon U.S. strike forces. But while these uncertainties were identified, there was no discussion of how uncertain they were, nor of how much these differences might affect the validity of the estimates that were provided of the levels of damage we and our allies might sustain in a nuclear war.

The fourth question was "How crucial to the outcome would be the question of whether the U.S. or the USSR struck first?" The reply was that if the U.S. attacked preemptively, we would clearly prevail, although we would still be greatly damaged by the Soviet retaliatory attack. The brief discussion proceeded quickly to observe that although U.S. policy precluded preventive war, circumstances might justify U.S. initiative, and that U.S. planning provided capability to take the initiative. Even so, however, plans were "drawn up to permit the U.S. to prevail, even though placed in a retaliatory role." But the ability to prevail in a retaliatory role, it was emphasized, was dependent upon the warning and the timeliness of the decision to react, because these would determine the survivability and effectiveness of our capability to retaliate. Then came a summary statement that the U.S. would clearly prevail if we struck first, but if placed in a retaliatory position our success would depend on timeliness of our response. It is obvious that although this answer provided no numerical suggestion of the magnitude of damage we might sustain, even though there were plenty of estimates to draw from, it was far less reassuring than the summary judgment previously expressed and repeated in the covering memo of the JCS. In fact, it came close to saying that unless we struck preemptively, the prospects were far from good.

The fifth and last question was, "If present plans are altered so as to concentrate upon destruction of the Soviet nuclear strike force by bringing a greater part of our own force to bear on exclusively military targets, what would be the answers to the first three questions above?"

The answer was that the effect on the Soviet nuclear strike force was highly dependent upon whether the U.S. initiated or retaliated, and would not be significantly affected by greater concentration on military targets. Greater concentration on military targets would therefore *not* significantly alter expected damage to the American and Allied civil societies nor would it change much else except that it would fail to damage war supporting industries in Russia and China to the desired extent

I can only guess how much credibility was accorded these responses by those in the White House who had requested the information.

Acheson's Berlin Paper

Less than a week after this latest version of risks to be

considered in event of nuclear war, Acheson completed the draft of his policy proposals concerning Berlin. The very next day it was transmitted to the White House under cover of a Memo for the President. The covering memo simply said, "Attached is a preliminary version of my report on Berlin. I will revise this report in the light of discussions with you and the Secretaries of State and Defense. Recommendations and Conclusions, which could serve as a draft policy directive, will be included in the final version of the report."

Acheson, having been handed the ball, obviously intended to run with it. But although his paper was an impressive exercise in strategic dialectic from the point of view of, and based on, the assumptions he took for granted, it was destined to arouse major apprehensions, both military and political. Brought in initially as the grey eminence to make policy for the new administration, Acheson's NATO study of three months before had in fact been accepted as the best expression of current American policy.

It would be hard to exaggerate the level of anticipation or the degree of importance accorded by the Defense Community to the developing Acheson report on Berlin. Dozens of studies had been prepared to provide information for Acheson to work with, and despite misgivings in many places concerning some of Acheson's views, his prestige was so great that most officials and staff members believed that whatever Acheson put on paper and submitted to the White House would become the basis of our policy. There might be minor revisions here and there, but, like the NATO paper of three months before, it would be adopted in essence as our national policy on Berlin and form the basis of a policy directive. It was rather long as such reports go, my summary notes on its contents running to 15 pages. Dated June 27, it was delivered to the White House the following day under cover of a brief memo in which Acheson volunteered to discuss its contents with the President and the Secretaries of State and Defense. Instead of this arrangement, however, the report was made the subject of consideration of the NSC meeting of June 29.

The Acheson Report began with a Foreword that amounted

to a declaration of doctrine from which its specific proposals flowed logically. The issue was defined as far more than the city of Berlin, or even the German question as a whole. "The whole position of the U.S. is in the balance." It was a conflict between Khrushchev and the U.S., and nothing could be accomplished by concession, by logic or negotiation until it had been demonstrated to Khrushchev that what he wanted was impossible. Any concessions or negotiations before such a demonstration were dangerous because they would weaken our position and increase his demands.

Acheson proceeded next to describe the nature of the "demonstration" that would be necessary. West Berlin, he reasoned, had always been protected from the Soviets by their fear that interference with the city would lead to war, war specified as meaning nuclear war.

"If Khrushchev now contemplates and later embarks upon a course of interference, it means his fear of war resulting (from this action) has declined." But the "capability of the U.S. to devastate the Soviet Union has not declined...The decline of effectiveness of the deterrent, therefore, must lie in a change in the Soviet appraisal of U.S. willingness to go to nuclear war over the issue which Khrushchev reiterates his determination to present... The problem is how to restore the credibility of the deterrent."

The established policy of merely threatening to use nuclear weapons was self-defeating, Acheson argued. If Khrushchev, not intimidated by that threat, permitted the East Germans to close traffic into West Berlin, we would either have to go to war or give in. If we sent a small Allied patrol down the Autobahn, and then a battalion size force, and both of these failed, as they would if the East Germans used their full forces against them, we would have to accept defeat or go to nuclear war. Or the East Germans might simply wave the battalion on into West Berlin while controlling other traffic on unacceptable terms. With current policies and forces, we would either have to accept the situation, or plunge into nuclear war so long as the Soviets believed we would not go to all-out war to prevent blockage of Berlin.

"Thus we would have suffered the worst of both worlds," Acheson argued. "We would have started nuclear war without having had the benefit of the deterrent effect which our determination to start the war rather than submit would — if known — have had on Russian decisions."

This brought Acheson to his basic conclusion. "We are thrown back on the necessity of devising, and starting quickly, a course of conduct which will change the present apparent Russian disbelief that the U.S. would go to nuclear war over Berlin rather than submit..." And this in turn required a decision, taken in advance, to accept that risk. "Nothing could be more dangerous than to embark upon a course of action of the sort described in this paper in the absence of a decision to accept nuclear war rather than accede to the demands which Khrushchev is now making..."

Acheson acknowledged uncertainty as to how far Khrushchev might go. "All that can safely be said is that Khrushchev probably would not incur the certainty of nuclear war over Berlin if he could see far enough ahead that war was certain. But, given his background and the inherent obscurity of the situation, we cannot be sure than before events passed beyond control he would see that war was certain... There is a substantial chance, not subject to evaluation, that (the measures) outlined here would convince Khrushchev that what he wants is not possible without war, and cause him to change his purpose. There is, also, a substantial possibility that war might result... It is, therefore, essential to make an early decision on accepting the hazard, and preparing for it... Success depends upon the existence of a core of hard decision, understood in all its grimness and cost..."

There then followed a proposed program of specific measures, under the headings of Preparations, Role of Negotiations, *Casus Belli*, and Possibilities and Consequences of Failure, that Acheson set forth as the means to accomplish the objectives outlined in more general terms in his Foreword. They assumed the issue would be joined when the East Germans (the German Democratic Republic, GDR), following a separate peace treaty with the USSR, took control of all access to West Berlin and closed the Autobahn. Presumably this would be at the end of the six month deadline for such a treaty that had been set by Khrushchev on June 4. By that time the U.S. should be in a state of improved readiness. Both nuclear and non-nuclear military forces, of both the U.S. and our NATO allies, should be brought to a state of advanced readiness without being provocative. Public opinion — American, Allied, and worldwide — should be prepared for a possible crisis. Civil defense measures, possibly including a fallout shelter program, should be undertaken, and there should be a long-term military buildup. Numerous supplementing measures were suggested, including development of naval countermeasures as a sort of counter-harassment, trade restrictions, and clandestine support of dissidence in East European satellite states. There should be no serious negotiation so long as Khrushchev believed the power balance favored him, but diplomatic gestures should be made for propaganda purposes and of a kind to make it easier for Khrushchev to retreat if he wished to do so.

There was a series of graduated responses to readily imaginable East German hindrances and denials of access to Berlin, each accompanied by enhanced general readiness measures and each timed to allow the Soviets to weigh the consequences of opposing the still stronger efforts to reopen access that would follow. The climax was to come with the long-proposed battalion probe and — if this was turned back, after an interval in which the Soviets would have an opportunity to negotiate — a conventionally armed force would be committed large enough to defeat anything the GDR alone could hold off. The JCS had estimated this would require seven divisions supported by four air wings. Some of the complexities and variables in the manner and timing of deployment of such force were briefly discussed. How much would be initially committed, how much held in reserve, for example, and how rapidly would the initial force need reinforcement.

Finally: "At some point, either at the end of one to two weeks or later, if the seven-division force were to be reinforced, a judgment would have to be reached that we had done all that was feasible to convince Khrushchev that the U.S. would, and indeed must — in order to preserve its army, its allies and itself — use nuclear weapons. Thus the last stage of deterrence would have been reached, if previous preparations and uses of force had not produced an acceptable settlement of the issue."

At the end of the paper, Acheson said that the program might fail if some of our allies would not associate themselves with us, or if general nuclear war was precipitated by miscalculation, especially out of pressures by either our SAC or the Soviet strategic force to attempt to strike preemptively, or, very simply, by flat refusal of the Soviets to be deterred. Although this final section had promised to discuss both the possibilities and the consequences of failure, there was somehow no discussion of the latter.

Rebuff of the Acheson Proposals

Instead of accepting the report, the NSC decided that a comprehensive analysis of its over-all implications should be provided by regular contributions from the State and Defense Departments, which in turn would be assembled and coordinated by a newly formed Interdepartmental Coordinating Committee. Departmental contributions were to be delivered to that Committee by July 6, and the Committee's report should be made to the President and the NSC at its meeting scheduled for July 13. This action almost completely bypassed Acheson, and very probably was a major factor in the animosity toward Kennedy that Acheson displayed in the immediately subsequent period. Conceivably as a sop, Acheson was asked to produce still another paper during the next month entitled "Berlin Political Program". But this was never submitted directly to the President, rather to the Secretary of State, and through the latter was circulated to the Secretary of Defense and the JCS. But although Acheson completed the paper on July 31, it did not reach primary recipients until August nor was it turned over to staffers until August 11. By that time events had overtaken it, and it had become largely irrelevant. Acheson, star performer for the first half of 1961, was to have no significant role in later developments.

The "comprehensive analysis of the overall implications" of the Acheson proposals to be undertaken by the Interdepartmental Coordinating Committee very shortly gravitated into concentration upon five major areas of concern. What should be the size, nature and timing of the longer term defense buildup? What did a more intensive examination reveal about the requirements and specific tactics of the possible military operations? How could we increase the chances that our allies would cooperate fully, and what should we do if they did not? What civil defense measures should be undertaken? Where should authority be lodged for making decisions involved in any sequence of actions from minor probes to possible ultimate recourse to nuclear weapons?

Emphasis on General Buildup as Keystone of Strategy

It was almost immediately clear that the White House placed greatest emphasis on strengthening and enlarging our defense posture in general and on a long term basis. The issues had become: how much, what kind, how fast, and in what manner? Accordingly, the Coordinating Committee asked Defense to prepare a proposed bill of particulars for what it originally described as a "partial mobilization" to increase flexibility and reestablish the credibility of our nuclear deterrent.

The order went forth on the very day of that NSC meeting (June 27) and passed through the Secretary of Defense's office to the JCS, where staff responsibility was assigned to J-5 (Policy). J-5 on a crash basis first came up with a proposal for partial mobilization of 559,000 military and 40,000 civilian personnel at a cost of $13.9 billion for the current fiscal year and $17 billion for FY 63. In a meeting with the Secretary of Defense on July 10, this was whittled down to $6.87 billion. The original estimates by J-5 were very nearly identical to figures previously turned out in response to a request for costing out the buildup that would have been required for the Acheson Study proposals.

Following consideration of this and other proposals on July 13, the NSC by its NSAM 59 of July 14 asked the Secretary of State to prepare a report evaluating two alternative courses of action. The first alternative was for a request to Congress, two or three weeks later, for a $4 to $5 billion program, including necessary taxes, stand-by controls, other legislation as required, and a Declaration of National Emergency. The second alternative called for an immediate request for $1 to $1.5 billion, without controls or taxes, to be followed later by additional requests if necessary. In evaluating these alternatives it was specified that consideration should be given to the effect of each upon our military capabilities, Soviet reaction, and Allied unity. A discussion of how best to deal with our allies in the matter was requested. The Secretary of State was also asked to report, in coordination with the Secretary of the Treasury and the CIA, on the feasibility and effect of possible economic sanctions against the USSR, the GDR, and against the entire Soviet bloc if access to Berlin were blocked. The Secretary of State also asked to report on timing and tactics and political repercussions of the various measures, economic and military, under consideration.

Much of Acheson's conceptual framework of how the expected crisis would arise, after a USSR-GDR closure of Autobahn access, was accepted as basic assumption. But Acheson himself was no longer the center of activity, nor even a major participant.

There was, meanwhile, throughout July and the first fortnight of August, a crescendo of varied threats from Khrushchev and an ever-growing and ultimately panicky emigration of East Germans into West Berlin and West Germany as tension mounted. All this added to official concern in this country. But there is no record of anyone foreseeing the nature of the culminating dramatic action in mid-August.

NSAM 59

Because of the growing tensions, the White House did

not wait for the two to three weeks period of study of alternatives before deciding on immediate actions. Instead, only five days later, at an NSC meeting on July 19, the decision was reached to proceed immediately on a $3.2 billion program that, in the words of Defense, would not involve early and massive mobilization of reserves (which might be more provocative than prudent), yet would lead to both immediate strengthening of readiness and contribute to a permanent increase in our defense establishment.

The decision was communicated to involved agencies the same day (July 19) under the heading of "Documents Prepared in Response to NSAM 59 of 14 July 1961." This was far from a coherent, closely reasoned paper leading logically to its conclusions. It was, rather, a hodgepodge, a 91-page compilation of undigested and uncoordinated contributions from participating agencies. They were in most cases the raw staff studies from disparate agencies that obviously had not been reviewed, nor even completed, let alone coordinated on an interagency basis. Nowhere in the document — the NSAM 59 — was there an exact, full statement of either the Coordinating Committee recommendation or the Presidential decision. There was no comprehensive statement of the mix of the many ingredients of policy: size and nature of buildup; military strategy and tactics concerning possible Autobahn harassment or closure; economic, naval and other assorted countermeasures under consideration; and policy toward both tripartite and NATO allies. There was discussion from various perspectives of issues involved, but no explicit, comprehensive statement of their resolution. Indeed, the $3.2 billion figure adopted did not occur in any of the Annexes devoted to the requested analyses of the $4 to $5 billion and $1 to $1.5 billion alternatives. Rather, it came in a later attachment to that report, added after its first typing. It evidently represented a last minute compromise figure submitted by the Secretary of Defense. It seems reasonable to infer that the White House decision represented a resolution of the matter that may have been hasty so far as that particular moment was concerned, yet which conformed closely to what had previously been intuitively preferred, but not definitely adopted until it seemed clear that no overwhelming contrary evidence had been turned up.

Gross inconsistencies and contradictions abounded within and among the separate Annexes. For instance, although in one place an "evaluation of likelihood of Allied military contributions" provided a very gloomy forecast of potential Allied participation in a strong conventional probe, success of such a probe was elsewhere indicated as dependent upon our allies' doubling their current commitments. This was coupled with statements that our allies were reluctant to adopt such a policy yet insistent upon participating actively in any possible adoption of it, but they were on the whole ill prepared to follow through even if they approved it. French divisions were described as poorly equipped for assignment to duty on the continent. West German divisions were most likely to be assigned, but their effectiveness was described as dubious. Italy had two assignable divisions but they were not fully equipped. The U.K., very reluctant to consider any commitment to conventional action, had but one third of a division in place and would need to increase this to four full divisions. Yet our allies would have to provide three-fourths of the total increases required for the large-scale probe that ever since the Acheson report began had been favored as the desired final gesture before resorting to nuclear weapons.

Most official thinking had indeed been tied to that Acheson assumption of the way the confrontation would develop, and had been accepted more or less as a working hypothesis by J-5 (the Policy directorate of the JCS to which primary action on NSAM 59 had been assigned). However, J-3 (the Operations directorate) had concurrently addressed the problem and produced a staff study arguing that the course of events that might lead to the decisive confrontation was inherently unpredictable, and that, therefore, buildup plans and contingency strategies should not depend upon any imaginary scenario of how the crisis would come about. To do so would obscure the real issues and might inhibit rather than facilitate making the required decisions. Rather than tie specific preparatory actions to the assumptions of the large probe as a final demonstration of resolve we should make clear our intentions to risk all by the general strengthening of our own military posture and of the posture, equally, of our NATO allies.

Here there was acceptance of the posited $4.5 billion figure and of the longstanding, but never attained, NATO buildup goals. These views were belatedly approved as JCSM 486-61 on July 18 and forwarded to the Secretary of Defense. Although not a part of the material originally considered by the NSC on July 19, they very probably contributed to the unexplained compromise figure of $3.2 billion in NSAM 59.

On July 20, the very day after the NSC decision to proceed along the general lines of a strategy based on a general and long term military buildup, Kennedy dispatched personal letters to de Gaulle, Macmillan and Adenauer, and directives to our ambassadors to NATO and all NATO capitals to inform their foreign ministers of American views and intentions, and to appeal for their cooperation and support. This amounted to a preliminary move toward a four-power Foreign Ministers Conference in Paris to be held from July 27 to August 10 to discuss the Berlin crisis and attempt to coordinate policies of the four nations most immediately involved. Most of the work of that conference would be delegated to a Working Group largely dominated by representatives of the defense ministries of the four nations.

EUCOM Objection to Acheson Probe Strategies

As consideration of actions to be taken moved further away from imagined scenarios conceived out of the abstract and toward more concrete details, objections to the strategy inherited from the Acheson report continued to accumulate. On July 20, JCS requested Norstad, in his capacity as USCINCEUR, to update and elaborate on estimates, tentatively supplied in early June for Acheson's use, of forces required to restore ground access to Berlin against the opposition of GDR forces acting alone. Four days later a report was transmitted, with a covering letter that argued that the large scale probe would be impractical in application. Beyond the three-

and-a-half page covering letter summarizing CINCEUR's views, there were over 30 pages of order-of-battle intelligence on the GDR forces and Soviet forces within the GDR, maps of airfields, radar defense installations, surface-to-air missile sites, natural obstacles and likely road block sites, with an analysis of the more effective tactics that might be employed against a probe. Finally there was an estimate of the total American forces required to overcome GDR resistance, provided we had the full cooperation of our allies, which was regarded as highly unlikely.

The covering letter said commitment of West German troops to the probe into East Germany would undoubtedly result in Soviet intervention, although use of West German troops for purely defensive purposes within West German territory would probably tie down East German forces without the adverse implications that would accompany their use in East German territory. Implementation of the probe would materially reduce the general war posture of EUCOM forces unless strategic reserves from the States were moved in before the forces already in Europe were committed. Neither ground nor tactical air forces could be equipped to operate for both nuclear and conventional combat. It had to be one or the other. If equipped and operating conventionally, they would be completely at the mercy of nuclear forces thrown against them. A relatively small probe could clearly establish Soviet intentions and a large-scale probe could be effective only if there were a sequence of events gradually leading up to it, involving both American and other NATO forces and including preparations for general war on a NATO-wide basis. Any decision to commit a force sufficient to prevent defeat by a satellite should recognize the probability of Soviet intervention and the clear-cut possibility of general war. With Soviet occupying forces already astride the Autobahn at Magdeburg, any major engagement between American and GDR forces along the Autobahn was difficult to visualize. The assumption of Soviet non-intervention was invalid. The cooperation of NATO, especially West Germany, France and the U.K., was absolutely essential, although highly questionable. Limiting probe operations to the axis of the recognized access route would make the probe forces extremely vulnerable. (To avoid this, it was clearly implied, would require an operation not clearly distinguishable from general invasion.)

On July 24, NSAM 62, classified Top Secret, signed by McGeorge Bundy, was dispatched to the affected agencies, clarifying NSAM 59 by spelling out the specific steps to be taken in pursuance of the decisions taken at the NSC meeting of July 18. And the next day Kennedy announced publicly the steps being taken: the request to Congress for additional funds of $3.2 billion; an increase in the Army's authorized strength from 875,000 to one million men; increasing the Navy and Air Force by 29,000 and 63,000; doubling or tripling draft calls; increases in air and sea lift; increasing non-nuclear arms procurement, etc. Then in addition to anything spelled out in the NSAM, Kennedy added:

> We have another sober responsibility. To recognize the possibilities of nuclear war in the missile age without our citizens knowing what they should do and where they should go if bombs begin to fall would be a failure of responsibility. In May I pledged a new start on civil defense. Last week I assigned, on the recommendation of the Civil Defense Director, basic responsibility for this program to the Secretary of Defense. Tomorrow I am requesting of the Congress new funds for the following immediate objectives: to identify and mark space in existing structures... to stock these shelters... to increase their capacity... to improve our air raid warning and fallout detection systems...

Near the end of the speech, Kennedy concluded:

> Three times in my lifetime our country and Europe have been involved in major wars. In each case serious misjudgments were made on both sides of the intentions of others, which

brought about the great devastation. Now, in the thermonuclear age, any misjudgments on either side about the intentions of the other could rain more devastation in several hours than has been wrought in all the wars in human history.

This statement was addressed even more to the Kremlin than to the American public. Clearly, the speech embodied the core of the Kennedy strategy. He was employing, while not acknowledging it, the Dulles strategy of Massive Retaliation, the game of chicken as theoretically elaborated by the think tank theorists of the late fifties. Except that it sought to provide an easy way out for Khrushchev without compromising our position in Berlin, it amounted to an application of the basic premises of the Acheson formulation. But the relationship with Acheson had already cooled. Moreover, Acheson interpreted Kennedy's expression of willingness to talk *before* the military demonstration as a signal of weakness and irresolution that would weaken the credibility of the nuclear threat. He allowed condescending grumbles suggesting Presidential weakness to become public knowledge. But Kennedy was in effect repeating much of the formula that had worked to relax tension in the Laos crisis four months before. Berlin was nearer home and vastly more important to both sides. Initiation of a fallout shelter program was intended, I believe, far more to add credibility to the nuclear deterrent than to save lives in event of war.

I remember well my own ambivalent reactions at the time. There was one Adam Yarmolinsky who was serving as a sort of general-purpose trouble shooter for Defense Secretary McNamara at the time who was assigned to oversee the development of the shelter program. As one who had worked on problems in this area I was called in to a few hurry-up meetings to consider proposed operating details of the program. Yarmolinsky was a gnome-like, low-key chap who was obviously very bright and whom I knew to be held in high esteem by McNamara and the Boston-Cambridge intellectual contingent that came in with Kennedy. But he had no special qualifications for dealing with this particular subject nor did most of the others he had gathered to advise him. I did not stay long with the group, but while I was with it I became convinced that many procedures and practices being decided upon were impractical or unworkable or grossly inadequate, and that because these evident deficiencies did not appear to bother Yarmolinsky, what was wanted was the gesture. I thought I knew enough about the attitudes of those whose advice counted to believe there was a significant chance that nuclear war might come. But there was a sort of fatalism, or eerie ambiance — something that at least never seemed explainable in rational terms — about people's attitudes. It existed as much among those with real knowledge of the dangers, and whose business it was to be concerned about such matters, as among the populace at large who had little or no real comprehension of what was involved.

If Khrushchev was impressed by the Kennedy program, it did not reduce his bluster. In response to earlier news leaks of White House consideration of a military buildup, the Soviets had already announced restoration of higher levels of defense spending that had been cut back in January. And Khrushchev dealt threateningly with John J. McCloy, who was then in Russia as Presidential Advisor on Disarmament.

In highly emotional language, Khrushchev told McCloy that in his July 25 speech Kennedy had in effect declared "preliminary war" and had presented an ultimatum which, if not accepted, would mean war; that he had consulted his Defense Minister and General Staff, had asked them to make necessary increases in Soviet defense; and Russia would never back down. He added that if war came, it would be won by the nation with the biggest rockets and the Soviets had these. Later he claimed the Soviets had 100 megaton bombs.

On July 27, two days after the Kennedy speech, the foreign ministers of the four powers immediately involved in Berlin convened in Paris. There was discussion of the old problem of the probe, a proposed transition of LIVE OAK from an exclusively planning group into an operational one, and of the means of coordinating among the four allies the various countermeasures other than military action that might be taken in the event of the expected interference with access to Berlin. Previously the non-military countermeasures, some of which might be taken in remote areas of the world far from Germany, had been discussed mainly by the four power ambassadors and their functionaries meeting in Washington. Now it was felt these should be closely coordinated with the sort of planning centered in LIVE OAK of measures and procedures to be used when our access to West Berlin was interfered with.

The Foreign Ministers met August 5-6 and their Working Group, which gathered on July 27, remained in session until August 10. But while they aired all the perceived major issues, they resolved little.

A draft directive on military planning for Berlin prepared by the Defense Department's office of International Security Affairs (ISA) was taken up for discussion by the Working Group but immediately ran into sweeping objections from Norstad, much the same as those he had voiced before. He criticized both its tone and substance and, at the invitation of the group, submitted a counterproposal. Norstad wanted a wider range of countermeasures to choose from in case of forcible obstruction of allied traffic instead of such emphasis on a large-scale conventional ground probe, because of uncertainties concerning the particular circumstances in which such obstruction might occur, and because he judged our allies reluctant to commit themselves to such a strategy except under very special conditions. Such large probe contingency planning as there might be should be undertaken on a tripartite basis, even with full NATO participation, rather than as a unilateral exercise, as it had seemed to be heretofore. He still believed that, so far as use of force might be considered, the 1959 strategy which assumed that a small-scale probe was sufficient to determine Soviet intentions, was the best strategy. Perhaps the gist of Norstad's proposals was expressed in concluding observations that because any military operations risked rapid escalation, military plans should always retain as their essential aim the survival of the Western allies. They could not, therefore, envisage commitment of capabilities to the detriment of their overall capacity to defend NATO against a larger Soviet threat.

And because of the possibility that any military efforts to persuade the Soviets to re-open access might lead to a response that would expand the conflict, any such efforts initiated in the NATO area *should come under NATO control at the outset.*

There were other efforts to settle upon tactics that might be applied by the U.S. on its own initiative without alienating our NATO allies. Faced with Norstad's arguments, General Gray, the JCS representative on the quadripartite working group, advised the JCS that there was urgent need for a basic document setting forth *national* tasks that the U.S. might undertake in a Berlin crisis, "national" evidently intended to mean unilateral. This led to a hurry-up study by the Joint Strategic Survey council which after going through all of the customary statements of objectives and anticipated phases of crisis over Berlin, sought to find areas of the world where we could harass or damage the Soviets and where we would not be at the great disadvantage we faced in Berlin and Germany.

On August 8, two days after the conclusion of the Quadripartite Foreign Ministers Conference, Secretary of State Rusk reported to the NATO Advisory Council on the agreements reached at that conference. There was really little to report. They had agreed to ask NATO to bring force levels in fact up to the levels previously agreed upon, and to make first echelon troops combat-ready. There should be a unified effort to develop popular support for the Western position within NATO and in the uncommitted world. NATO nations should be prepared to impose a total embargo upon the Communist Bloc if access to Berlin were denied. And NATO should be prepared on the substance of a stand it would take in negotiations when the crisis developed.

And with this the NATO Advisory Council adjourned, after expressions of support for the proposals submitted by all except Portugal, which did not comment.

The Building of the Berlin Wall

The most dramatic single event of the Berlin Crisis was the sudden and unexpected building of the Berlin Wall on the night of August 12-13. The drama of that act was fully appreciated immediately, but not all the consequences. Despite forewarnings of something of the sort, it had not been foreseen because we were concentrating expectations completely on other ways in which the culminating crisis might arise. There had been abundant accounts of the flight of East Germans into the over-crowded émigré reception center in West Berlin, and also of the ever more stringent measures imposed by East German authorities to stem the flow. It was widely agreed that this "hemorrhage" of labor — such was the way it was often described — above all of skilled and professional workers, was creating such a politically explosive situation that the regime would inevitably fall if it went on much longer. But no one is on record as having predicted the Wall.

Nor was the Wall's significance understood at the time. Almost certainly, the seething unrest within the GDR was forcing Khrushchev's hand. Whether or not the erection of the Wall was an act of desperation, it marked a turning point in the crisis. It shifted tension to the city itself, where our position was weak and the issues not entirely clear. Our occupying garrison there, always an elite corps, was scarcely more than a hostage surrounded by vastly superior forces, 200 miles from reinforcement, resupply or rescue. The status of East Berlin as part of a conquered city occupied by all four allied powers, but in practice ruled exclusively by compliant East Germans backed by Soviet tanks, was less clear-cut than stoppage of Allied traffic on the Autobahn. It was therefore a more awkward issue to deal with for those not directly involved.

Harassment of Western traffic into West Berlin by rail, air, and Autobahn would continue for years. Most of this was routine annoyance to keep us mindful of our exposed position in Berlin. But Berlin itself now became the main scene of confrontation, and not the Autobahn, as so much of our contingency planning had assumed. And much of the Kremlin's choice of issues was clearly designed to exploit differences among the three Western occupying powers, and within NATO as a whole.

The early reactions of American officials to the first reports of the Wall seem well summarized by Paul Nitze, who was close to the center of Washington's Berlin policy and decision-making at the time, and whom I interviewed not long afterward. Nitze recalled that while in Paris a fortnight before for the Quadripartite Foreign Ministers meeting, there had been some discussion of what the Russians might do to cope with the problem of the flight of émigrés from East Germany into Berlin. The idea of a blockade, or even some sort of wall was mentioned. (There was, after all, the precedent of the patrolled, barbed wire barriers separating East Germany and Czechoslovakia from West Germany.) But "the intelligence boys thought it unlikely," and "the consensus of the top level group was that the Russians would not move into the erection of a barrier or a wall, or instituting a blockade in the immediate future."

Like most of official Washington, Nitze was on vacation the weekend the Berlin Wall went up. Returning immediately to Washington, he called the Joint Strategic Survey Council into what became almost continuous session for the next two days trying to decide what action to recommend to McNamara to propose to the President. In Nitze's words, "One of the clear things that stood out was that nobody from our forces in Europe recommended any action." This, by itself, had not been very persuasive to Nitze, who recalled that his first impulse was that we should, somehow, do *something*. According to Nitze's memory, there were two considerations that led them to the decision to do nothing drastic. First was their appraisal of Russian intentions. "We took quite seriously the fact that the Russians had moved up two divisions to the outskirts of Berlin in deepest secrecy, and that our fellows hadn't found out about the movement until the action actually began," Nitze recalled. (Later intelligence estimated it was *three* divisions, not just two.) "It was our view that if this had been merely a bluff they would have moved these divisions with full fanfare to let us know they were there. This movement in deepest secrecy could be read as being a serious intention of the Russians to back up the East Germans in the event there were a fracas ... The East Germans had elements of three divisions in Berlin ... In any case they had clearly overwhelming military power in the immediate area..."

The other consideration came from appraising the immediate consequences of the only immediate step they could think of, which was to knock down the footings of the wall, which was being constructed right on the boundary. "If we knock that down and they move back a quarter mile and we knock that down, we're talking about occupying the eastern sector of Berlin in order to prevent their erecting some sort of protected area within (their own territory) ... It was our view you couldn't go that far without having a very serious fracas right there. That they would resist with force and that ... we couldn't defend on the spot and would have to raise (the conflict) to the all-German level at least ... What I remember most clearly is that we were persuaded that this was serious business on the part of the Russians, and you darn well had to get yourself in a position where you could deal with a continuation of serious power plays where they really intended to fight rather than back down..."

The Berlin Wall was a drastic, immediate, dramatic act whose enormity was almost immediately apparent, although it was of course not fully accomplished over night. It took a bit more time to complete construction of the barrier, to mount its sentry posts and gun emplacements, post guards and lookouts, and issue regulations and establish procedures for enforcing them. The Underground kept running, a rapidly dwindling few commuters continued to go back and forth with special passes. But to Berliners the immediate jolt was enormous. Our first response took the form of a formal U.S. protest, dated August 17 and delivered that day to the Moscow Ministry of Foreign Affairs. It was a legalistic protest, stipulating that closure of the occupation sector boundary was a flagrant violation of the quadripartite agreements of 1949 concerning the occupation of Berlin, and that the U.S. could not admit the right of East German authorities to enter the Soviet sector of Berlin. The U.S. flatly rejected the Warsaw Pact justification that had accompanied the action, protested "solemnly", and concluded that: "This unilateral infringement of the quadripartite status of Berlin can only increase existing tensions and dangers."

To this protest the Soviets replied the next day, with such promptness and detail as to suggest their reply had been prepared in advance, that West Berlin had become a center of Western espionage activities and of West German militarist and revanchist plotting and that the actions closing it off were taken in the interest of the German people and had the full support of the USSR.

Even before this diplomatic exchange, Willy Brandt, the mayor of West Berlin, addressed a letter to Kennedy dated August 16, transmitted by Embassy telegram to Washington and at the same time, either deliberately or by indiscretion, leaked to the German press. Brandt's letter declared that the events of August 13 had destroyed the remnants of the quadripartite status of Berlin, and that the Allied commanders there had limited themselves to "delayed and not very vigorous steps."

He warned that this created a crisis of confidence within West Germany and boosted self-confidence in East Germany. He proposed that the Western Powers reiterate their guarantee of remaining in West Berlin and insist upon re-establishment of the four-power status of all of Berlin and, finally, strengthen the U.S. garrison there. On the same day that our Berlin Mission transmitted Brandt's letter, it advised Washington that 200,000 West Berliners had staged a protest rally despite bad weather; that their prevailing mood was cynical and pessimistic; that the common belief was that the West, including West Germany, had written off the quadripartite status of Berlin; and that following the GDR takeover of East Berlin, Communist takeover of West Berlin was only a matter of time. The status of Berlin, rather than Western access to it, was becoming the immediate issue, but adjustment to this phase of the shifting crisis was partial and slow.

The White House, less consumed by staffing rigmarole and contingency planning, responded immediately. On the very next day, Kennedy announced Vice President Lyndon Johnson's departure for Berlin to assure West Berliners of American determination to preserve their freedom and their ties to the Western world. The following day (August 18), the White House announced that the President had ordered the movement of a reinforced battle group of about 1500 men to proceed by Autobahn to West Berlin to strengthen our garrison there. That move was accomplished on August 20, with great apprehension, but there were no holdups.[3]

These moves helped considerably to improve West Berliner morale, later to be boosted further by the August 30 recall from retirement of General Lucius Clay to serve as Kennedy's personal representative in Berlin. Clay was a hero to most West Berliners for his defiant leadership during the Berlin Blockade of 1948. His presence as presidential emissary was later to cause some chain of command problems, however. It resulted in the two American commands in Berlin not always being fully coordinated, and Clay's more aggressive instincts did not always coincide with standing instructions and prescribed procedures that our own military garrison, and the missions and garrisons of our British and French allies, were under orders to obey.

Although these measures gave reassurance to West Berliners, the mood in this country was probably more gloomy in the month following the erection of the Berlin Wall than at any other time until the grand climax, more than a year later, in what we generally think of as a different affair — the Cuban Missile Crisis. There were many reasons for the gloom. There seemed to be no way to restore the quadripartite status of Berlin, which in a practical sense had long been largely gone, but now was brought out as an issue by the cruel drama of the Wall and the thousands of family separations and personal tragedies it brought about. Khrushchev was as threatening as ever, and had launched a propaganda campaign to resolve the issue by making Berlin an open city, which might sound good to some, but surely would have meant its rapid absorption into East Germany.

Deepening Gloom

Two new National Intelligence Estimates were published on August 24, both bearing bad tidings. NIE 11-10-61, "Soviet Tactics in the Berlin Crisis", began with the conclusion that by means of the Wall the Soviets had accomplished two goals by a single action and were now ahead of schedule. (Always in this period we assumed the Soviets had a time-table of progressive actions leading up to their separate peace treaty at the end of the year, which would precipitate the final crisis by turning over the Autobahn to East Germans who in turn would deny us access.) They had reduced the refugee flow to tolerable proportions, thereby stabilizing the East German regime, and at the same time destroyed the four-power occupation status of the city. Moreover, the estimate concluded that Khrushchev had probably advanced his timetable, and by reacting strongly to American moves, had increased the involvement of Soviet prestige and was now professing that the issue had come to transcend the problem of Germany and Berlin. He said Western refusal to join in a peace treaty amounted to an attempt to break up the Soviet bloc. By claiming a challenge to Soviet power and prestige, Khrushchev sought to convey that the USSR could not draw back from a crisis in which reason and prudence would otherwise dictate restraint.

To this suggestion that Khrushchev might be in a position where he would not withdraw without having his way, there were added new estimates of Soviet military strength in NIE 11-A-61, "Main Trends in Soviet Capabilities and Policies." This was less fearsome, but hardly reassuring. The Estimate concluded that so far as overall defense expenditures were concerned, the publicized military budget increases of early July (in response to American military budget increases) had been achieved in part by merely uncovering previously concealed military expenditures. In terms of strategic striking strength, more definitive studies were under way, but tentative estimates were that as of mid-1961 the main weight of a large-scale nuclear attack against distant targets would have to be borne by long range aviation. Although this downgraded the *missile* threat, the NIE stated that "We believe the USSR has sufficient nuclear weapons to support massive nuclear attacks against targets in America by its Long Range Striking Forces." Moreover, the "Soviets now have available a wide spectrum of fission and thermonuclear weapons which is probably adequate to meet their basic requirements. We estimate that at present the Soviet stockpile probably includes nuclear weapons in the range of tested yields from about 1 KT to about 8MT..."

As for conventional forces, "Soviet forces in East Germany represent a powerful armored striking force of 10 tank and 10 motorized rifle divisions, with well over 5,000 tanks and supporting artillery and other units ... These forces are combat-ready, and generally at a high state of readiness which reaches a peak in early autumn ... Soviet forces stationed in East Germany are equipped with dual capable weapons and carriers. There is some evidence that nuclear weapons are presently stocked in East Germany..."

An even more important paper of the same day (August 24) was a memo addressed by Nitze to McNamara, subject "Berlin Buildup". It was the first formal expression of a mood that had been growing for several weeks, and as such became a landmark in the evolution of our Berlin policy-making. Later developments suggest that it was more alarmist than circumstances warranted, but it constituted, none the less, a coherent statement of the rationale for the stronger and accelerated actions we were immediately to undertake. The memo began by observing that the restrained, gradual military strengthening decided upon in July, which had been intended to leave the Soviets a graceful exit, had failed, as was evident not only by recent events in Berlin, but by increasing threats from Khrushchev, the latest in the form of a Soviet note of August 23 threatening air access to Berlin by any except military personnel. Moderation had failed, what preparations we had taken served only to induce Soviet charges of war mongering, and the Soviets had sped up their timetable. Among reasons for not calling up reserves before were the time limit upon service of reserves called up without a declaration of war, and fear that such a call-up might alarm our allies. Nitze argued that the Soviets' accelerated timetable meant the time for mobilization had already arrived, and that our allies would now be more reassured than alarmed by it. He concluded gloomily that if we did not mobilize immediately, we should do nothing to enlarge our commitment, such as sending General Clay, and we should enter negotiations promptly to get the best deal we could get, which he specified would probably include negotiation of access rights with the GDR and of *de facto* recognition of absorption of East Berlin into the GDR. (The latter was already largely accomplished.) Otherwise the only alternatives were to break down the barriers in Berlin, engage in hot pursuit if our air access were disturbed, with every intent of nuclear follow-up if our initial steps were opposed, or prompt negotiation but with the intent of nuclear follow-up if our minimum demands were not granted.

The very next day, August 25, the Pentagon Public Affairs Office put out a news release announcing that Secretary of Defense McNamara, with the approval of the President, had directed the Army, Navy and Air Force to order 311 selected units from Reserve components to active duty in accordance with the program first announced on July 25. This was hardly the mobilization Nitze's memo appealed for. It comprised only 76,500 men, 46,500 Army, 6,400 Navy, and 23,600 Air Force. But it was a step in that direction.

Thirteen days later, on September 7, McNamara advised the President of additional steps that had been taken, and outlined a sequence of mobilizing measures he proposed taking over the next week and in subsequent stages during the last half of September, in October and in November. Already 10 fighter squadrons had been moved to Europe, including 4 squadrons of F-100s to France and Germany. Currently the Air Force was arranging deployment of another wing of fighters, plus six wings of bombers that would be moved to Spanish bases on September 12. On September 15, orders would be issued calling up reservists to report between October 15 and November 15 (when training areas would be ready), and this would raise the total call-up to 227,000. Movement of dependents of military personnel to Germany was to be suspended.

And, within a week, there was to be publication of a presidential letter to the American public describing the threat of nuclear war, especially fallout, recommending protective behavior and directing attention to a civil defense booklet being made available at the same time. Draft calls were to be increased in both September and October, and expiring Army enlistments to be extended for periods up to four months.

Kennedy had been made well aware of the trouble we were having trying to induce our allies to cooperate in the particular strategies we favored. On August 21, he had sent a memo to McNamara asking for a report on the status of contingency planning for the anticipated interference with traffic on the Autobahn or in the air corridor sometime that autumn. He was especially concerned about prospects of NATO participation in a conventional forces buildup, in what sort of response our quadripartite allies might join, and finally in more remote countermeasures such as naval blockade. Many groups in many places and at many echelons were working on the problem. There had been constant, indeed accelerated, paper shuffling, but little change in the attitudes of the national representatives presumably seeking some common ground. An old hand at LIVE OAK once remarked to me, "The Americans, being a nuclear power, want a conventional forces strategy. The Germans, being a land power, want a naval strategy. The French, having no forces except in Algeria but hoping to become a nuclear power, want a strategy of nuclear retaliation. And the British just want the problem to go away."[4]

There were of course some divergences and ambivalence *within* national establishments. Such differences reflected different service viewpoints, national interests, varied perceptions of vulnerability or of proximity to prospective battlefields, and different appraisals of the nature of the Soviet threat. There had been some progress since the Acheson report at the end of June in the sense that there was greater awareness of the different perspectives of the different partners. But the major effort to develop an agreed strategy at the meetings in Paris shortly before the Wall went up had ended with little or no real progress. So the effort had to be continued.

Within our American establishment, attitudes toward the large-scale probe strategy had been tempered. The reply to Kennedy's August 21 request for a progress report on contingency planning for a Berlin blockade had to be, in essence, that studies were still in progress, which meant that there was no effective agreement. Norstad, in his dual capacity as Commander in Chief of NATO and of U.S. forces in Europe, and also responsible for LIVE OAK planning, was critically important. Consistently, his communications to both military and political authorities in Washington reflected his appraisal of what we could convince our allies to cooperate with, and what they would balk at. From the beginning, when Acheson was asked to formulate Berlin policies, Norstad had discouraged commitment to the massive probe notion as too rigid, as impractical in a tactical military sense, and as a strategy our allies would not accept. By late summer, Norstad's views were gaining wider acceptance, and Kennedy was among those influenced by them. Less than a week after the Wall went up, Norstad had submitted to Washington a proposed draft of a directive to himself for a quadripartite contingency plan that would reflect the changed situation. Norstad's draft emphasized the allied concern for "the widest practical choice of realistic military measures to counter Communist aggressive acts." The proposal suggested alternate plans already developed or considered, including three levels of probes to determine Soviet intentions, ranging from the scarcely more than patrol-size operation code-named Free Style, through Trade Wind, to division-size June Ball, plus air corridor plans Jack Pine I and II and Q-Ball. But the general plan was to proceed with enough deliberation from one to another level of escalation (unless our hand was forced) to give our allies a voice in determining whether or not to proceed to the next step. And, as in previous recommendations, Norstad concluded with the observation that "Any military operation risks rapid escalation, therefore military plans should retain survival of our Western allies as an essential aim, and not commit capabilities to the detriment of the overall capacity to defend NATO territory."

There were to be no fully agreed-upon contingency plans until October, when an approach worked out by Paul Nitze of Defense and Foy Kohler representing State succeeded in finding enough common ground, at least on paper, to avoid strong disagreement. More on that later. Meanwhile, the whole problem of a big buildup of American forces in Europe emerged as an issue independent of the issue of military probes. The cost and problems of the buildup became more impressive as the reality of actions, as distinct from the mere consideration of plans, began to unfold.

These issues came to a head on September 7 when McNamara delivered his response to Kennedy's request of August 21 for a progress report. Kennedy immediately called in the Secretaries of State, Defense and the Treasury, and as a result of that conversation addressed a sharp inquiry the following day to the three departments. Kennedy's questions suggested he was far from convinced that the big conventional buildup in Europe advocated by those favoring the large-scale probe strategy would have the effects its proponents claimed for it. Specifically, he wanted to know:

1. What will the presence in Europe of six additional U.S. divisions accomplish (a) in meeting the Berlin situation? (b) in vitalizing NATO and strengthening the long-term defense of Western Europe?

2. Will an increase of our conventional forces in Europe convince Khrushchev of our readiness to fight to a finish for West Berlin or will it have the opposite effect? What other steps of all kinds may help to carry conviction on this point?

3. Supposing that we and our allies raise the ground strength of NATO to 30 effective divisions, what will we have accomplished? Specifically: (a) Can NATO then defend Western Europe against a massive conventional attack by the Soviet bloc? (b) Can we safely mount a corps-size

probe to reopen access to Berlin and at the same time present an adequate ground shield? (c) How long can 30 divisions be supported logistically in combat?

4. Since our current plan is to send only one (existing) division (to Europe), why is it necessary now to call up four divisions from the Reserve?

There were six more questions, asking for specifics on how more reserves could be used if called up and not sent to Europe; how such a buildup would reduce the logistic support, and thus combat capability, of forces already on the spot; whether Khrushchev could not add an equal or greater number of divisions to counter such a move; and finally, in a question directed solely to the Secretary of the Treasury, what would be the net annual cost, in gold, and what could be done to reduce that cost?

These questions brought forth divided answers from the Pentagon.

McNamara had referred the questions to the JCS, who in turn assigned them to J-5 (Policy) for staffing. On the major and underlying issue of the effectiveness and wisdom of the larger buildup of U.S. conventional forces in Europe, the Navy, Air Force and Marines were opposed, while the Army and the Chief of Staff of the JCS (four star Army General Lyman Lemnitzer) favored the large-force strategy. The majority reply, which noted that Norstad was generally in agreement, expressed fear that the larger force would more likely convey the message that we sought to delay the use of nuclears until most of Western Europe was overrun, that even this augmentation could not reopen access against determined Soviet opposition, and could not withdraw without adverse effects upon allies, that a much smaller force would be sufficient to ascertain Soviet intentions, and that deployment of the larger force would impair the capability of the existing NATO ground force to provide the shield that established NATO strategy assigned it. Lemnitzer expressed his disagreements with the majority view in a separate memo for the President. There were a few areas of agreement on details, but in such matters as appraisals of how the Kremlin might react — an obviously debatable matter — or how rapidly and effectively and in what manner the Soviets might deploy additional strength to counter a testing probe we might launch, which again depended upon how one interpreted inconclusive order-of-battle intelligence, the Chairman's judgment and that of the majority report were at considerable variance. Thus the President was still left with no agreement among his military men concerning what military strategy to employ. The Army and the Chairman of the Joint Chiefs favored one strategy, in many respects joined by the Assistant Secretary of Defense for International Security Affairs, Nitze, while the Navy, Air Force, Marines, and perhaps most importantly, our NATO Supreme Commander and Commander in Chief of all U.S, forces in Europe, and our European allies, favored another.

Non-Military Considerations Underlying the Choice of Military Strategy

Which would be the best military strategy depended most crucially on factors that were not, strictly speaking, military. Rather, it depended mainly on judgments of how Khrushchev and the Soviets would react.

That involved guessing what was in Khrushchev's mind, in the minds of his advisers, and in the whole opaque world of Kremlin decision-making. This in turn would stand to be influenced by what these parties believed to be American attitudes and intentions as they existed in the minds of Kennedy and his advisers. We were playing games to impress them, commonly calling our moves demonstrations of our determination to fight rather than grant their demands. They, in turn, were playing their own game, seeking by bluster and threat and occasional coaxing to tempt us to accept some apparent compromise that would in fact leave us in a still less tenable position, and seeking always to color the issue so that it would seem of little consequence to our European allies, and therefore deter us from taking actions we preferred for fear our allies would not follow.

In this game the side that best understood the other had a big advantage. On the surface, the Soviets appeared to have that advantage. We were, first of all, an open society in which little could remain concealed for long from eyes intent on learning what we were up to. Their society and government were almost the exact opposite. We could learn much through various kinds of observation, but much that was most important to know about could only be conjectured on the basis of scraps of information that generally were subject to varying interpretations. Equally important, perhaps, was the fact that they had a corps of experts who made a lifelong career of studying us. Their man, Gromyko, came to the U.S. in 1942 and has been prominent in dealing with us ever since. Dobrynin, their ambassador as I write this in 1981, has served longer in Washington than any other ambassador accredited to the U.S. By contrast, we change ambassadors every few years, and only a few of them could qualify as experts on Russia. We had a few experts on Russia, most notably George Kennan and Chip Bohlen. Kennan was shunted aside by Acheson, basically because he seemed to Acheson insufficiently anti-Soviet, despite his authorship of the famous "Mr. X" article in *Foreign Affairs* calling for a policy of putting constraints on Soviet expansionism. Chip Bohlen never fell into such disfavor and remained as an occasional interpreter and adviser during the Kennedy years. But there is no record of his playing a prominent role in assessing how much was bluff and how much was firm in Soviet declarations and moves concerning Berlin. Generally speaking, he was, somewhat like Kennan, inclined to ascribe some measure of Soviet aggressiveness and paranoia to their feelings of being surrounded by potential enemies. "Experts" on Russia and the Soviets come in many colorations, and presidents and secretaries of state tend to choose among such experts according to their own predispositions about the Kremlin. In turn, the coloration of the experts tends to determine the coloration of the highest official interpretation of Soviet motives. It seems probable the Soviet leaders do the same. We tend to think the Soviets are more hidebound by their ideology than we are; very likely they have similar notions about us. But it seems they still retain some advantage in gauging intents based on the greater level of specialization and the longer tenures of those on whom they presumably depend to interpret the real motives that underlie our gestures. State Department documents found their way into JCS files only on occasion, and accordingly I was never aware of all that our Moscow embassy was reporting. But from the White House and Defense Department documents I did see, I am convinced that recognized experts on Russia had comparatively little influence on the way we interpreted Soviet actions and declarations. Kennedy, like other presidents, secretaries of state, and JCS chairmen, seems to have depended far more on his longstanding, seat-of-the-pants notions of how to interpret Soviet intentions than on any other factor. Like most others, he chose experts on the basis of whether or not they agreed with his seat-of- the-pants inclination.

Beginnings of a Slow Unwinding

The period from the time of the building of the Wall into early November was filled with accelerated actions, diplomatic maneuvers, and almost frantic attempts to reach some working agreements on how the anticipated Soviet moves would be met, even though signs were accumulating that none of the most feared moves would ever materialize. In retrospect it seems reasonably clear that by tactics of threatening the very worst, Khrushchev ended up attaining his minimum objectives, although I knew of no one who recognized this at the time, nor were we prompt in recognizing that the first phases of the crisis were past. Stabilization of an entrenched, Stalinist-type Communism was accomplished in East Germany, and East Berlin was converted, in fact, into an indisputably East German city, even though we did not recognize the legitimacy of either. Perhaps the reason we were slow to perceive the significance of these developments was that the Soviets and their East German protégés continued to issue enough threats, annoyances, and carefully limited harassments, to keep us always fearful of the outbreak of a military conflict they never pressed hard enough to precipitate. We gradually accustomed ourselves to settling gratefully for the lesser loss.

The major rearguard actions covering the Soviet withdrawal after scoring their immediate gains were an acceleration of threats to interfere with air access to Berlin (a tactic that had already succeeded, as a diversion, in getting us to concentrate so heavily on an anticipated denial of Autobahn access), while they solidified their control of East Berlin. The latter involved actions that were riskier because they reached a point where American and Soviet tanks faced each other at point blank range at the Friedrichstrasse check-point, "Checkpoint Charlie", with NCOs' fingers on the triggers of tank guns that, with one false move, might have unleashed violence disproportionate to the immediate issue of unquestioned access of American officials to East Berlin. But even that situation developed after the Soviets had succeeded, through repeated previous annoyances to feel out our reactions to their probings, in learning the procedures our people were instructed to follow. And our extreme local vulnerability probably seemed a reasonable assurance that we would not initiate unexpected rash acts.

On the strictly political level there were repeated sessions of the Washington Ambassadorial Group (WAG) seeking inter-allied agreement on plans, sessions of foreign ministers and NATO ambassadors, special meetings between Rusk and Gromyko, and a couple of intercessions at the head-of-state level, especially by Kennedy to de Gaulle, seeking French support for our favored countermeasures strategy. All this on top of continuing work on contingency plans, where it seemed full agreement and cooperation could never be reached, at lower echelons — neither at the Working Group of the WAG, nor LIVE OAK, nor between the JCS and USCINCEUR, nor even within the JCS.

Meanwhile, there were lower-level probes by trusted agents that, so far as U.S.-USSR communications were concerned, may have been as important as any. In mid-July Nitze had first talked with the First Secretary of the Polish Embassy, Edward Kmiecik, in an exchange of views wherein Nitze told the Pole that

Khrushchev's threats sounded like those of Hitler, and the Pole told Nitze that the Poles and Russians worried about revanchist German influence on Western policy and about rumored increases in U.S. divisions in Germany. Two days later, on July 15, Nitze had lunch at the Metropolitan Club with Soviet Ambassador Mikhail Menshikov, who was just about to go to Russia for a four-week vacation. In that meeting, Nitze told Menshikov of his work at the end of WWII with USSBS and of his first-hand acquaintance with current studies (referring to but not identifying the WSEG Fallout study and WSEG 50) of the probable effects on Russia of attacks totaling 7,000, 10,000 and even 20,000 megatons. The sequel to this conversation came on October 7, when Nitze, with the concurrence of McNamara, Lemnitzer, Bundy, and the State Department, lunched with Menshikov at the Russian Embassy. In the course of this conversation, which Nitze later described as "pretty frank and brutal", Nitze took up the issue of the Soviet resumption of atmospheric testing and coincident threats directed against our NATO allies who were themselves unable to retaliate in kind, assuring Menshikov that the U.S. would consider an attack on them the same as an attack upon us. From this point Nitze elaborated further on the devastation of Russia that we had estimated would occur in event of war.

In all this, Nitze emphasized that our studies of the balance of nuclear forces indicated that our forces were preponderant, and that we had great confidence in that preponderance. Nitze's reason for such emphasis was that there was an impression prevailing in many quarters of the American government that although our strength was indeed overwhelming, and that the Russians themselves recognized we had superior nuclear striking power, the Russians were at least partially convinced that we were not aware of our own superiority. (It is an interesting conjecture how much the missile gap fear of 1959-60 contributed to this.)

This notion of the state of Russian appraisals of *our* estimates of the balance of forces had been stimulated a month earlier when Rusk cabled Ambassador Llewellyn Thompson in Moscow stating that our planners were in need of best estimates of the Soviet view of the U.S.-USSR power balance. Thompson's reply, which was received on September 9, was to the effect that the actual balance of forces was probably less important to the Soviets than their estimate of their own ability to convince the U.S. and the world that the balance was in their favor. Thompson elaborated that the Soviets had a fairly accurate idea of U.S. strength, were especially fearful of our solid fuel missiles, Polaris submarines, greater air and naval strength, and that they considered that any step-up of the arms race would be to their disadvantage. He added that Soviet moves in Berlin and East Germany had little to do with military factors, but rather were defensive in that Berlin had been exploited against them in the Cold War, making stability impossible in East Germany, which they considered essential to Soviet interests, and that the Soviets were generally less fearful of the U.S. than of the growing military capability of West Germany.

Immediately after the meeting with Menshikov, Nitze dictated a six-page memo to record what had transpired, indicating that he believed an impression had been made, and that Menshikov, in the end, "got to his serious point, (which was) that October or November would be the best time to work out an arrangement over Berlin." What sort of arrangement Menshikov had in mind is far from clear. In fact, it was not really clear what sort of message he was seeking to convey, or whether what he said in any way reflected what Nitze had told him. This may be viewed in retrospect as an early hint of Soviet readiness to reduce the level of tension, but we did not interpret it as such at the time, probably because pressures within the city of Berlin, in the air corridors, and in rail and Autobahn access to Berlin continued to arise from time to time. Nitze recorded that his only reply to Menshikov's suggestion of working out an arrangement in October or November was that the way to end the crisis was to call it off.

On that very same day, September 7, Nitze delivered a carefully calculated address to the United States Army Association at the Sheraton Park Hotel. This address was primarily intended to impress our allies, not just the Soviets, with the overwhelming strength of our nuclear striking forces, and our readiness to use them, if necessary, to defend not only ourselves but our allies. Speaking as he was to the Association of the United States Army, Nitze talked at some length of the great need for conventional arms, and of the steps being taken to increase them. But the point he wanted most to get across came near the end of the speech.

> In summary, first, we have great nuclear capabilities. We are not particularly impressed with the Soviet threat to develop nuclear weapons in the 100-megaton range. We are not interested in arms of a terroristic nature, but rather our nuclear capability is tailored to specific tasks. We have a tremendous variety of warheads which gives us the flexibility we require to conduct nuclear actions from the level of large-scale destruction down to mere demolition work. I could not, of course, give specific numbers, but I can say that the number of nuclear delivery vehicles of all types the U.S. possesses provides the flexibility for virtually all modes and levels of warfare.

Recovery of Confidence in Our Strategic Forces Strength

These publicized and unpublicized representations of the strong comparative position of the U.S. in strategic weapons resulted from a comprehensive re-evaluation of the strategic balance going on behind the scenes in our intelligence establishments. Neither the Army as an institution nor Army General Lemnitzer as Chairman of the JCS had ever accepted the supposed Soviet superiority advertised by the missile gap issue. In discussing this with me at a later date, Lemnitzer indicated clearly, although without ever making an explicit statement involving direct criticism of Kennedy, that he attributed the "missile gap" and the intelligence estimates supporting it to "politics". And he indicated in fully explicit terms that he had endeavored, ever since the January NIE, to have a reappraisal that would disclose the error of the earlier estimates and not credit the USSR with a superiority that was really ours. (WSEG 50 would have gone a long way toward accomplishing that, but the problem was to get the judgment incorporated into a study that would be blessed at highest levels and land face up — in summary and dramatic form — on the President's desk as the most authoritative statement possible.)

The frenzy of intelligence activity to produce a new national estimate was no secret to insiders, nor was the general direction that a new set of estimates would take. But the final negotiations between competing and conflicting agencies, and the final wording of the piece of paper approved for White House eyes took until September 21, when NIE 11-8/1-61, "Strength and Deployment of Soviet Long Range Ballistic Missile Forces", was published. This estimate stated:

> New information providing a much firmer base for estimates of the Soviet long range ballistic missiles has caused a sharp downward revision in our estimate of present Soviet ICBM strength but strongly supports our estimate of medium range missile strength.
>
> We now estimate that the present Soviet ICBM strength is in the range of 10-25 launchers from which missiles can be fired against us, and that this force level will not markedly increase during the months immediately ahead.

From this beginning, the estimate evolved through a series of revisions based less on any new intelligence than on what we were learning from our own experience about the enormous technical problems involved in deploying, and above all maintaining in a state of readiness, the liquid-fueled missiles of that era. Moreover, anyone familiar with the intelligence sources and processes at that time was in a position to know that both current estimates and future projections were based on incomplete and rarely conclusive wisps of evidence interpreted through whatever one's judgment was of Soviet intentions, capabilities, and competence, and in technical aspects, by analogy with our own experience (which might be very different).

The concluding paragraph of the NIE conceded that the Soviets were capable of inflicting severe damage to European and peripheral areas but belittled their capability against U.S.-based SAC. The concluding paragraph included these words:

> ... Although Soviet propaganda has assiduously cultivated an image of great ICBM strength, the bulk of the USSR's present capability to attack the U.S. is in bombers and submarine-launched missiles rather than in a large ICBM force. While the present ICBM force poses a grave threat to a number of U.S. urban areas, it represents only a limited threat to U.S.-based nuclear striking forces.

There was of course an Air Force dissent, which was as much to be expected as the Army's unhappiness had been in the earlier, higher, estimates. The Air Force did concede, however, that the current Soviet ICBM force was not substantially higher than the maximum range of the "agreed" NIE.

An interesting sidelight is that it took only four days, from September 21 to 25, for the gist of the TOP SECRET NIE to appear in Joe Alsop's syndicated column. Not only did Alsop disclose the substantive significance of the NIE, although none of the exact numbers, but also the impression that was then developing among American officials that since the Soviet threat against the U.S. was not so great, the problem was now centering on the fact that Khrushchev held, not us, but our-West European allies hostage to his objectives in Germany. Evidently the official who leaked the story to Alsop managed to enlist Alsop's help in conveying that impression of the situation. For, in Alsop's words:

...the Soviets are now credited with possessing ... close to 200 (medium range) ballistic missiles ... that can reach targets in all of Western Europe except the Iberian Peninsula.

...with utmost brutality and arrogance, Khrushchev has boasted of his ability to destroy the Western European nations, and has called these nations his "hostages." But Khrushchev has never specifically boasted that he could "destroy" or "annihilate" the United States...

...He has been using terror tactics. But he has been able to use terror tactics — with considerable success in some quarters, unhappily — because the Western alliance, like all alliances, is more politically vulnerable than Khrushchev's unitary, authoritarian empire...

...in the contest of will ... the trouble is that, as now organized, the contest has more than two participants. On one side the Soviet Union stands alone. On the other side, President Kennedy stands at the head of the Alliance of the West.

For the present, what is chiefly important is to make Khrushchev understand that if he pushes the Berlin crisis to the ultimate crunch, the great power that the United States still possesses will not remain unused.

The struggle over the status of East Berlin, dramatically initiated in mid-August by the construction of the Wall, continued with growing intensity through September and October. Then, although never formally resolved, it lapsed into a minor role as a bone of contention. Our policy, very simply, was to continue to observe the charade, while uttering occasional futile protests, that East Berlin was still merely the Soviet-occupied sector of the entire city, which would remain occupied by four powers until such time as a formal peace treaty with *all* of Germany would enable Berlin to revert to the new Germany. Meanwhile East Berlin would remain under Soviet control within the central jurisdiction of the inter-allied control of the entire city, because, so the formal fiction went, the East German government had no authority there, and officials of American and other Western occupying powers had the right to move into and within East Berlin free from any control or hindrance from the East Germans. Most of this had long since eroded away. The central authority had become a sheer fiction commemorated by the ceremonial rotation of national heads of the Kommandatura, where no real power was exercised. The real government of the city was in the hands of the all-German governments of both West and East Berlin.

What the Soviets and their East German protégés wanted, short of getting full control of all of Berlin, was to make East Berlin into an undisputed integral part of East Germany. The tactics of the Soviets were to nibble away until they achieved their goal, if not *de jure*, at least *de facto*. We were a giant, but so situated that we could not advantageously respond to minor annoyances in kind. Their game was to erode the agreed provisions for the occupation of East Berlin by a series of ploys to which it would be awkward for us to respond effectively without bringing on a crisis vastly greater than whatever seemed the issue immediately at stake. Our highly vulnerable, exposed position in Berlin made this fairly easy to do. Their only great concern was to avoid provoking us to a point where we might unleash global war. They could generally learn, from the behavior of local troops and officials, how far they could safely proceed by minor annoyances, and how we would very probably react to any initiative they took.

Aside from the factor of local military vulnerability in an exposed, forward position, our situation was weak on two other counts. There was little we could do to react to a Soviet probe without the cooperation, or at least the acquiescence, of our allies, who were generally skittish about anything that might appear risky, and whose approval would take valuable time to get in any case that had not been fully anticipated. And so as far as actions in East Berlin were concerned, we were aware that while we might knock down a barrier, we could not force the Soviets to keep a crossing open. So long as the Soviets and the East Germans did not permit movement into and within East Berlin in a manner satisfactory to us, and in accord with mutual commitments developed out of the Potsdam agreements, nothing short of invading and taking over the administration of East Berlin would accomplish this. Our lack of foresight in the initial arrangements at the end of World War II had committed us to an untenable position.

Within days after the Wall appeared on August 13, evidence began to accumulate indicating that access to East Berlin from the west would soon become an issue. This posed the problem of reaching agreement, in advance of some crucial incident, on how we should best respond to some serious obstruction of access. Above and beyond the difficulties of our extreme local vulnerability and precarious political position with respect to our allies was the fact that the Soviets and East Germans could pick the time, the place and the exact nature of the incident whereby they could challenge our right of access to East Berlin. A fairly comprehensive set of instructions was issued on August 26 to Norstad for the guidance of our Berlin Brigade, which would be the American action party in event of any serious incident.

These instructions began by stating that American policy was to "demonstrate our legal right of entry into East Berlin," but that a clear distinction must be observed between our right of access to East Berlin and right of access to West Berlin. Access to East Berlin was important, but not so vital that it must be maintained by combat, except self-defense of our forces. If fired upon, our forces should defend themselves but withdraw to West Berlin. If fired upon in West Berlin, they should return the fire only so long as they were under fire. No line of action should be initiated to maintain U.S. right of access to East Berlin which might result in a situation from which they would have to withdraw with consequent loss of prestige. However, our right of access to West Berlin was of such importance that it should be maintained even if it entailed combat. Continuing the instructions on the level of guiding principles, it was stated that while we did not concede that either the USSR or the GDR had legal authority to restrict our access, for 'practical' purposes our rights of access would be considered satisfied if just one entry point remained open for unimpeded movement into East Berlin. (This was of course the Friedrichstrasse entry point — "Checkpoint Charlie" — all other entry points having in fact been blocked off a fortnight before.)

The Exhaustive Search For Countermeasures: An Exercise in Futility

It was anticipated that there could be four types of obstacles to access. In case of "administrative" resistance, the instruction was to ask for a Soviet officer, and if none appeared, to proceed, if possible, without violence, but if not possible without violence, to withdraw. In case of "passive" (easily removable) obstacles, instructions were to remove them and proceed. In case of obstacles removable only by bulldozer or tank, instructions were to withdraw and ask instructions (which in effect returned control of further local action to Washington). In case of obstruction by either mobs or East German troops, the same procedures were to be followed as in the case of "administrative" obstacles.

On the purely diplomatic side, instructions issued by State to Minister Lightner in West Berlin were to deliver a protest to the Soviet commanding officer in East Berlin in the event of obstacles to access, with the understanding that follow-up protests would be delivered by Western ambassadors in Bonn, acting as residual High Commissioners in Occupied Germany, to the Soviet ambassador in Bonn. State wanted this protest to be kept in diplomatic channels rather than being handled by Norstad acting as Supreme Commander of NATO forces. Lightner commented in his reply that the French were without instructions and refused to participate, although the British in West Berlin had instructions that were apparently not in conflict. However, he wondered how a protest could be delivered to the Soviet commanding officer if East Berlin were cut off. Press statements might be useful if the issue were clear-cut, but protests at the local level were of little use unless very prompt, and were becoming counterproductive (i.e., serving mainly to demonstrate our inability to *do* anything). Protests at the Moscow level were sometimes helpful, but if unheeded or not followed up, they impaired prestige.

Much-discussed restrictions on trade were again considered, but again the problem was that they would have little effect without the full cooperation of West Germans and all NATO allies (mostly ranging from reluctant to opposed), and in any case remote countermeasures lacked effectiveness as retaliation against local aggressions. There were numerous local complications, mostly trivial, some of moderate importance, suggesting potential approaches or problems. There were Czech and Polish missions in West Berlin that might be harassed, but what good would it do? There was the Soviet honor guard at the Soviet War Memorial in West Berlin that might be denied access, but what good would that do? More significantly, there were the Soviet air controllers, whose continuing service was useful if not vital. The concluding judgment, related directly to what might be accomplished by military action, was a recommendation that use of force should be confined to keeping Friedrichstrasse open "come hell or high water, distressing as this arbitrary limitation is." The search for countermeasures got this far and no farther. The one redeeming ray of light in all this was that, gradually, we were learning that the Soviets were playing a game, a dangerous game perhaps, but a game in which they hoped to win all they could without making it deadly.

Harassment of Americans going into East Berlin gradually increased through September and early October, the main Soviet tactic being to direct the East German police — *Volkspolizei*, known as Vopos — who under occupation agreements had no jurisdiction, to inspect identification documents. To permit this amounted to acknowledging their authority, and of course Soviet authority would be slow to appear to end delays and embarrassment. Such incidents extended from Berlin to the Autobahn. No one was ever delayed more than a few hours, but the annoyance was great and the symbolism was distressing. There were protests at the level of

Berlin, then Bonn, finally Moscow, to no conclusive effect.

As October went along, the issue of access to East Berlin became more tense, and more confusing so far as policy was concerned. The little game of probes to assert our right of access became more serious, the response to those probes toughened, with new devices of hectoring and evasion, and our own actions and policies became more uncertain because of divided counsels both within our American establishment and between the U.S. and our allies. Having established General Clay as his personal representative in West Berlin, President Kennedy was receiving advice and recommendations from Clay that were often at variance with what State, Defense, and Norstad were telling him. Clay and the JCS were all in favor of using tanks to demolish any obstacle the East Germans might erect at the Friedrichstrasse checkpoint, whereas our tripartite partners in Berlin, as well as our other NATO allies, were all dubious of such policy to various degrees, and above all were opposed to delegating authority to do this without consultation that would extend back all the way to their foreign ministers. Clay's presence as a restorer of West Berliner morale was welcomed by all, but as a policy advisor with direct access to Kennedy his influence was sometimes feared by those who considered the full cooperation of our allies indispensable, because his counsels were commonly on the bolder side.

On October 18, following a White House meeting, Kennedy had Bundy send out, as a supplement to earlier instructions on Berlin, a directive labeled NSAM 107, "Friedrichstrasse Crossing Point," intended as policy guidance on Berlin for the highest levels of State, Defense and the CIA. NSAM directed that: "If the Friedrichstrasse crossing point is closed either by unacceptable demands or the erection of a barrier, we would run 2 or 3 tanks up to the checkpoint to demolish whatever was barring our entry ... and then have them withdrawn and stationed nearby..." This was to be followed by a prescribed protest procedure. But the directive concluded with the big qualifier, "This course of action is subject to the agreement of the British and French." Such agreement was never forthcoming.

Just four days later, the American Minister in Berlin headed into East Berlin ostensibly to go to the theater, was stopped by Vopos demanding he show identification, which he refused, asking to see a Soviet officer. When none came he proceeded until stopped again by Vopos, with the same results. He then called for American M.P. escort, and with them toured East Berlin. Later he repeated the tour with escort, then issued a protest to the Soviet Provost who admitted delay in providing identification photos to East Germans, but insisted they had the right to patrol, and in turn protested the invasion of East Berlin by armed American patrols.

Beginnings of the Tank Confrontation

The next move in the game came the following day when a privately owned vehicle with U.S. forces license plates and a civilian driver was turned back by Vopos. There were, of course, many variations that might have been undertaken as probes, but largely at Clay's urging it was decided that the stopping of a vehicle bearing U.S. military license plates with a civilian driver was an appropriate measure to test Soviet intentions. Accordingly, on October 26, the Commander of the American Berlin Brigade notified the Soviet Commandant of East Berlin that an American-licensed vehicle with civilian occupants would attempt to enter East Berlin via the Friedrichstrasse checkpoint at ten minutes past five that afternoon and asked that a Soviet official be present to check their documents, stating that if no Soviet official were there, the vehicle would proceed, regardless. If harassed, the U.S. would insist on armed patrols. When the car arrived, no Soviet official was there. When the occupants refused to show their credentials to the Vopos, who refused to call a Soviet officer, the car proceeded, with an armed escort, for a tour of East Berlin, then returned and was escorted back through the checkpoint by U.S. troops. Only after that action did the Soviet Commandant reply. He declined to send Soviet officials to check identification, and warned that further acts of force would be met by Soviet countermeasures.

The very next day the sally into East Berlin was repeated.

And within ten minutes of their return into the American sector, Soviet tanks, eventually ten in number, arrived at the crossing point, directly confronting the American tanks only 100 to 200 yards away until they withdrew to a tank park nearby. The issue was joined, and the game was becoming dangerous.

Strong protests were lodged in Moscow. Moscow, unyielding, replied with protests against the American armed intrusions into East Berlin, warning in strong tones that force would be met by force. For about a month American and Soviet tanks were never far from the checkpoint, and for much of the time, too close for comfort. But without the fact being advertised, just as the tank confrontation began, the White House decided, according to secret advice it communicated to our Moscow embassy, that our probes already undertaken had "served their purpose", and that "further probes by U.S. personnel wearing civilian clothing in official U.S. vehicles and using armed guards or military escort will be deferred." The Secretary of State was directed to take the public position that our probes had demonstrated Soviet responsibility for the unilateral actions of the Communists in turning East Berlin over to the GDR illegally, and had demonstrated our unwillingness to recognize GDR authority over American official personnel. General Clay, the JCS, and apparently Norstad, continued to believe we should not abandon the policy of crashing down on illegal obstruction at Checkpoint Charlie, but they were issued specific instructions *not* to take such action. Lesser, unescorted, unarmed probes continued, and tension remained, but the major fuse had been removed.

It is unclear what, precisely, may have been all the reasons why Kennedy called off the armed probes and forceful entry. Almost certainly he was much influenced by the failure of the British and French to support stronger measures. Obviously, it would have been extremely awkward, to say the least, to take such action unilaterally. All of the official documentation suggests this was the main reason if not the only reason. But recognition that East Berlin already had, in all reality, if not in formalized legality, become a part of East Germany, and that what we were disputing was merely symbolism, and in our vulnerable extended position hardly worth the gamble of a world war, must have played some part in his thinking. Even Clay had openly conceded that the issue of access to East Berlin was "intrinsically unimportant" and mattered merely as "an insidious first step."

At this point, the West Berlin Crisis of 1961 was really past, but the bureaucratic momentum of the long effort to develop contingency plans for the sort of situation we had, from the first, assumed would produce a decisive confrontation, rolled on. Through these October days when the issue of American official access to East Berlin, unhampered by Vopo molestation, made the newspaper headlines, the longstanding issue of Allied access to West Berlin continued to preoccupy the United States at high levels, as it sought an agreed policy concerning actions to be taken if and when the Soviets interfered with or denied entry to West Berlin. Since Acheson began his studies of the issue early in the year, thousands of man-hours had gone into the development of scores of varied policy proposals, but no comprehensive contingency plan had ever emerged that did not arouse opposition strong enough to prevent adoption by at least one of the parties whose approval was essential. Acheson had faded from the scene. But at the working level, attempts to develop acceptable contingency plans were an ongoing activity at LIVE OAK, within two branches of the JCS and sometimes within the office of the Chief of Staff himself, within the office of Assistant Secretary of Defense Nitze and within State. Whatever proposals emerged from one of these would first be scrutinized by each of the others, often by the Washington Ambassadorial Group or by special meetings of the foreign ministers concerned, and finally at the level of heads of state.

Origins of NSAM 109: The Nitze-Kohler Formula

Despite the difficulties, an agreed statement of guiding policy, along with the outlines of contingency plans, began to emerge in October. It involved a measure of compromise among proponents of differing strategies, a measure of fuzzing up some issues where explicit agreement remained unattainable, and some apparently tacit approval of a proposal that was never committed to paper for all to see. Although later on there was the usual large number of contributory participants, the individuals who devised the basic formula almost single-handedly were Nitze of Defense and Foy Kohler of State.

Kohler was notable as an expert on both Soviet and European politics, who at the time was Deputy Under Secretary of State for European Affairs. The initiating occasion was the preparation of a draft memo for Secretary of State Rusk to use in a meeting with President Kennedy on October 10. In anticipation of this, Nitze and Kohler, drawing obviously from the great number of countermeasures that at one time or another had been proposed, began by drawing up three charts, or graphs, on which they entered proposed actions by categories ("political", "economic", "naval", "military") in a sequence ranging from the merest local protest to all-out war. They called the three graphs Horse Blanket, Pony Blanket and Poodle Blanket. The Horse Blanket attempted to be as nearly all-inclusive as possible, the Poodle Blanket was the most summary and abbreviated, and the Pony Blanket was half way between the two. What went forward to Rusk and Kennedy was just one of the Blankets, a 2-page summary covered by a 4-page memo that expressed the leading strategic concepts underlying the recommended "Sequence of Actions in a Berlin Conflict." These actions would be the components of a phased sequence of varied countermeasures, with pauses between phases to allow time for the Soviets to consider the greater risks they would face if the crisis were permitted to advance to the next stage.

The memo began with "a major consideration" that was crucial because it marked the beginning of a retreat from the most widely advocated American proposal planning for a strong conventional ground probe before resorting to nuclears. And from this it followed that the conventional arms buildup and large-scale reinforcement plans that had been a centerpiece of our strategy since July were no longer judged necessary, and perhaps not even desirable. It was "conceded that, on the one hand, such military measures as small probes can be taken from existing posture with acceptable risk, and on the other hand that even the full planned NATO buildup would neither give us a non-nuclear predominance in Europe nor necessarily be a critical factor in the outcome of a general nuclear war." There were, however, many intermediate measures available to apply pressure and demonstrate intentions, the appropriateness of each depending upon circumstances. This provision — that the adoption of listed countermeasures would need to be decided upon according to circumstances — was critically important. It permitted listing and consideration of countermeasures as possibilities that would have met with strong objections from some allies if included as an agreed component of contingency plans. At the same time it provided an appearance of unanimity that could hardly be said to exist in reality.

There followed a pro and con discussion of the advantages and disadvantages of immediate reinforcement of forces already on the spot, the main issues being whether or not it would provoke the Soviets into either over-compensating or accelerated reaction, whether or not the gain from hastened reinforcement would compensate for the disruption of a more orderly buildup, and its effect upon our NATO and quadripartite allies. There were no strong recommendations, but the tenor of the discussion could not be called favorable to dramatic moves to reinforce. And there was a reminder that time was running out on Khrushchev's "ultimatum" of June.

The tabular summary intended for the eyes of Rusk and the President, entitled "Sequence of Military Actions in a Berlin Conflict," was the guts of the proposal, but represented the abbreviated version informally called the Poodle Blanket. It defined four hypothesized contingencies, and briefly outlined recommended responses with an added terse comment.

Contingency I was Soviet-East German interference with ground or air access short of definitive blockage. The recommended response was to execute contingency plans including a platoon probe on the ground or a fighter escort in the air and continue using unblocked mode of access. This was judged without risk unless the Soviets wanted war, and the risk of war would not be increased by such action.

Contingency II was defined as a situation wherein, despite such Allied response, the Soviets and the GDR continued with apparent determination to maintain significant blockage. Recommended response, if this occurred *before* substantive reinforcement of NATO: non-military countermeasures should be undertaken simultaneously with mobilization and forward deployments, meanwhile continuing the use of any routes to Berlin not blockaded by force. If the situation developed *after* reinforcement, one or more of the military actions outlined in III should be initiated after further appropriate non-military countermeasures.

The commentary on these options was that the current shortage of readily available forces imposed a choice between delaying action while reinforcing and acting immediately with more modest forces. Either course of action had drawbacks, but the more prompt action was considered preferable because, it was argued, delay would weaken deterrent credibility, erode Allied resolve, and threaten the viability of Berlin.

Contingency III envisioned a situation wherein the Contingency II actions had failed to restore Berlin access. In this case, a nonnuclear but expanded force with strong air support should probe the Autobahn "in sufficient strength to demonstrate intent to reopen access," accompanied by expanded non-nuclear air action to gain local air superiority including attacks on ground installations involved in interference with access and, away from the immediate scene, worldwide maritime control and blockade. The commentary on these measures was that they should impress the Soviets with the danger of irreversible escalation, and on the other hand, that although local military success was not impossible, overpowering a determined Soviet conventional resistance with conventional weapons was not feasible. The naval countermeasures exploited Allied superiority at sea but there were political handicaps because of the lack of their direct relationship to Berlin.

Contingency IV addressed the situation wherein, despite Allied use of all of the above non-nuclear actions, the Soviets continued "to encroach upon our vital interests." At this stage we should initiate, and continue if necessary, selective nuclear attacks, at first for the primary purpose of demonstrating our will to use them, later for tactical advantage such as preserving the integrity of Allied forces previously committed. And if this failed, go to general war. On this the commentary was that the timing of initiation of nuclear weapons, and determination of the scale of their use, was not ours alone to decide, and that our initial restrained employment, whatever its nature and intent, might trigger an unrestrained counterattack.

It seems noteworthy that on October 6, the very day that the Poodle Blanket policy proposal was completed and signed by Nitze and Kohler, Gromyko discussed Germany and Berlin with Kennedy in the White House, in the final round of a series of talks the Soviet foreign minister had been having in Washington, previously with Secretary of State Dean Rusk, but with Kohler present at all of them. According to dispatches sent out to our immediately concerned embassies, Kohler concluded that the Soviets appeared to understand that their current course was dangerous, that it had been established that negotiations on Germany were to be between the USSR and the West, not between East Germany and the West, that the USSR time limit had been relaxed (although this was not yet formally acknowledged), that the West was not yet in "a negotiating position", and that continued contact with the USSR was desirable to explore possible means of preventing the USSR from acting unilaterally. And on October 16, only ten days later, Khrushchev, addressing the Soviet Communist Party Congress, declared, "If the Western powers display readiness to settle the German problem, the question of the time limit for the signing of a German peace treaty will not be material; we shall not insist that the peace treaty be signed before December 31." Khrushchev was obviously retreating from the position he had taken in the ultimatum of June 4, at least so far as time limits were concerned, and we had taken note of this. But although by stabilizing the

Ulbricht regime in the GDR and making East Berlin in all reality a fully East German city, he had achieved his minimum objectives, he had by no means renounced his demands for eventual Western recognition of the German Democratic Republic, which at the time was believed would eventually lead to the incorporation of West Berlin into the GDR.

The Nitze-Kohler "Poodle Blanket" had been presented to President Kennedy on October 10 at a meeting attended by Rusk, Kohler, Bundy, McNamara and Deputy Secretary of Defense Gilpatrick. With no substantial change except to shift the four sequential contingency proposals from a tabular to textual format, and to specify all military as "allied", the President approved the draft for circulation for comment to State and Defense before final acceptance as a statement of U.S. policy.

Specifying that the military actions be Allied could have been Kennedy's own idea, but this may have been in deference to the views of Norstad and State, known to be generally sensitive to what we could and could not convince our allies to go along with. State offered no significant comments of record, but Gilpatrick, acting for McNamara, immediately requested formal JCS comment and also prepared a letter to Norstad asking his reaction to the document as a basis for detailed contingency planning. Defense Department participation in preparation of the Horse Blanket-Pony Blanket-Poodle Blanket opus had been in the office of the Assistant Secretary of Defense for International Security Affairs, and there were often significant differences between that office and the JCS, and often between the collective view of the JCS and that of Chairman Lemnitzer and the Army. ISA, Lemnitzer and the Army tended generally to be more friendly to the large conventional ground probe strategy whereas the Navy and Air Force were more skeptical of its feasibility. State and Norstad tended also to be skeptical, though for more political reasons; they doubted that our Allies could be induced to accept it.

The collective JCS response was assigned to J-5 (Policy), and a few of the comments, hurriedly assembled and forwarded on October 13, included a few proposals that might be charitably viewed as eccentricities deriving naturally from some of the national fixations that flourished during the preceding decade. For instance, one point emphasized in the basic memo stated that "... positive action to oppose Communist aggression in any geographical area will be evidence of the determination of the U.S. and will influence the Berlin situation. The JCS have examined the present situation and have agreed that intervention in SE Asia is militarily desirable to counter Communist insurgency. This action should have the effect of making our determination unmistakably clear to the Soviets."

This recommendation was not accompanied by any statement indicating awareness of our advertised shortage of military forces, of the undesirability of dispersing strength, or of longstanding reluctance of many Army men to get bogged down in Asian jungle warfare. At another point the old "Unleash Chiang Kai-shek" motif recurred. As a measure to precede resort to nuclears, the recommendation was seriously advanced to "Release the GRC (the Taiwan government) for unrestricted air operations against the Chinese mainland, initiate blockade, unrestricted mining, ASW (anti-submarine warfare), ship seizure actions." In this there was no hint of any awareness of the major break in Sino-Soviet relations and ensuing enmity that our experts had been aware of for a year and a half, and that was by now becoming common knowledge. (There was of course one school of thought — apparently still not extinct — for whom the Sino-Soviet antagonisms were not real, but merely a dark and deceptive plot to mislead the U.S. and the non-Communist world.)

On October 23, Kennedy approved the Pony Blanket proposal as NSAM 109, "U.S. Policy on Military Actions in a Berlin Conflict." Finally there was a formally approved American policy to supplant the relic of the late Eisenhower years, NSC 5803 of February 7, 1958, "U.S. Policy Toward Germany," which the Kennedy administration had been intent on replacing ever since the election, first having assigned responsibility for the change to former Secretary of State Acheson.

The New U.S. Policy: NSAM 109

On the face of it, NSAM 109 prescribed very little. Rather, it explicitly allowed for the adoption of military measures, described generally in very elastic terms, *provided* the situation called for them and *provided* our allies agreed to them. This was the main difference from NSC 5803, which had implied that the next step beyond the rebuff of a mere platoon probe would be general war (which, despite the implication, in all likelihood would *not* have followed without intervening measures of some sort). The wording of NSAM 109, which included only minor changes from the original Poodle Blanket proposal, ran as follows:

> The President has approved the following statement of U.S. policy on military actions in a Berlin conflict:
>
> In the event military force is applied in the Berlin situation, it is the U.S. policy that the nature and sequence of such use should preferably be:
>
> If Soviet/GDR administrative or other action interferes with Berlin access by ground or air but is short of definitive blockage, *then* the tripartite powers should execute Berlin contingency plans, to include tripartitely agreed probes of Soviet intentions by a platoon or smaller force on the ground and by fighter escort in the air: they should continue to use fully any unblocked mode of access.
>
> If, despite the above tripartite actions, Soviet/GDR action indicates a determination to maintain significant blockage of our access to Berlin, *then* the NATO Allies should undertake such non-combatant activities as economic embargo, maritime harassment, and U.N. action. Simultaneously, they should use fully any unblocked access to Berlin.
>
> If, despite the above Allied actions, our

Berlin access is not restored, the Allies should take appropriate further action to clarify whether the Soviets/GDR intend to maintain blockage of air or ground access, or both, while making clear our intention to obtain re-opened access. *Then* embark on one or more of the following expanded military courses of action:

A. European Theater

1. Expanding non-nuclear air action, against a background of expanded ground defensive strength, to gain local air superiority. Extend size and scope as necessary.

2. Expanding non-nuclear ground operations into GDR territory in division and greater strength, with strong air support.

B. Worldwide

Maritime control, naval blockade, or other worldwide measures, both for reprisal and to add to general pressure on the Soviets.

IV. If, despite Allied use of substantial non-nuclear forces, the Soviets continue to encroach upon our vital interests, *then* the Allies should use nuclear weapons, starting with one of the following courses of action but continuing through C below if necessary:

A. Selective nuclear attacks for the primary purpose of demonstrating the will to use nuclear weapons.

B. Limited tactical employment of nuclear weapons to achieve in addition significant tactical advantage such as preservation of the integrity of Allied forces committed, or to extend pressure toward the objective.

C. General Nuclear War.

There it was. The language permitted enough latitude of interpretation to accommodate a wide range of differences in the matter of specific actions. It made everything contingent upon tripartite and Allied agreement (unless the United States at some juncture decided to act unilaterally). It delegated the critical task of determining crucial action proposals to contingency planners, who of course would develop plans in accord with instructions from above, and it would be those in ultimate authority who would decide whether any action was to be taken, and if so, which one. So there was not, in fact, any commitment. But there was nominal agreement, within the American establishment, on a statement of general policy that did not, on the face of it, prescribe actions that our allies would almost surely resist. And it provided an acceptable charter to those agencies responsible for developing plans for the anticipated contingency. Reduced to barest essentials, the unresolved issues that remained concerned the use of tactical nuclear weapons and, in general, were confined to what were often referred to as the "discontinuities", the points, that is, at which it was assumed the situation would pass from one of the four phases to the next. Of these, the most important, of course, was the discontinuity from conventional to nuclear measures — from III to IV. And while this might be summarized in very simple terms, everything about it was both immensely complex and also near the core of all the gravest concerns that both haunted and divided all who were involved.

The more crucial and controversial issues concerned use of tactical nuclear weapons, feasibility of graduated escalation, and triggering of general war or preemptive strikes against strategic forces. One could only theorize about these matters, and there were almost as many theories as theorists, or at least as many as there were interested groups. There was no relevant experience. The weapons that might be involved were untested in combat situations, as were, also, those to whom their actual use would be delegated. Everything would depend, moreover, not only on intelligence that in any case would be subject to some significant margins of error, but, vastly more important, on guesses concerning the reactions in time of unprecedented crisis of foes we knew much too little about, and who probably did not themselves know how they would act in some hypothetical future crisis. There could not be really complete assurance of the behavior of allies, or even of ourselves, when the last minutes arrived of an either-or situation and the issue was whether to go nuclear. And lurking in the back of most minds, almost surely, and almost surely in the back of the minds of those on *both* sides, was the terrifying notion that, *if*, after all this, there is going to be nuclear war, we had better get in the first blow. This was, in the end, the key issue. But it could not be explicitly discussed. Yet some assurance of the sort usually conveyed by explicit agreement was necessary. That was to be provided, later, by a sort of sleight-of-hand.

The immediate task following presidential approval of NSAM 109 was to attain some form of allied agreement, both quadripartite and NATO. The annual meeting of NATO was approaching as well as the expiration date of the still not formally rescinded Soviet "ultimatum". Norstad was recalled for consultation and on November 7, in a meeting with Kennedy, he reported his reactions both to NSAM 109 and to the general military buildup that had been under way since July. According to a memo for record, Norstad was "not particularly impressed" with the potential effectiveness of either the military mobilizations or the concurrent non-military measures indicated for phase II. As for the two additional divisions then planned for movement to Europe, he said they would not enable his forces to do more than they could do with the forces already there, although they could perform the same tasks better and longer. He did assure Kennedy he was confident he could persuade our allies to adjust to U.S. policy, but in its present form NSAM would arouse misgivings in NATO, particularly among the Germans. He said, however, he was preparing instructions for his SHAPE planners which would be consistent with American policy and acceptable to the allies.

The Allied Agreement: The Uses of Ambiguity and Sleight-of-Hand

Meanwhile Nitze and his group in ISA were preparing a memo on "Rationale of U.S. Military Policy in the Berlin Crisis From the NATO Standpoint", on which JCS comment was requested. This memo amounted to an explanation of a draft paper to be used as a "basis for restricted discussions with our principal allies to assist in bringing them to convinced and understanding support of our plans, programs, and actions." Here came the sleight-of-hand. It was a touchy, highly sensitive document because it dealt with matters we hoped would be properly understood by our best allies but which we did not wish to be explicit about, and hesitated to commit to paper for the eyes of any except a small handful of our highest in command, and our most trusted allies.

In partial explanation, the introductory remarks noted that "German comments have stressed nuclear preemption; it appears that their point, otherwise better omitted, must be met, or they can be expected to hammer on it in a variety of ways."

The draft itself, entitled "NATO Military Policy in the Berlin Crisis", began with statements of "Considerations of General Nuclear War and Policy Conclusions" that suggested forcefully some of the major concerns of those who were formulating policy. Current analyses of the probable results of general nuclear war led to judgments, it said, that, although they should be accepted cautiously, *had* to govern our decisions because we had nothing better. They were that the West had a preponderant advantage both in nuclear striking power and in capacity to survive a surprise attack. The Soviets could deliver comparatively few weapons on North America in any case, and in the best case Western superiority would be overwhelming. Soviet counter-damage would be "severe, but not so serious as to endanger (U.S.) national survival." However, the Soviets probably could seriously damage NATO Europe even after a full-scale preemptive attack, and to this extent their claim that NATO Europe was their hostage was valid.

On the other side, the acknowledged Soviet preponderance of conventional strength made it impossible for the Allies to oppose Soviet aggressions successfully by conventional means, and local and conventional military opposition to the Soviets could successfully serve but one purpose, which was to confront the Soviets with the clear choice between ceasing aggression and nuclear war. But even tactical nuclear weapons may trigger general nuclear war at low levels of engagement, and so therefore, "It might be advisable to strike first strategically rather than engage in large scale tactical nuclear war." Attaining goals without nuclear war remained as the NATO objective, but the Soviets should be regularly reminded of Western nuclear superiority and of "Western readiness to engage in general war for our vital interests..." But because public emphasis on the fact that "as action policy, the West will make every effort to strike first when the general situation demands general war" was destabilizing, the "declaratory policy," in contrast, "would focus on our nuclear superiority, our ability to survive a Soviet first strike with dominant nuclear forces intact, and our readiness of fight nuclear war in defense of our vital interests". Here was a sort of ambiguity that left little doubt of what was left unsaid.

This draft was given the unqualified blessing of the JCS by a formal memo on November 15, which described it as a "well developed, forthright summation of U.S. assessments, concepts and policies," and added that: It adequately reflects the basic concepts of U.S. military policy with respect to Berlin and could serve as a basis for discussion with selected allies on occasion.

Which it did, following approval by McNamara and Kennedy. Chancellor Konrad Adenauer, accompanied by his Defense Minister Franz Josef Strauss, spent four days in Washington from November 21 to 25, and in conversations with Kennedy recited the longstanding German skepticism over the effectiveness of the projected 30 conventional division NATO force, as well as over the preferred American tactic of gradually escalating military actions. Agreement was reached on enough of the issues to assure that the U.S. and the Federal Republic of

Germany could present a common front, especially in those areas where there might be negotiations with the Soviets. It is not explicit in the available records of the meetings that Kennedy actually used the ISA paper, although it seems probable he did, because Adenauer was sufficiently reassured to bring an end to the habitual German objections to our contingency planning proposals.

In follow-up actions just before the regular NATO December meetings, McNamara and Nitze made the contents known to the defense ministers of Britain and France, and Strauss's deputy, in a somewhat theatrical maneuver. Getting these officials alone where there was no chance of note-taking or making a record, McNamara read the paper aloud to them, letting them look over his shoulder as he read, then quickly withdrawing it. Such was the sleight-of-hand. Other NATO nations were, for the time being, left in the dark.

By this time — early December — the 1961 phase of the Berlin crisis was receding, and everyone knew it, although there were few who did not fear it would erupt again at any time. And it did, in February-March of 1962, as a test of our nerves over air corridor access. We were becoming much less jumpy about it by then, because we were learning from experience that the Soviets were just playing their game of seeking, by every conceivable annoyance or threat they believed would not provoke us into drastic reaction, to extort concessions they had no legal or moral right to ask, but which we found it difficult to deny because of our highly vulnerable, exposed position in Berlin.

There continued to be nasty little holdups on the Autobahn and on the railroads into Berlin, many minor tragedies along the Wall and in the no man's land separating West from East Berlin. The minimum Soviet objectives of solidifying their control of East Germany and East Berlin had been largely assured, if not fully accomplished and formally acknowledged. It is not clear how much more, or how much less, they could have gained, had our policies and actions varied within the compass of what was responsibly considered. It is a reasonable speculation that had we been either more aggressively defiant of Soviet moves, or readier to concede their demands, that a vastly different resolution of the issues would have occurred. The rapidly spreading unrest in East Germany in the period before the Wall was highly explosive, and that situation, combined with the generations-old Russian fear of invasion, especially by a militaristic Germany, might very easily have led the Kremlin into risks it would not have undertaken under any circumstances considered less threatening. We might therefore have precipitated the general war everyone dreaded by taking steps that prevented stabilization of East Germany. On the other hand, had we seemed less resolute, the Soviets might well have sought to extend their grip on Germany by measures that would have ignited the German hatred of the Russians and precipitated violence that could quickly have become uncontrollable, and in this way have led to general war. Obviously, this is conjecture. But it can hardly be called mere conjecture that people on both sides who had the power to initiate nuclear war were considering, in all seriousness, taking steps that, from all we know, would have led us into that general war. We were that close to it.

For all the thousands of hours of agonized study and reflection, the net difference between NSC 5803 and NSAM 109 is difficult to find. The latter amounts to little more than a return to the Dulles doctrine of massive retaliation, after a year of soul struggle in futile search for a way to adapt it to a world in which both sides have the power to retaliate massively.

We were hung up on the horns of two dilemmas. One was our militarily indefensible commitment in Berlin. The other was the then unresolved, still unresolved, and probably forever unresolvable problem of devising military strategy in a world committed to the institution of warfare while possessed of weapons that, if used, would prove suicidal.

DOOMSDAY POSTPONED?

by Diana Johnstone

It was the Berlin Crisis that first aroused high-level awareness of the dangers of using nuclear weapons to deter or offset the superiority of Soviet conventional forces in Europe. Whereas public alarm was raised to an all-time high over the Cuban Missile Crisis, some experts believe the Berlin Crisis was more dangerous.[1] The close call helped top leaders reach the common sense conclusion that an exchange of nuclear strikes would mean mutual suicide. This became known as the "MAD" (Mutual Assured Destruction) doctrine which in the early 1960s was tacitly accepted by both Washington and Moscow.

Paradoxically, MAD almost seemed to have provided a happy ending to the issue. Mutual Assured Destruction implied that nuclear conflict must be ruled out forever.

Unfortunately, the story did not end there.

In reality, MAD was not so much a doctrine as a moment of recognition. On May 6, 1962, less than a year after the Berlin Crisis and months before the Cuban Crisis, Robert McNamara delivered a confidential speech to NATO ministers in Athens in which he backed away from any commitment to counter Soviet aggression in Europe with nuclear retaliation. Most European leaders had welcomed the "massive retaliation" doctrine, which they took to be a protection, and did not want to see it abandoned. The ideas were expressed publicly in the "No Cities" speech delivered in Ann Arbor on July 9 of the same year. "No Cities" expressed the desire to avoid getting drawn into the city-destroying strategy of World War II in any future conflict using nuclear weapons. The timing of these speeches, falling between the two major crises of the early 1960s, shows the impact of the Berlin scare. McNamara was trying to wiggle out of the dilemma brought to light by the recognition that using nuclear retaliation against the Soviet Union to counter Soviet conventional forces in Europe could be catastrophic for *both* major nuclear powers.

McNamara's Ann Arbor speech stressed the irrationality of nuclear attack. "First, given the current balance of nuclear power, which we confidently expect to maintain in the years ahead, a surprise nuclear attack is simply not a rational act for any enemy. Nor would it be rational for an enemy to take the initiative in the use of nuclear weapons as an outgrowth of a limited engagement in Europe or elsewhere." He didn't say so, but that meant it would *not be rational for the United States* to take such an initiative – which had been the implicit policy up until the Berlin Crisis.

McNamara went on to warn that: "the mere fact that no nation could rationally take steps leading to a nuclear war does not guarantee that a nuclear war cannot take place. Not only do nations sometimes act in ways that are hard to explain on a rational basis, but even when acting in a 'rational' way they sometimes, indeed disturbingly often, act on the basis of misunderstandings of the true facts of a situation. They misjudge the way others will react, and the way others will interpret what they are doing. We must hope, indeed I think we have good reason to hope, that all sides will understand this danger, and will refrain from steps that even raise the possibility of such a mutually disastrous misunderstanding."

This amounted to an implicit declaration of the MAD doctrine, although the term was not used.

McNamara made this more explicit in his September 1967 "Mutual Deterrence" speech in San Francisco. "It is important to understand that assured destruction is the very essence of the whole deterrence concept. We must possess an actual assured-destruction capability, and that capability also must be credible. The point is that a potential aggressor must believe that our assured-destruction capability is in fact actual, and that our will to use it in retaliation to an attack is in fact unwavering."

MAD thus depends on a sort of "trust" in reverse. Since we cannot trust others not to commit total destruction, we must expect them to trust that we will.

And yet, even as McNamara moved away from "assured destruction" as irrational, he was still looking for a less apocalyptic way to use nuclear warheads as battlefield — or "tactical" — weapons that would spare both the USSR and the United States the loss of their cities. However, the lack of targeting accuracy and the huge development costs ruled out such a program. Nuclear weapons were forgotten as the United States got bogged down in Indochina.

Indeed, the public has been largely reassured by MAD that there is no serious threat of nuclear war because, as McNamara stressed, it would be totally irrational.

Unfortunately, that may be a serious illusion. The development of tactical nuclear weapons has continued unabated. All major weapons systems have their ardent supporters, in the armed forces and in the strategic planning community, who are just itching to watch them wipe out the latest designated enemy.

In the early 1980s, the presence of opposing Soviet and U.S. missiles aroused a massive protest movement among Europeans who realized that they would find themselves in the target area. These anxieties were dispelled by Mikhail Gorbachev's historic move toward conciliation with the West.

Unfortunately, the collapse of the Soviet Union, which provided the unforeseen opportunity for putting a decisive end to the threat of nuclear war, was exploited instead by the American "War Party" to impose a new arrogance, based on belief that "winning the Cold War" proved the United States to be invincible. This triumphalism revived the euphoria felt by Truman when he realized that he enjoyed a monopoly of nuclear destructive power.

The 1990s were a period when a new security structure could have been built, based on the trust shown by Russian leaders – and betrayed by the United States. Violating oral assurances, the United States moved to push NATO up to Russia's borders. The "anti-missile shield" with its potential for facilitating a U.S. first strike was revived and stationed close to Russia, using the insultingly transparent excuse that it was meant to "deter Iran". At the same time, the idea spread that smaller and more accurate nukes could be used as "normal" warheads in any war the United States chooses to wage.

Both political and technological developments have made the possibility of nuclear war far more likely than it ever was before.

The Death of MAD

The shifts of political power in Washington have drastically increased the dangers. In March 1992, *The New York Times* revealed the initial version of the Defense Planning Guidance for fiscal 1994-99 from the office of Paul Wolfowitz, then undersecretary of defense for policy. This document was prepared by a group including Defense Secretary Dick Cheney, I. Lewis "Scooter" Libby, Richard Perle, and among others RAND's star nuclear doomsday strategist Albert Wohlstetter. Known as the Wolfowitz Doctrine, it was a virtual manifesto of neoconservative policy aims. The gist of the doctrine is to use U.S. superpower status not merely to oppose enemies – there weren't any serious enemies to be seen at the time – but to "prevent the re-emergence of a new rival".

"The doctrine establishes the U.S.'s leadership role within the new world order", the paper proclaimed. "The U.S. must show the leadership necessary to establish and protect a new order that holds the promise of convincing potential competitors that they need not aspire to a greater role or pursue a more aggressive posture to protect their legitimate interests.

"The doctrine announces the U.S's status as the world's

only remaining superpower following the collapse of the Soviet Union at the end of the Cold War and proclaims its main objective to be retaining that status."

It is significant that once Communist rule collapsed, the ideological pretext for war preparation evaporated. Others were found. The adversary is no longer a hostile ideology, but merely any nation big enough or strong enough to represent an eventual challenge to all-powerful America. Despite initial protests, over the past two decades this viewpoint has come to dominate Washington's approach to the world.

The doctrine stated the U.S's right to intervene when and where it believed necessary, thus unilaterally nullifying national sovereignty, the very basis of international law.

To describe this as imperialist is to miss the point of its essentially destructive nature. This doctrine, composed by intellectuals who were also close advisors to Israel, resembles the Israeli policy of maintaining its status as regional power by weakening its neighbors. But concerning the United States, the doctrine is applied to the whole world. The first results have been seen in Middle Eastern wars. The wars against Libya and Iraq, nations with no adequate means of defense, were not properly "won" by anyone, but succeeded in reducing to chaos two rivals of Israel and Saudi Arabia, Washington's closest allies in the region.

As the Wolfowitz Doctrine stated, "Our first objective is to prevent the re-emergence of a new rival, either on the territory of the former Soviet Union or elsewhere that poses a threat on the order of that posed formerly by the Soviet Union. This is a dominant consideration underlying the new regional defense strategy and requires that we endeavor to prevent any hostile power from dominating a region whose resources would, under consolidated control, be sufficient to generate global power."

This makes it clear that even as the Soviet Union was collapsing, the neoconservative camp saw Russia as the potential adversary in the new strategy of rival prevention.

Initially, in the 1990s, no great effort was needed to weaken Russia, as the nation declined drastically under the confused leadership of the alcoholic Boris Yeltsin, easily manipulated by his "friend" Bill Clinton and various U.S. advisors.[2] Naively believing that the United States was a "partner", Russia dismantled and abandoned most of its strategic nuclear arsenal in hopes of ongoing disarmament treaties.

It was only as Russia began to recover under the leadership of an able President, Vladimir Putin, that the vast nation once again could fill the chronic need of the United States for a significant enemy. In his landmark speech to the 2007 Munich Security Conference, Putin boldly stated his belief that "the unipolar model is not only unacceptable but also impossible in today's world." This rejection of U.S. world hegemony was enough to confirm Russia's new status as number one enemy, no longer for reasons of ideological differences but simply by aspiring to independence from U.S. hegemony.

The new cold war against Russia intensified dramatically in the winter of 2013-2014, when U.S. Assistant Secretary of State for European and Eurasian Affairs Victoria Nuland handed out snacks to anti-Russian protesters in Kiev before backing the violent regime change in February 2014 which imposed her chosen candidate Arseniy Yatsenyuk as prime minister of Ukraine. The prominent role of Nuland, a former advisor to Dick Cheney, former spokeswoman for Secretary of State Hillary Clinton and wife of leading neoconservative theorist Robert Kagan, made clear that the neocon influence in Washington remained decisive under the Obama presidency. The troubles provoked on Russia's doorstep in Ukraine, and Russia's inevitable defensive reaction,[3] became the pretext for an all-out Western propaganda campaign portraying Russia as an expansionist aggressor threatening to invade NATO member states. These accusations accompany an unprecedented Western military buildup on Russia's borders, including a new particularly threatening new generation of nuclear weapons.

In reality, Russia is targeted not for what it has done, but like the mountain that must be climbed "because it is there", Russia must be opposed simply because it is there. China suffers from the same fault. It is big, "re-emerging", independent: another potential rival that must be held in check.

When Barack Obama first came to office in 2009, he was advocating "a nuclear-free world" – a promise cited by the Nobel committee justifying its haste in awarding the Peace Prize to the novice American President only months later. If U.S. leaders were willing to live together on the planet as equals with Russia and China, there would be no overwhelming obstacle to their proceeding jointly to achieve worldwide nuclear disarmament for the benefit of all humanity. But since U.S. leaders have decided that their "exceptional" power must dominate the world, their nuclear arsenal becomes indispensable. The link between national hubris and the capacity to carry out nuclear destruction is crucial.

Contrary to Obama's 2009 promises, his administration has been going ahead with plans to spend billions of dollars precisely on what they call "revitalizing" the U.S. nuclear arsenal with thousands of improved warheads and delivery systems. It is not only Obama's promises that are being broken. It is also the commitment made in the 1968 Nuclear Non-Proliferation Treaty by nuclear powers to work toward total nuclear disarmament. The United States continues to put non-proliferation at the top of its agenda, as seen in the years of pressure against Iran's hypothetical nuclear program, while failing carry out its own side of the agreement. However, it is clear enough that current U.S. leaders consider treaties as ways to police other countries, not themselves.

The U.S. nuclear arsenal is *dual use* – it can serve its much-advertised purpose of deterrence, as well as its unspoken purpose of launching a preemptive strike.

This arsenal is composed of a triad of strategic bombers, intercontinental ballistic missiles (ICBMs) and missile-launching submarines (SSBNs). They are all being "revitalized", that is, provided with greater accuracy and flexibility in ways that enhance their preemptive strike capacities.

"The same nuclear triad", observe Keir Lieber and Daryl Press, "could be used in an offensive attack against an adversary's nuclear forces. Stealth bombers might slip past enemy radar, submarines could fire their missiles from near the enemy's shore and so give the enemy's leaders almost no time to respond, and highly accurate land-based missiles could destroy even hardened silos that have been reinforced against attack and other targets that require a direct hit. The ability to destroy all of an adversary's nuclear forces, eliminating the possibility of a retaliatory strike, is known as a first-strike capability, or nuclear primacy."[4]

First strike has always been the essential issue. The meaning of MAD was that the United States no longer dared launch a first strike against the Soviet Union, as it had against Japan, because the Soviet Union could strike back. But after the collapse of the Soviet Union, the Soviet deterrent was allowed to deteriorate. The United States pursued modernization, while ostensibly pursuing nuclear disarmament by retiring obsolete weapons to make way for more accurate replacements. Once the United States attains nuclear primacy – meaning first strike capacity – MAD is as dead as a doornail.

"The improvements to the U.S. nuclear arsenal offer evidence that the United States is actively seeking primacy," Lieber and Press wrote. "Such improvements only make sense if the missiles are meant to destroy a large number of hard targets."

> If the United States' nuclear modernization were really aimed at rogue states or terrorists, the country's nuclear force would not need the additional thousand ground-burst warheads it will gain from the W-76 modernization program. The current and future U.S. nuclear force, in other words, seems designed to carry out a preemptive disarming strike against Russia or China.
>
> The intentional pursuit of nuclear primacy is, moreover, entirely consistent with the United States' declared policy of expanding its global dominance. [...] To this end, the United States is openly seeking primacy in every dimension

of modern military technology, both in its conventional arsenal and in its nuclear forces.

The fact that a whole array of upgraded nuclear weapons are to be stationed in Europe, facing eastwards, makes it obvious that the new military buildup clearly targets Russia. There is the new Long Range Standoff cruise missile, designed to deliver nuclear explosives by air or drone on targets up to a hundred kilometers away. It will be able to deliver the new B61-16 warhead, a forward-deployed bunker-busting bomb theoretically able to decapitate enemy States (the most rapid means of regime change). With a force of 50 kilotons, four times the Hiroshima bomb, it is to be mass produced at a cost of $20 million dollars each. Its main novelty, the supposed "dial a yield" ability to deliver explosions of varying strengths on demand - more sophisticated electronics that can go wrong. It is meant to replace the B61 warhead currently stationed in Italy, Turkey, Germany, Belgium and the Netherlands.

NATO governments are being put under pressure to spend billions in order to perfect their nations' position as ideal targets for Russian retaliation. A score of nuclear warheads are already stationed at the Kleine Brogel airbase in Belgium, which the United States is "modernizing". Belgium is exhorted to spend four billion euros to buy 40 U.S. F-35 jets, a compendium of potential high tech glitches whose nuclear weapons sorties would be totally under U.S. control.[5] The Lockheed-Martin F-35 has been a bonanza for the company's top executives and stockholders, and the costs of trying to fix it are likely to rise.

The United States is simultaneously restructuring the Büchel airbase in Germany to fit them to receive the new nuclear bombs. In 2009, the Bundestag adopted a resolution demanding that the United States withdraw all its nuclear weapons from German territory, but this is being ignored.

The Federation of American Scientists estimates that the U.S. now deploys roughly 200 ready-to-fire nuclear warheads in Europe. In addition to the twenty stationed respectively in Germany, Belgium and the Netherlands, and fifty in Turkey, Italy has the most, with seventy stationed on two bases, Aviano and Ghedi Torre. The numbers are surely scheduled to rise.

The B61-12 can be fired vertically to strike targets a hundred kilometers away, guided by satellite. These supposedly "tactical" weapons thereby are also *strategic* weapons, which can be used either to obliterate enemy forces or the enemy's command and control centers. The U.S. leads its NATO allies in annual nuclear bombing exercises called "Steadfast Noon" at its various satellite airbases in Europe.

Orchestrated by hysterical anti-Russian propaganda in the West, this military buildup can leave no doubt to Russian leaders that the West is actually preparing to wage all-out nuclear war against Russia. Predictably, Russia is responding by it own military buildup, including nuclear weapons and delivery systems. The arms race is very much on again. Russian defensive measures will be loudly interpreted as "threats", thus providing new grist to the Russophobic propaganda mill.

There are a few high level critics of these plans. Former assistant secretary of defense Andrew C. Weber, a former director of the Nuclear Weapons Council, calls the modernization "unaffordable and unneeded".[6] Weber and former Defense Secretary William Perry signed an October 15, 2015 Washington Post op ed calling on President Obama to scrap plans to build the "standoff" nuclear cruise missile whose capacities risk tempting a future president to contemplate "limited nuclear war". Even a strong advocate of the buildup, retired vice chairman of the Joint chiefs of staff Marine Corps General James E. Cartwright, acknowledges that the upgrading makes use of the weapons "more thinkable".

Such mild objections appear unable to stop the momentum of long-term weapons systems planning. So much money and so many careers are committed to the so-called "modernization", a term suggesting some sort of inevitability.

In contrast to the days of MAD, current nuclear weapons planning seems not to be inhibited by the thought that the United States itself might suffer. U.S. planners can consider that if used in, say, a war against Russia in Ukraine or Georgia, both the fallout and the Russian counterstrike will come down on the European allies, not on the United States. By hyping up the imaginary Russian threat to "expand" into NATO land, U.S. officials mean to scare Europeans into consenting to a form of defense that ought to scare them much more.

Europeans are supposed to be reassured by the ten billion dollar a year anti-missile defense systems the United States is erecting in Rumania and Poland. But former Pentagon testing office director Tom Christie told journalist Andrew Cockburn that "None of the interceptors we currently have in silos waiting to shoot down enemy missiles have ever worked in tests."[7]

However, as Lieber and Press observe, "the sort of missile defenses that the United States might plausibly deploy would be valuable primarily in an offensive context, not a defensive one – as an adjunct to a U.S. first-strike capability, not as a standalone shield. If the United States launched a nuclear attack against Russia (or China), the targeted country would be left with a tiny surviving arsenal – if any at all. At that point, even a relatively modest or inefficient missile-defense system might well be enough to protect against any retaliatory strikes, because the devastated enemy would have so few warheads and decoys left."

The great thing about these super high tech weapons systems is that even if they don't work, they are paid for by taxpayers' money, stockholders get their cut, and Congress members get their campaign donations.

In contrast to the Soviet Union, the United States has always maintained its "right" to carry out a nuclear first strike. This has never changed and was reaffirmed by Defense Secretary Ashton Carter at a meeting with airmen on September 27, 2016 at Kirtland Air Force Base in New Mexico.[8] The doctrine of nuclear deterrence that leaves open the possibility of launching a "first strike" before an enemy attacks will remain the basis of U.S. policy even as new generations of nuclear weapons are introduced, he said. "That's our doctrine now, and we don't have any intention of changing that doctrine," he emphasized.

Logically, proclaiming a first strike posture is not a deterrent position. Given the great advantage to the side that strikes first, this declaration actually amounts to an incentive to the other side to strike first if a crisis arises. Faced with an aggressive U.S. buildup in tactical nuclear weapons coupled with a first strike policy, a potential adversary is put in a "use them or lose them" situation regarding their own nuclear forces.

This situation leads Lieber and Press to warn that "deterring nuclear conflict will be much more difficult in the coming decades than many analysts realize."[9]

Speaking on September 26 at the Air Force Global Strike Command base in Minot, South Dakota, Defense Secretary Carter accused Moscow of "saber-rattling" and boasted that: "Across the Atlantic, we're refreshing NATO's nuclear playbook to better integrate conventional and nuclear deterrence." Such talk can only sound threatening to Russian leaders who are planning to do nothing that needs to be deterred. Carter was there to praise the Pentagon's plan to spend 348 billion dollars renovating the "nuclear triad" of strategic bombers, missiles and submarines, all outfitted with nuclear weapons, which he described as America's "bedrock of security" and "the highest priority mission of the department of defense".

Moreover, Carter declared, "for all Americans, and for that matter, all people all over the world, the bedrock of security you provide has enabled millions and millions to get up in the morning to go to school, to go to work, to live their lives, to dream their dreams and to give their children a better future."[10]

As if human life itself depended on the unholy trinity of the U.S. death machine. And this dependence will go on and on, Carter said, requiring us to continue to invest in all three legs of the triad for our children and our children's children.

In July 2016, the Chairman of the Joint Chiefs of Staff General Joseph Dunford branded Russia an "existential threat" to the United States. Where is the evidence that Russia has either the intention or the ability to cause the United States to cease to exist? Or is the United States an existential threat to the whole world?

The Johnstone memoir of a past era illustrates the tendency

of military planners to think only in terms of how much it takes to destroy the enemy. That has not changed. And this tendency is promoted by the War Party made up of neoconservatives and liberal interventionists completely committed to the United States' exceptional mission to dominate the whole world, by whatever means necessary. Complicit mass media stoke fears of evil enemies, preparing the Western public to accept wars that are being planned in an atmosphere of secrecy tightened by drastic repression of "whistle blowers".

The arrogance of power has made today's leaders in Washington more aggressive and reckless than during the Cold War against the Soviet Union. MAD was sinister, but forgetting the MAD fear of retaliation is even more frightening.

In recent years, Washington war planners have gone from MAD to madness.

The Political Relationship of Forces

The widely unforeseen results of the November 2016 elections raised the question of whether a change in Presidency could be enough to bring about a fundamental transformation of U.S. foreign policy. Although foreign policy was not a major issue in the campaign, the two candidates differed sharply, notably on relations with Russia. Contrary to both Hillary Clinton and the entire Washington policy-making elite, Donald Trump promised to meet with Vladimir Putin for the purpose of normalizing relations between the two leading nuclear powers.

This upset could appear to amount to a reprieve. The rush toward nuclear war was apparently stalled. But all the elements remain: the weapons themselves, the developing plans to use them, and above all the ideological dominance of the belief that U.S. hegemony must be maintained by all means – with nuclear weapons the ultimate of those means. The entire careers of Washington intellectuals and military planners have been devoted to the project of maintaining a "unipolar world" by crushing rivals. They show no sign of giving this up. Even more disquieting, the unprecedented public denunciation of the President elect, largely on grounds of his alleged negative attitudes toward women and minorities, does not bode well for building popular support for whatever peace-making efforts he may undertake.

It is not clear whether a lull in hostilities between the two major nuclear powers can be used to take significant steps toward a world without the threat of nuclear annihilation, or whether it will serve to allow the War Party to regroup its forces for a counterattack. The answer depends on a how successfully an outsider President can deal with institutions impregnated with an ideology which he rejects.

The incredible imbroglio in the Middle East has led not so much to "isolationism" as to a common sense objection that the United States needs to have one main enemy at a time, rather than simultaneously fighting and supporting all sides, as was resulting in Syria.

But the United States remains armed to the teeth, with a foreign policy that is enemy-centered, even if the main enemy shifts from Russia to the "Islamic State", an uncertain entity prone to metamorphosis. Iran remains high on the Washington enemy list, the attitude toward China is ambivalent, and U.S./NATO moves in recent years have provoked Russia into a new military buildup, including nuclear weapons modernization, which will not be easy to reverse. The Russian sense of Western betrayal during the disastrous Yeltsin years has slowly but surely created deep and lasting distrust.

For seventy years, the United States has striven to maintain nuclear supremacy as its ace in the hole. The pursuit of nuclear primacy is in itself the confirmation of a dualistic world view in which *we* are good enough, and *they* are bad enough, to justify *our* capacity to destroy *them*. The status of nuclear weapons in military planning reveals the official U.S. attitude toward the world far more eloquently than speeches.

So long as its dualistic mindset persists, the war machine is always able to train its Manichean sites on yet another "existential threat".

U.S. world hegemony is showing itself to be unattainable. The choice is fundamental. Pursue the quest for absolute domination leading toward absolute destruction. Or recognize reality, and work for the first time, to build a peaceful international structure with other nations as partners, rather than as vassals or enemies. Working seriously for nuclear disarmament would be both the symbol and the basis of a new world order based on cooperation rather than fear.

ENDNOTES

Foreword

1   <https://consortiumnews.com/2016/10/07/key-neocon-calls-on-us-to-oust-putin/ >

The Dangerous Seduction of Absolute Power

1   Gove Hambidge, *The Prime of Life*, Doubleday, Doran & Company, New York, 1942 ; p. 179.

2   Ibid, pp 78-79.

3   Henry A. Wallace left the Department of Agriculture to become Vice President of the United States during Franklin D. Roosevelt's third term, from January 1941 to January 1945, despite opposition from segregationist Southern Democrats. In 1944, they succeeded in replacing Wallace by Harry S. Truman to be Roosevelt's running mate only months before Roosevelt's death in April 1945. This change turned out to signify the slow death of the New Deal and prepared the way for the Cold War. In a last ditch attempt to save and extend the New Deal, Henry Wallace ran for President as Progressive Party candidate in 1948 on a platform advocating universal health insurance, an end to the Cold War, an end to segregation and full voting rights for black Americans.

4   Hambidge, pp 102-103.

5   Ibid, pp 79-81.

6   Gar Alperovitz, *The Decision to Use the Atom Bomb*, pp 352-3.

7   James Franck, Donald J. Hughes, J.J. Nickson, Eugene Rabinowitch, Glenn T. Seaborg, J.C. Stearns, Leo Szilard.

8   At the end of the Potsdam conference with Churchill and Stalin, Truman issued a statement concluding: *"We call upon the government of Japan to proclaim now the unconditional surrender of all Japanese armed forces, and to provide proper and adequate assurances of their good faith in such action. The alternative for Japan is prompt and utter destruction."* That statement was clearly designed only to be used to claim afterwards that "Japan was warned". In fact, "prompt and utter destruction" sounds like a description of what the United

States was already doing, and there is not the slightest mention of the atom. Even more ridiculously futile were leaflets dropped on Japanese civilians announcing the devastation with which they were already all too familiar. <http://blog.nuclearsecrecy.com/2013/04/26/a-day-too-late/> Leaflets warning of atomic bombs were dropped only *after* the Hiroshima and Nagasaki bombings.

MEMOIR OF A HUMANIST IN THE PENTAGON

PART I
Chapter 2

1   British slang for reconnaissance, pronounced rekky.

PART II
Chapter 4

1   In 1957, Hugh Everett became director of WSEG's Department of Physical and Mathematical Sciences. This was the same year in which, as a graduate student in physics at Princeton, he invented the highly contested "many worlds" interpretation of quantum mechanics. [D.J. footnote]

PART III
Chapter 2

1   SIOP was the acronym for Single Integrated Operations Plan. Until the late fifties each of our varied forces and commands that would be involved in bombing had its own operations plan which was developed to fulfill its assigned responsibilities under a general, overall war plan. But it had become apparent that when one got down to operational details there were many duplications, inadvertent omissions, and confusions in specific assignments and missions. As a result, beginning some time in the late fifties, annual operations plans were undertaken that were aimed to assure coordination of all of our varied strike forces: from the U.S., from Europe, from Asian bases, from fleets in the Pacific, the Mediterranean, the Atlantic, and from submarines beneath the surface of the seas.

2   The NESC was an occasional, ad hoc, high level group that from the late fifties through the sixties bounced back and forth between the Pentagon and the NSC. It was activated from time to time when the White House or the Secretary of Defense wanted a study or a position

paper on some pressing national security issue, and for one reason or another, chose not to turn for it to whatever agency had regular staff responsibilities in that area. The personnel of NESC varied from, one occasion to another, and consisted mainly of supposed experts on loan from CIA, State, varied military services, Civil Defense or the Office of Emergency Management (in any of its many names and shapes over the years), the AEC, RAND, and indeed wherever truly knowledgeable, prestigious, or fast talking persons might be found. NESC performed no basic research. Rather, it drew on previously completed or specially assigned impromptu studies by regular agencies, and on that basis developed judgments and policy proposals presumably better than had the staff work been assigned, instead, to the group or agency with established responsibility in that field.

3   The movement of this group was as elaborately prepared as short notice allowed. The instructions of CINCUSAREUR were that early on August 19 a chosen task force consisting of a Battle Group drawn from the 18th and 8th infantry Divisions, plus one towed 105 mm howitzer battalion and one combat engineer company were "to demonstrate intent to reinforce Berlin", not to probe Soviet intentions, although they should be prepared to react if harassed or opposed. In case of procedural delays at check points, they were to request accelerated procedure. If denied passage without forceful resistance they were to set a one hour deadline, and report, then remove or crash through the barrier and proceed, if there were no added resistance. In event of lightly defended obstacles or harassing fire, they should take appropriate defensive action, proceed, and ask instructions. If opposed by superior force, they should try to hold ground and report, but were authorized to disengage and withdraw if in danger of being cut off or losing forces. In all cases they should report hourly. As these instructions suggest, the movement was followed with suspense at every command post and headquarters all the way back to Washington. The movement turned out to be completely uneventful. Having been advertised in advance, lack of incident probably had some significance. But it could be interpreted to suggest the Soviets did not want a confrontation, or alternatively, that they preferred the confrontation to occur elsewhere or at another time. Appraisals of the gravity of the situation over the following fortnight were in any case far from hopeful.

4   For one of the enclosures of WSEG 50, I had asked Arnold Wolfers to write a paper summarizing the attitudes of our NATO allies toward our nuclear deterrent strategy and general military posture. Professor Emeritus of International Affairs from Yale, at the time associated with the Johns Hopkins Graduate School of Foreign Affairs in Washington,

Wolfers was a frequent State Department consultant and one of the most knowledgeable people anywhere on the subject. The piece he wrote was not startling, but significant and eloquent. Among its main points were these: There was growing apprehension among our NATO allies, especially France, that the credibility of our nuclear deterrent was eroding because of the growing capability of the Soviets to inflict serious nuclear damage upon the U.S. There was a disturbing ambivalence among our allies. They wanted the protection of our nuclear umbrella but were fearful they might become the battleground for a war between the two superpowers. Although fearful of nuclear war, they were resistant to suggestions to increase their conventional forces, sometimes arguing that instead of increasing the credibility of our nuclear deterrent, the conventional forces buildup would, instead, suggest to the Soviets that when crisis came we would be afraid to unleash our nuclear forces, and they, with their superior conventional forces, would easily overrun Western Europe.

Doomsday Postponed?

1   "William Y. Kaufman, the analyst most directly involved in elaborating the Athens strategy [see below], claims that Berlin was the most dangerous of all potential nuclear crises, more dangerous than Cuba." *Getting MAD, Nuclear Mutual Assured Destruction, Its Origins and Practice*, edited by Henry D. Sokolsky, Strategic Studies Institute, U.S. Army War College, November 2004.

2   Described by Strobe Talbott in his 2003 book *The Russia Hand*.

3   Faced with a U.S.-controlled government in Kiev aspiring to join NATO, Putin protected Russia's main naval base in Sebastopol, Crimea, by sponsoring a peaceful referendum in which the overwhelming majority of Crimeans expressed their desire to return to Russia – a popular desire which existed since Khrushchev arbitrarily transferred this historic Russian territory to Ukrainian administration in 1954.

4   Keir A. Lieber and Daryl G. Press, "The Rise of U.S. Nuclear Primacy", *Foreign Affairs*, March/April 2006.

5   "Pentagon Tester: F-35 Still Has Serious Problems", Popular Mechanics, August 24, 2016. <http://www.popularmechanics.com/military/weapons/a22530/pentagon-tester-f-35-combat-testing-delays/> The "vastly overpriced" F-35 "among myriad other deficiencies, cannot fly within 25 miles of a thunderstorm", observed Andrew Cockburn in the June 2016 issue of *Mother Jones*.

6   William J. Broad and David E. Sanger, "As U.S. Modernizes Nuclear Weapons, 'Smaller' Leaves Some Uneasy", *The New York Times*,

January 11, 2016.

7   "Behold the Pentagon's Amazing, Nuclear-Powered ATM", *Mother Jones*, June 2016.

8   <http://www.military.com/daily-news/2016/09/27/first-strike-nuclear-doctrine-wont-change-carter.html>

9   Lieber and Press, "The New Era of Nuclear Weapons, Deterrence, and Conflict", *Strategic Studies Quarterly*, Spring 2013.

10   <http://www.defense.gov/News/Transcripts/Transcript-View/Article/956079/remarks-by-secretary-carter-to-troops-at-minot-air-force-base-north-dakota>

GLOSSARY
OF ACRONYMS

AEC   Atomic Energy Commission

ASD/ISA   Assistant Secretary of Defense for International Security Affairs

BEW   Bureau of Economic Warfare (later FEA)

BMEWS   Ballistic Missile Early Warning Station

CBI   China-Burma-India theater (World War II)

CDNI   Committee for the Defense of National Interests (U.S. creation in Laos)

CEP   Circular Error Probable

CINCPAC   Commander in Chief of Pacific Area

CINCUSAREUR   Commander in Chief of U.S. Army Forces in Europe

CINCUSAFE   Commander in Chief of U.S. Air Forces in Europe

DDR&E   Defense Directorate of Research and Engineering

DGZ   Desired Ground Zero

ECA   Economic Cooperation Administration

FBIS   Foreign Broadcast Information Service

FEA	Foreign Economic Administration
GDR	German Democratic Republic
ICBM	Intercontinental Ballistic Missile
ICC	International Control Commision (to monitor 1954 Geneva Accords on Indochina)
IDA	Institute for Defense Analysis ("civilian" WSEG)
ISA	International Security Affairs (Defense Department)
J-3	Operations Directorate of the JCS
JCS	Joint Chiefs of Staff
JICA	Joint Intelligence Collection Agency (of the CBI)
NSAM	National Security Action Memorandum
NESC	Net Evaluation Subcommittee
NIE	National Intelligence Estimate
NMCC	National Military Command and Control Center
NORAD	North American Air Defense Command
NSA	National Security Agency
ONR	Office of Naval Research
ORO	Operations Research Organization (U.S. Army)

PEO	Programs Evaluation Office (U.S. agency in Laos)
PV	Physical Vulnerability
RAND	Research and Development (U.S. Air Force)
SAC	Strategic Air Command
SACEUR	Supreme Allied Commander in Europe
SEAC	Southeast Asia Command
SWNCC	State-War-Navy Coordinating Committee
TAC	Tactical Air Command
USCINCEUR	United States Commander in Chief, Europe
USSBS	United States Strategic Bombing Survey ("uzzbuzz")
WAG	Western Ambassadorial Group
WSEG	Weapons Systems Evaluation Group

INDEX